MRS. SATAN

Books by Johanna Johnston

RUNAWAY TO HEAVEN: *The Story of Harriet Beecher Stowe and Her Era*

MRS. SATAN: *The Incredible Saga of Victoria C. Woodhull*

MRS. SATAN

THE INCREDIBLE SAGA
OF
VICTORIA C. WOODHULL

BY

JOHANNA JOHNSTON

G. P. Putnam's Sons   New York

PRINTED IN THE UNITED STATES OF AMERICA

To
W. W. W.

FOREWORD

THIS book is not fictionalized biography, except as its chief subject did some fictionalizing herself. Victoria Claflin Woodhull and, almost equally, her sister, Tennessee Claflin, struck even their contemporaries as incredible. "It would be thought that one such woman in a family was sufficient," the New York *Times* commented in 1872. "That there should be two such, jointly working at the same time, would surpass belief, did not the fact stare one in the face."

The bibliography at the end is a partial listing of the hundreds of sources consulted and checked against each other for facts about their lives, the lives of those who affected them, and the opinions of their contemporaries about them. Every conversation and every quotation in the text has been taken verbatim from a contemporary source. (The chapter headings are quotations from Victoria, or from those close to her.) Physical descriptions and reactions are based on the same sort of record.

Chief acknowledgment must be made to Emanie Sachs, who first tracked down what facts are available about the Claflin sisters' early lives and who was able to talk to men and women who had known the sisters, or to the children of such people. Her biography of Victoria Woodhull, *"The Terrible Siren"* (Harper & Brothers, New York, 1928), is an invaluable sourcebook for any study of the lives of both sisters. Her personal kindness in the preparation of this book is also gratefully acknowledged.

7

The biographer would like to thank also all those who have aided in the search for primary source material for this study; among them are Norma Westneat, who helped make the resources of Sterling Memorial Library and the Beinecke Rare Book Library, both at Yale University, yield various riches; and the staff of the New-York Historical Society Library, especially Shirley Beresford, chief of the reading room, and Thomas Dunnings, Jr., newspaper librarian.

And to everyone else who, in the 1870s, 1880s, 1890s and early 1900s, made note, one way or another, of the pain, wonder or love inspired in them by Victoria Woodhull, the biographer offers the gratitude of one who finds in such fragments evidence of the living responses that truly fill out the shape of a character.

JOHANNA JOHNSTON

CONTENTS

Illustrations follow page 96.

MRS. SATAN

1 § *I Anticipate Criticism . . .*

THEY burst upon the scene proclaiming principle. For Victoria Claflin Woodhull and her sister, Tennessee Claflin, it was not enough to be the first women ever to have their own brokerage office on Wall Street, hailed as "Queens of Finance," and "The Bewitching Brokers." Principle had to justify their unprecedented achievement.

"All this talk of women's rights is moonshine. Women have every right. They have only to exercise them. That's what we're doing," Victoria insisted. She was a beautiful woman whose cheeks flushed in moments of excitement and whose blue eyes shone with compelling intensity.

Tennessee said, "I despise what squeamy, crying girls and powdered, counter-jumping dandies say of me." She was always more flamboyant in her language than Victoria, and she proclaimed principle with smiles, sparkling glances and all sorts of quick, unexpected gestures.

Principle drove the sisters on to even more astonishing activities and ever more sensational headlines. Victoria announced herself a candidate for the Presidency of the United States. "I anticipate criticism," she said, "but I trust no one will question my sincerity." Tennie, quick to emulate Victoria, declared herself a candidate for the state legislature.

Principle inspired the sisters' lively and radical newspaper, *Woodhull & Claflin's Weekly*. Principle burned in Victoria as she addressed a Congressional committee and won the startled respect of its members. Principle gave her irresistible eloquence as she held a national convention of suffragists spellbound.

Free love was a matter of principle too. "Yes, I am a free lover," Victoria cried to a throng of three thousand in New York's Steinway Hall. "I have an inalienable, constitutional and natural right to love whom I may, to love as long or as short a period as I can, to change that love every day if I please."

For millions of Americans in the latter half of the nineteenth century such a proclamation was final proof that principle had nothing to do with the activities of Victoria Woodhull and her sister. To them, the two women were simply wantons, lost to shame, gluttonous for notoriety.

But there were others, a surprising number of them, actually, who did not agree, at least so far as Victoria was concerned, and who saw her as she saw herself—a heroine of the social revolution.

Within this minority there were many who were ready to swear that it was only a sense of mission that led Victoria, "The Wicked Woodhull," to reveal a scandal about America's most beloved preacher, the Reverend Henry Ward Beecher. The repercussions of that act ruined her, lost her and Tennessee the fortune they had made, lost Victoria the respect and prestige she had won—lost her, it seemed, everything. She must have guessed it would be so. She had a cluster of cool, rational friends about her who could have told her so if she did not sense it herself. But she went ahead, and Tennessee, her faithful shadow, went with her, true to principle, whatever the cost.

It was as though, once having found principle as a guide to action, Victoria Claflin Woodhull was obsessed by it. There had been so many years without it, years of racketing from one place to another, seeking her destiny and finding only confusion. There had been, even before the wandering years, such an absence of something—she did not know what—that when she found it she could not let it go.

From her father neither she nor any of his children received the slightest clue that anything in the world was worth pursuing except financial advantage and personal safety. He was running a gristmill in the little town of Homer, Ohio, when Victoria was born on September 23, 1838. But milling was not especially his trade any more than half a dozen other occupations were. He preferred activities of a speculative nature and was particularly pleased by anything that called for scheming, some kind of clever deception, or, best of all, litigation.

Known generally as Buck, Reuben Buckman Claflin, and his twin brother, Samuel, were born in 1796 in Sandisfield, Massachusetts, the first two of thirteen children of Robert and Anna Claflin. One can learn from genealogical records that the Claflin line in America had been founded five generations earlier by a Scottish mercenary soldier, who spelled his name Macklothlan, and who came to the New World in 1661. Beyond that, Buck Claflin's background is obscure. He and his brother were five when their parents left Massachusetts for the wilds of northern Pennsylvania. There Buck Claflin spent his childhood, but by early youth he was wandering southward toward the more interesting activities centered in the river towns along the Susquehanna. He was a tall, lean fellow, with a big, bony nose and a jutting chin, sightless in one eye from an early accident with bows and arrows while playing Indians. With his remaining eye he saw sharply and shrewdly enough, however, and his quick wits, his talent for judging both cards and horses were soon developed by association with the boatmen and raftsmen, the gamblers and horse traders who roistered in the river towns. For a while he kept a store. Then, in the early 1820s, having acquired a string of horses, he made his way to Selingsgrove, home of a landed Pennsylvania family named Snyder. John Snyder, the son of Simon Snyder, who had been governor of the state for three terms, hired Buck to take charge of his stables.

In Selingsgrove, Buck Claflin met Roxanna Hummel, a young woman who worked as a maid for the Snyders. The daughter of Jake Hummel, a local tavern keeper of German descent, Roxanna spoke with an accent, was unlettered, homely and small. But she had a quick tongue, a fiery temper and a confidence in her own opinions, visions, superstitions and religious convictions which obviously appealed to Buck. In 1825, Reuben Buckman Claflin and Roxanna Hummel were married.

They lingered in Selingsgrove for several years. Two boys were born and given the curious names of Hebern and Maldon. Two daughters were more prosaically named Margaret Ann and Polly. Then the family moved to another little Pennsylvania town, stayed briefly, moved again and yet again. Two more babies were born and died in infancy. One winter the house in which the Claflins were living was destroyed in a blizzard and Buck joined his brother who was working on the river as a raftsman. A commission from John Snyder to see about a disputed tract of land in Ohio rescued him from that hard life and sent him and his family to Marietta. From Marietta the Claflins moved on to Streetsboro, Ohio, where Buck ran a tavern briefly. After that came the move to Homer, the acquisition of the gristmill, and, in 1838, the birth of Victoria, Buck and Roxanna's seventh child, the fifth to survive.

Homer was an insignificant settlement among the rolling Ohio hills and fields, forty miles north and east of Columbus but quite removed from any of the bustle of that growing metropolis. A few homes, a general store and post office, a church, a log school building and the mill made up the village, which existed only to service the farmers round about. Life still had a backwoods simplicity to it in Homer: no main road ran through the town, no stage stopped there, but real pioneer difficulties were long since past. Indian mounds dotted the vicinity but any living Indians had been gone for almost a quarter of a century. The townsfolk were settled, ordered people who followed the pattern of their days—keeping house, tending store, splitting wood, shoeing horses, going to church—without any more dramatic alarms than periodic epidemics of ague.

That was the pattern, that is, for everyone except the Claflins, who were soon bristling against the quiet, respectable background like a bramble patch. They moved into an unpainted, ramshackle house on the edge of town near the gristmill. They filled the house well enough by themselves but soon they were joined by Buck's river-boating brother and his family. With these arrivals, the house spilled over. There were beds and pallets everywhere, in the parlor and cellar as well as more likely places, and they were rarely made. Roxanna cared nothing for housekeeping, in itself an affront to the town's busy housewives.

The noise the Claflins made was another source of irritation. They were a shouting, accusing, quarrelsome clan. Uninhibited shrieks and yells were forever echoing out from their dwelling, Roxanna's voice as loud as any. Buck Claflin, home from the mill or one of his other haunts, was often apt to add to the tumult by roundly whipping any child who happened to annoy him. Braided withes were kept limber for the purpose in a barrel of rainwater.

But Roxanna Claflin had an almost mystic sense of family unity as well as a high tolerance for dissension. "Break bread—now we must all break bread together," she would insist when a quarrel had spent itself. She would force embraces and reconciliations and then dramatically bless the reunited combatants, referring to herself as their "holy mudder in Israel."

This necessity for family loyalty, forced on them by their mother, was one of the chief convictions acquired by Victoria and her brothers and sisters during their childhood. Whatever the pain or provocation, members of the family had to be privately forgiven sooner or later, and in any outside difficulties they had to be fiercely supported and defended. The need to preserve family solidarity would stay with Victoria all her life, often at dismaying cost to her other ambitions.

The eighth Claflin child was born in Homer in 1841, a girl, and once again Roxanna showed her erratic taste in names by calling the child Utica, nor was it ever explained whether the name was inspired by that of a nearby village, the larger town in New York, or was just a group of sounds Roxanna found pleasing. A ninth baby was born a couple of years later and died. Then, in 1846, came the last of Buck and Roxanna's children, the little girl whom Roxanna exotically named Tennessee Celeste.

All of the children, with the exception of Maldon, were unusually handsome, fair-skinned, straight-limbed, clear-eyed. Victoria was a beautiful child with great blue eyes, a mop of silkily curling brown hair and a delicate profile. For the townspeople it was a source of some wonder that the lanky, vaguely malevolent-looking Buck Claflin and the pinched-faced Roxanna should have created such good-looking offspring. For Roxanna, already obsessed by self-importance, the beauty of her children was simply an outward and visible sign that she and her children were different from other people, hedged in by none of the rules and restrictions to which others were subject. When she made clothes for the children, she tried to make the clothes different too, to further emphasize their special status.

But the differentness of the Claflin young, as it manifested itself in their loud, self-assertive behavior, won them little love among their neighbors. Nor did Roxanna help matters by publicly taking up the cudgels for them when she felt they had been rebuffed in some way, making a scene in the church after they had been sent home from Sunday School for disruptive behavior, haranguing the teacher at the school if they were chastised there.

It was not held against Roxanna that she was addicted to the revival meetings periodically held either in the church or at some campsite in a nearby woods. Evangelical revival meetings, fervent as they might become, were a respectable and enlivening aspect of religion in those years, championed by no less a figure than New England's famed Congregational minister, Dr. Lyman Beecher. Beecher had himself migrated with his family from Connecticut to Cincinnati, Ohio, in the early 1830s to help fix the religious complexion of the West by means of those emotional purges. Nor was anyone in Homer too much dismayed by Roxanna Claflin's extravagant religious ecstasies on such occasions when she made her way, whirling and babbling in tongues, to the mourners' bench.

What did annoy her neighbors was the way in which she carried the same extremes of behavior into her everyday life. She often prayed loudly in the back yard for the souls of everyone within earshot. Somewhere—perhaps back in Pennsylvania, working for the Snyders—she had heard of the new technique of mesmerism, and when any of her children fell ill she doctored them by hypnotism. These curious excesses cast a further shadow of suspicion around her.

Buck Claflin had his own ways of sparking uneasiness. He ran the mill casually and was knowledgeable enough about various other matters so that local farmers sometimes consulted him about surveying problems or the merits of a horse. He made friends with local political figures to such purpose that he was appointed Homer's postmaster during the James K. Polk administration. But his fondness for taking matters to law on the slightest pretext, his sharpness in any kind of deal made most residents wary of him and a few, who had tangled with him to their sorrow, preferred to avoid him entirely.

"Sinners, repent!" Victoria would cry sometimes when she had managed to gather a few neighborhood children around her. The missionary urge, the desire to preach, to teach, to lecture from a little above others was strong in her from her earliest years. Standing on an old Indian mound near the Claflin house, she would harangue her audience with phrases and images remembered from the revivals she attended with her mother. "Repent or know the burning flames of hell."

But the children would soon grow restive and Victoria, quick to sense their mood, would have to shift to a lurid tale about Indian scalpings. Even so, her audience would gradually drift away. She was too intense—and one of the crazy Claflins anyway —and so made the children as uneasy as her father and mother did their parents.

Tilting her chin, Victoria would let them go. She could play with her younger sister, Utica, or with the baby, Tennie. Best of all was one recourse with which she could always win the excited attention of her family. Taking after her mother, who saw all manner of things while in the throes of a religious experience, Victoria was clairvoyant. She began manifesting the talent at the age of three. A neighbor died and soon thereafter the little girl fell into a swoon which lasted for several hours. Waking, she reported that the spirit of the neighbor had carried her off to the otherworld, where she had seen angels, beautiful flowers and all sorts of wonderful sights. Sometimes Victoria played with the spirits of the baby sisters who had died before her birth. Now and then she saw the devil, a tall man with his face hidden behind a red silk handkerchief but a cloven hoof plainly visible instead of a booted foot.

Her most dramatic visitor, however, was the spirit of a noble-looking man in a white Grecian tunic.

"You will know wealth and fame one day," this apparition promised her. "You will live in a mansion in a city surrounded by ships and you will become ruler of your people."

The prophecy did not seem incredible to Victoria, nor to any of the Claflins when she related it to them. Imbued as they were with the idea that they were different, it seemed quite reasonable that for one or all of them all human desires should be gratified. Time passed and in the rush of daily drama the destiny awaiting Victoria was half forgotten by the rest of the family. Victoria did not forget it. The knowledge that she was going to know wealth and fame someday and become a leader was a shield against all the rebuffs and humiliations she might suffer as one of the alarming, unreliable Claflins.

Buck Claflin had the idea of insuring the mill against fire sometime in the late 1840s. The procedure was not so routine in those years as it later became and attracted some attention. A great deal more attention was attracted when the mill caught fire one Sunday night and quickly burned to the ground.

Various circumstances about the blaze aroused suspicion. The mill had been unused and empty since the Friday before the fire. On the Saturday before, Buck had taken off on foot for a nearby town, stopped there briefly and started back toward Homer. Then he had stopped in the town which was Homer's nearest neighbor and taken a room for the night. Sometime before midnight, however, he became uneasy and told the landlord he must get home because he had a presentiment that his mill was on fire.

When he arrived in Homer on a borrowed horse, he found his presentiment true and his neighbors taciturn, glancing at his wife and sons with scarcely veiled suspicion. The next day, when he began taking steps to collect his insurance, he was greeted with sharp questions. He discovered that in this new crisis old grievances were being remembered as well. He began to hear whispers about tar and feathers. Abruptly, Buck Claflin dropped his claim and quietly left town.

A week or so later, some of the town's more practical citizens put on a benefit bazaar so that his abandoned family might be sent on its way to join him, wherever he might be.

For several years after that the Claflins wandered from one little Ohio town to another, living here and there as Buck's fortunes dictated. There were deals, trades, fleeting partnerships, lucky card games and not such lucky ones.

The strange thing was how little the harshness and crudity of this disorganized life seemed to touch Victoria. Her older sisters, Margaret Ann and Polly, handsome young women by this time, had a bold way about them and their tempers flared as loudly as ever. But Victoria, growing to be twelve, thirteen and fourteen, kept the quiet, quaint manner that had been hers since babyhood. She had no example of a lady on which to model herself. She might easily have picked up the piercing whine of her mother's voice or the showy emotionalism of her sisters, but her speech was soft and her emotions revealed themselves more in the increasing gravity of her gaze than in any outbursts. "Someday you will know wealth—fame—" Perhaps the prophecy had its own inspirational value.

The Claflin peregrinations ceased for a while in Mt. Gilead, Ohio, a little town not far from the Homer they had fled. Margaret Ann, who had been married for some time to a respectable and well-to-do young man named Enos Miles, had settled there. Polly's good looks were winning her the attention of an equally reputable young man of the area, Ross Byrnes, whom she would ultimately marry. Buck brought most of the rest of the family to a halt there also. Maldon, always the butt of his mother's tirades because he was the ugly duckling, ran away to work on the railroad. Young Tennessee, the baby, had been sent some time before to stay with relatives in Pennsylvania.

Soon, however, word came from these relatives that Tennessee, aged only five or six, was showing remarkable signs of second sight. She frightened playmates by "reading their minds." She had told a farmer where he could find a lost calf. She had predicted a fire in a seminary so accurately that there had been a good deal of uneasiness until an investigation proved that the little girl (luckier than her father in a similar case) was innocent of complicity. There really should have been nothing to surprise the Claflins in the news. Tennessee was simply following the pattern of both Victoria and their mother, winning attention and creating drama as she did so. The operating factor was that the times had suddenly become much more propitious for spiritualistic phenomena.

All sorts of strange fads, fancies and grandiose but serious plans for the perfecting of mankind were abounding in America during these years. Poets, writers and philosophers were busy trying to build practical utopias in New England and elsewhere. Horace Greeley, editor of the New York *Tribune,* was among those backing the scheme of the Frenchman Charles Fourier for dividing mankind into phalanxes of 1,620, in which groups entirely new rules for the conduct of life were to be practiced. Greeley also both practiced and preached vegetarianism and the benefits of graham flour. Phrenology, the analysis of human character by a study of the conformations of the head, was considered a serious science by many. Women, for the first time in history, were holding meetings and demanding certain rights for themselves. Some were wearing bloomers as a symbol of emancipation, and Lucy Stone was making headlines by refusing to take the name of her husband, Henry Blackwell. Abolitionists were pursuing their persecuted course and many who had rejected their radical stand were feeling a new uneasiness about slavery thanks to an astonishing novel, *Uncle Tom's Cabin,* written by Lyman Beecher's daughter, Harriet Beecher Stowe. Temperance lecturers were roaming the land, and in New York City, Phineas T. Barnum had a Moral Lecture Room close at hand to his embalmed "Feejee Mermaid."

Very little of all this agitation filtered into the life that the Claflins knew. They had heard of phrenology and gibes about women wearing pants. Most of the rest of the stir was on a level well above their sphere of activity.

But there was one other great general preoccupation that did touch them. In the late 1840s, a wave of interest in spiritualism had begun building, attracting serious, sober, educated men and women as well as the ignorant and superstitious. The interest swelled almost to a mania with reports about two young sisters, Kate and Margaret Fox, in Rochester, New York, who could summon mysterious rappings from walls and furniture to answer the most difficult and unlikely questions. The validity of their performance was questioned by a few, but Horace Greeley was only one of the responsible public figures who believed in them implicitly. By 1850, the sisters were holding profitable seances in New York. By 1852, they had toured widely, as far west as Cincinnati, Ohio, collecting medals, awards, honors and a great deal of cash as they went.

Two young girls who heard and saw things ... Suddenly, Buck Claflin seemed to waken as if from a trance and to realize the riches that lay disregarded and unexploited at his very feet. He hurried to Pennsylvania, made a few quick dollars there by advertising Tennessee as a child fortune-teller, and then traveled back with her to Mt. Gilead so that he could combine her talents with those of Victoria. Soon he had set both of the girls to work in the parlor of a Mt. Gilead boardinghouse, tipping tables, summoning spirit music and conducting seances.

It was not an unhappy time for Victoria. She was utterly serious about her clairvoyant powers and always would be so. If her father took no such committed view as she and if he were continually urging her and Tennie to help along the effects they were evoking, and if sometimes she did encourage various phenomena, it made no difference in Victoria's basic belief in herself. And the attention she and Tennessee won with their mysterious activities could have been only pleasing.

She was also getting acquainted with her youngest sister for the first time. Tennessee, a pretty, light-hearted child, was full of foolish, laughing ways when she was not solemnly invoking spirits. Victoria, so earnest herself, was charmed by the laughter and filled with a sense of protectiveness for the little girl. In return, Tennie looked at Victoria with admiring eyes and whatever Victoria did she tried to do also.

"I anticipate criticism," Victoria would say years later. She would say it calmly, for she had known criticism all her life. It was a natural and normal stimulus to her. There was criticism after the seances began. Residents of the boardinghouse complained about the strange noises and occasional shrieks that emanated from the parlor when Victoria and Tennessee were holding forth. But Buck could always find a new location for the meetings. There were always enough people who were awed and impressed to make the exhibitions deeply satisfying. And for the two sisters the ties of affection that would last all their lives were being formed, and Victoria was finding in Tennessee the first and most loyal of all her followers.

But Victoria was almost fifteen by this time and blossoming into a loveliness that eclipsed that of her older sisters. Her great blue eyes, her delicate features and rose-petal skin, all enhanced by her disarming, ladylike air could not fail to catch the attention of local youths. Whatever tentative exploration she may have begun in the realm of sex was soon cut short, however. Her youthful beauty brought her a proposal of marriage which her parents, at least, felt was too good to turn down.

2 } *I See Our Futures Linked ...*

MEN would help Victoria all her life, gladly devoting themselves and their talents to her interests, happy to assist her in her climb toward destiny. The one exception, the one man who seemed only to further the confusion of her early life and add to its miseries, was Canning Woodhull, her first husband.

Woodhull, the son of a good family in Rochester, New York, had studied medicine in the East and then gone to Ohio, planning to set up a medical practice there. Residents of Mt. Gilead, remembering him later, recalled a friendly and sensitive young man with a great love of children.

Victoria told a different story. Years later, she gave an account of her first marriage to one of her lovers, Theodore Tilton, when he was preparing a biography of her. It was a lurid tale that she told Tilton, full of desperate revelations and confrontations. Further embellished by Tilton's prose style, the story became almost a parody of the kind of Dickensian melodrama which was popular at the time. But however Victoria's memory may have distorted actual events and however Tilton may have exaggerated the distortion, what Victoria was remembering was plainly not happiness.

Canning Woodhull stopped the young girl on a Mt. Gilead street one day and, according to Tilton's recital, spoke winningly. "My little chick, I want you to go with me to the Fourth of July picnic."

Victoria was "elated at the promise of a little pleasure," for she had painted a black picture for Tilton of herself as a four-teen-year-old drudge, enslaved by cruel parents to an unending round of household tasks. But after promising her parents to earn enough money to buy a pair of new shoes for herself, and after doing so by selling apples (that was what she told Tilton), she won their permission for the excursion.

On the way home from the picnic, Woodhull broached the subject of marriage. "My little puss, tell your father and mother I want you for a wife." Victoria remembered herself as "quivering with anger," though why she felt anger rather than maidenly surprise and hesitation, she did not explain.

Perhaps the hurt that lingered came from her father's quick readiness to dispense with her clairvoyant talents and carry on the spiritualist sessions with Tennessee alone. Her parents, she told Tilton, "thought it a grand match," and did everything they could to further Woodhull's suit. And so, in 1853, when she was not yet sixteen, Victoria Claflin was married to Canning Woodhull and departed from whatever roof was sheltering her to live with him in his lodgings.

If she had had any hope that love and marriage might give a new direction to her life, shock and disillusionment came swiftly. Three days later, Canning Woodhull stayed away all night at a house of ill-repute and the young bride "learned to her dismay that he was habitually unchaste and given to long fits of intoxication."

Still, Victoria made an effort to be a good wife. Not long after their marriage, the couple paid a visit to Woodhull's family in New York. Perhaps it was instructive for Victoria, instinctively so ladylike, to observe the ways of the Woodhull gentlewomen. If so, she made no reference to anything like that later. Instead, her narrative rushed on to tell of increasingly somber events after she and her husband returned to the Middle West.

Drinking more and more, and there is no doubt that Victoria's charge in that direction was based on fact, Canning Woodhull was less and less able even to contemplate medical practice. They lived, one assumes, on some small income from his family. And they began moving from place to place, just as Buck Claflin had done after leaving Homer.

They were in Chicago when their first child was born in 1854, a boy whom Victoria named Byron. It was bitter winter and the sixteen-year-old mother had no other attendant during the ordeal of childbirth than her half-drunken husband. A few weeks later, Woodhull deserted her for a month. She learned that he was "keeping a mistress in a fashionable boardinghouse, under the title of wife." Dressed, as she recalled it, in a calico dress without undergarments and wearing "india rubbers without shoes or stockings," Victoria set forth to find her husband and beg him to return to her.

Woodhull, his mistress, and all the boarders were gathered at dinner when she arrived. Standing before them in her shivering disarray, she told her story so movingly that the listeners "literally compelled the harlot to pack her trunk and flee the city, and shamed the husband into creeping back like a spaniel to the kennel which his wife still cherished as her home."

A change seemed to come over Victoria after that. First her father, then her husband, had dictated the circumstances of her life. And her husband, well-born, well-educated, had shown himself as lacking in any kind of principle or direction as her father. "Wealth—fame—a mansion—" that had been the prediction, but no one to whom her fate had been submitted had led her any closer to it. She began taking charge of her life herself.

The prophecy had also mentioned a "city surrounded by ships." Perhaps that was what turned her thoughts now to San Francisco, a city whose harbor was full of steamships, sailing vessels, every kind of ship from every nation, in the fifth year after the discovery of gold in the California hills.

Somehow she got herself, Canning Woodhull and the baby to California. Presumably they went by sea. If they had made the long, dangerous overland trip, surely some memories of its hardships would have been recalled for Tilton and the world. Arrived in San Francisco, the town that had mushroomed from a population of nine hundred to more than a quarter of a million in a period of months, she found a brawling, sprawling,

jerry-built city of saloons, hotels, stores, opera houses, sur-
veyors' and assayers' offices—every kind of attraction and service
to cope with a tidal wave of men, dirty, worn and suddenly rich,
or hoping to be—but no mansions.

Stepping forward as the breadwinner for the first time since
her marriage, Victoria got a job as a cigar girl in a saloon. Having followed in her father's course for so long, she should not
really have been overcome with shock at the rough manners
and language of a San Francisco bar. But relating the experience
to Tilton years later, Victoria said that the rude remarks of
the customers caused her to blush so much that the proprietor
told her that she was "too fine" for the work. Her innate air of
refinement also had the proprietor pressing a twenty-dollar
gold piece into her hand and then personally escorting her to
the hotel where she and Woodhull were staying.

She tried to earn money next by working as a seamstress, an
occupation that seems never to have impinged on her life
before or after. Chance brought her as a customer the actress
Anna Cogswell, who, like so many other theatrical people, had
been lured to the gold-rich city. Miss Cogswell, looking at the
sad and lovely face of the young woman surrounded by yard
goods, suggested that she might do well on the stage, mentioned
the fact that she headed her own repertory company and urged
Victoria to stop by the theater for an audition. Soon Victoria
was playing small roles in Miss Cogswell's presentations.

The theater offered beautiful young women, talented or no, a
chance for wealth and fame in those years, as it always has.
Why its opportunities did not appeal to Victoria as a means of
achieving her destiny is a mystery. Perhaps it did not offer
enough scope for her missionary urge, her need to deal with
people directly, as herself, and to cry, "Sinners, repent."

She was on stage one night as a minor figure in a ballroom
scene of the popular drama *The Corsican Brothers,* when she
suddenly seemed to hear the spirit-voice of Tennessee calling to
her, "Victoria, come home!" She seemed to see her mother and
Tennessee, arms outstretched, beckoning to her. Abruptly, and
quite heedless of any demands of the drama, Victoria ran from

the stage. She did not pause to change from her pink silk costume or delicate slippers but hurried just as she was out into the foggy streets and to her hotel. The next day, she, her husband and baby were on a steamer bound around the Horn for New York.

In the world of politics, national affairs and issues of the day, to which Victoria paid no attention—which went on somewhere else entirely so far as she was concerned—the Kansas-Nebraska bill had been passed to allow the settlers of each state self-determination in the matter of permitting or prohibiting slavery. "Bleeding Kansas" had become the battleground of antislavery and pro-slavery men. Lyman Beecher's fifth son, Henry Ward Beecher, already famous as America's most persuasive preacher, was winning new honor among the foes of slavery by using his pulpit at Plymouth Church, in Brooklyn, to plead for funds with which to purchase rifles for the antislavery men. "Beecher's Bibles" these guns were being called, after the misleading label "Bibles," stamped on the boxes in which they were shipped. Theodore Tilton, a very young man, only three years older than Victoria, was listening to Beecher with the hero-worshipping wonder of a born idealist. Tilton was just starting on a journalistic career, working as a reporter for Horace Greeley's *Tribune.* He deeply admired his towheaded and eccentric editor, appreciating his brilliance as a newspaperman as well as his many and varied enthusiasms. But to Tilton, Henry Ward Beecher was becoming a demigod, a man of eloquence, sentiment and passion, and a man who dared act on his beliefs as well as preach them.

To Victoria Claflin Woodhull, The Reverend Henry Ward Beecher was a name, nothing more. The world in which he and Tilton lived, the world in which Beecher's sister, Harriet, was writing another antislavery novel, *Dred,* the world in which the slavery question was now stirring the deepest emotions in men and women both north and south was not hers.

After traveling around two continents and then overland to join her family, Victoria found that no crisis or disaster had inspired the spirit-call to come home. Tennie was the same loving, admiring little sister that she had always been. Her mother was the same, welcoming her with raptures but soon lapsing into complaint. Her father was perhaps a little more cheerful. He had discovered that Tennessee had the gift of magnetic healing as well as second sight and was happily launched on a new career with her. Billing Tennie as "The Wonder Child," he had organized those members of the family who still surrounded him into a sort of traveling medicine show. Salves and potions concocted by Roxanna were sold. Hebern, a handsome young man, alternated with his father as pitchman and general medical advisor to all comers.

There was undoubtedly a place for Victoria with this family group if she wanted it. She had given up any hope of support from Canning Woodhull; he, like young Byron, was just another child who leaned on her for support. She might easily have decided to join Tennie, her mother, father, Hebern and Utica, and contribute her talents to the general welfare.

Instead, she heard spirit-voices counseling her to use her clairvoyant talents on her own. She should go, the voices told her, to Indianapolis, and announce herself there as a spiritualist physician. Off she went, with Woodhull and the little boy.

She did well in Indianapolis in this new role, according to Tilton's biography, "reaping a golden harvest and golden opinions as well." But Byron fell from a second-story window one day and was so badly injured that for some time he lay near death. At last he recovered physically but with permanent damage to his brain. He would remain for the rest of his life a "near-idiot." Nursing him, seeing and advising her patients, caring for Canning Woodhull in his sobering-up periods, Victoria dragged through the weeks and months. She prayed, she said later, for another child, "a daughter, to be born with a fair body and a sound mind."

Her prayer was finally answered in 1861. Tilton records that her daughter was born in New York City, but why Victoria happened to be there at the time was not explained. The Civil War had begun. The city was buzzing with recruitment, parades of volunteers, the waving of flags. Victoria seems to have turned a blind eye to it all. Her daughter was fair and sound, just as she had hoped she would be. In a burst of exoticism outdoing all her mother's efforts, Victoria named the child Zulu Maud. Nor did she, who loved to explain things symbolically or allegorically, ever give any explanation of that more than mildly curious name. Zulu Maud the child was and Zulu Maud she would remain, for all of her long, patient and loving life.

Soon after the child's birth, Victoria and her little family were back in the Middle West again. Guns and cannon were thundering to the south and east; there were raids and threats of raids in the border states; young men were leaving towns everywhere to join the army; news of casualties found its way everywhere also. Victoria never spoke of how these events may have touched or affected her. She never referred to the war in later years. Tilton's biography of her brushed past the years of conflict as though they had not been.

What records there are for those years have to do with Tennessee's career as it was reflected in handbills and advertisements, testimonials and letters to the editor in the newspapers of one city or town after another.

In 1859, Buck Claflin had his entourage in Columbus, Ohio, and was advertising Tennessee as "this young lady [who] has been traveling since she was eleven years old, and who has been endowed from her birth with a super-natural gift to such an astonishing degree that she convinces the most skeptical of her wonderful powers. . . . She can see and point out the medicine to cure the most obstinate diseases."

By 1863, Buck had traveled on with his "wonderful child" to Ottawa, Illinois, and had discovered the profits in anything claimed as a cure for cancer. He advertised himself in Ottawa as "Dr. R. B. Claflin, AMERICAN KING OF CANCERS," and guaranteed cures "in all cases where patients live up to directions." But Tennessee was still the main attraction, the child who had "so astonished people through her wonderful cures and mysterious revelations during her travels in the United States."

Business went so well in Ottawa that Buck was able to rent an old hotel as a "cancer infirmary." Glowing testimonials from Tennessee's gratified patients were printed in the paper. Then there came a disclaimer from one of the patients so quoted. She had never written the testimonial, she informed the editor. Miss Tennessee Claflin had not cured her, as claimed, but had made her much worse. A group of doctors decided to investigate the cancer infirmary and soon were reporting their shock at finding the patients neglected and the quarters filthy. Then the ex-patient who had repudiated Tennessee's claims died of cancer. And Tennessee was indicted for manslaughter.

"Sudden Disappearance of Tennessee Claflin," the Ottawa *Free Trader* headlined one day in June, 1864. And Tennessee, Buck, Roxanna, Hebern and Utica were on the road again.

Cincinnati, Ohio (no longer the home of the Beecher clan, which had made its way back to New England some years before), was the next stopping place for the Claflins. Soon Victoria with her husband and two children had joined them there.

Principle—if there was little of it in Victoria's life there seemed to be none at all in Tennessee's. Perhaps Victoria had a hope of offering her lovable but foolish younger sister some protection from the more extreme of their father's exploitations. Perhaps she was seeking also, after so much lonely wandering, for the admiring affection which Tennessee offered so freely. Whatever had brought Victoria to Tennessee's side, after this reunion she stayed there. From now on, for Victoria, the family as a unit would be the whole family, Tennie and her mother and father, brother and sisters, as well as her husband and children—a group only infrequently broken up.

People who lived near the house that the Claflins rented in Cincinnati would recall later how they had seen Roxanna Claflin and her two daughters, Victoria and Tennessee, stirring some concoction in a kettle in the back yard and of the way the sight had roused uneasy reminders of the three witches in *Macbeth*. But cancer salves and potions were no longer advertised after Victoria joined the Claflin group. Instead, a sign in the front window of the house read simply: "Tennessee Claflin and Victoria Woodhull, Clairvoyants."

Troubles continued, all the same. And now more than the noise, the quarreling and the general unconventionality of the Claflins were disturbing the neighbors. An aura of illicit sex was beginning to surround the Claflin daughters. Utica, at twenty-three, was almost as beautiful as Victoria but with the same sort of quick temper as her oldest sisters, Margaret Ann and Polly. Tennessee, almost twenty, was delightfully pretty, and with every flick of her skirt, every wink of her eye, she deepened neighborhood suspicions. And a number of strange men did call at the house after dark.

Charges were lodged with the police that the Claflin residence was a house of assignation. Then, before anything was done about that, Tennessee's name was suddenly figuring in an adultery case in the Cincinnati courts and shortly thereafter she was featured in a blackmail suit. It was time to leave Cincinnati.

The Claflins traveled next to Chicago, where Victoria and Tennessee again advertised themselves as mediums. In this city, Tennessee impulsively plunged into marriage with a young sport named John Bartels. She did not take his name, feeling perhaps that her own, inscribed on so many bottles and jars of elixirs, had a commercial value that outweighed any less savory associations it had acquired in Ottawa and Cincinnati. But Tennessee married was the same Tennessee she had always been, with the same free and easy way with men. Neighbors in Chicago began making the same kind of complaints to the police that had been made in Cincinnati.

In the summer of 1865, after the war had ended, Victoria hired a wagon and took Tennessee, John Bartels and Hebern on a trip through Missouri and Arkansas to tell fortunes and conduct seances. They made a great deal of money on the trip and were somehow inspired on their return to Chicago to hire a band and outriders to accompany them to the doors of the Claflin dwelling. Flaunting their good fortune before the critical neighbors may have made them feel better but it did not improve the general climate of opinion. And it had not been all sunshine on the journey, for Tennessee and her husband had quarreled so bitterly over a ten-dollar bill, the source of which she would not reveal, that after their return to Chicago, Tennessee gave John Bartels his share of the trip's proceeds and he departed from her life.

Male callers at the Claflin house continued to upset the neighbors. Finally, unable to force any action from the police in connection with their worst suspicions, they swore out warrants against Victoria and Tennessee for fraudulent fortune-telling. Eviction papers were served on the Claflins. And Chicago was left behind.

Early in 1866, Victoria, Tennessee and the usual family group were in St. Louis, Missouri, and Victoria was announcing herself as a spiritualist physician. The pattern of her life seemed established—an endless series of flights from one town or city to another, an endless series of attempts to convey to someone the power and excitement with which her otherworldly voices and visions sometimes filled her. She was twenty-eight. Eighteen years had passed since the white-robed spirit had promised her "wealth, fame, a mansion—ruler of your people."

Tilton's biography of her picks up the story at this point, as Victoria's spirit-voices gave her the second fateful prophecy of her life.

A handsome, side-whiskered young man with an erect military bearing came to consult her one day. Victoria saw him walking across the darkened room toward her, watched him sit down in the chair provided. Then, before he could even tell her his problem, she went into a trance.

"I see our futures linked," she told the stranger. "Our destinies bound together by the ties of marriage."

Only after awakening from her trance did she learn that the

handsome stranger was Colonel James Harvey Blood, a man of standing in St. Louis. She learned also that there were obstacles to a linking of their futures on his side as well as hers. He, even as she, was already married.

But Victoria's spirits were guiding her truly, even so, for into her life at last had walked a man of principle.

3 § *Go to New York!*

COLONEL Blood believed in free love. Of all the fads, fancies and world-saving doctrines that were rife in the country at the time, only that one truly horrified the vast majority of Americans, causing their breaths to grow short, their faces to pale and words almost to fail them. Still, a few dedicated spirits, scorning the revulsion they inspired, were not afraid to declare that if man really was to be perfected his sex life must be reformed first of all. A group of such brave souls had pioneered a utopia of their own, the Oneida Community in New York, where it was held that "sexual intercourse should no more be restrained by law than eating or drinking." And here and there across the country there were others who saw a vision of a better life, who read Goethe's *Elective Affinities* and free-love pamphlets and managed as well as they could with their belief that men and women, bound to partners who had ceased to be, or had never been "true mates," were only following God's law if they broke the false ties when fate brought them face to face with a "spiritual affinity."

The free-love doctrine was not the only principle cherished by James Blood, a gallant, courteous, idealistic man. But it was the fateful one at his and Victoria's first, electric meeting. He may, perhaps, have had only an intellectual sympathy for the doctrine until then, a theoretical commitment. Listening to Victoria's astonishing message, then looking into her blue eyes, he faced the moment of putting his principle into action and did not fail the test.

They began to know each other during the course of a wagon trip on which they embarked soon after their meeting. James Blood simply broke every tie. He abandoned his wife and young daughter, left his position—he was City Auditor of St. Louis—dismissed his reputation. Victoria entrusted her children to the care of the family and ignored Canning Woodhull, who may have been alcoholically absent anyway. They took off in a covered van to travel through Missouri and the Ozarks, the same territory which Victoria had traversed so profitably a year before with Tennessee, John Bartels and Hebern.

Once away from the city, they stopped on the outskirts of any likely hamlet. Colonel Blood, giving up his last name and calling himself James Harvey, went forth into the settlement as an advance man to advertise the presence of the clairvoyant, Madame Harvey, who could read the past and the future and give advice on problems spiritual, emotional and physical. The response, just as Victoria had found it a year before, was eager and the money rolled in.

Traveling along the quiet backwoods roads in between such engagements, they could pull the wagon to the side and make love whenever they wished. And any lingering doubts that James Blood might have felt about his decision must have ended then. If love that was free was like this, then surely half the ills of the world would vanish when men and women allowed sexual honesty to reign.

They grew acquainted in other ways also. Soon enough, Colonel Blood learned how little education Victoria had acquired in her few years at the log cabin school in Homer. He discovered that she had read almost nothing in the years since and even wrote her name with difficulty. But he also discovered that her perception was uncanny. She followed him, or seemed to, in his discourses on any subject and then, her eyes shining, could herself begin to converse on the matter as though it had long been one of her chief studies. The quickness of eye and ear and the emotional sensitivity that made her a successful clairvoyant and reader of fortunes obviously served her intellect as well, given an opportunity.

Victoria told James Blood of how it had been prophesied that one day she would know wealth, fame, and become ruler of her people. James Blood was not disturbed by her conviction that this would indeed all come to pass. His visionary preoccupations had prepared him for all sorts of unlikely events in the future. Undoubtedly Victoria pointed out to him, as she would to many others, that across the sea another Victoria was already ruler of her people and no one thought that odd. It was an omen that her parents had named her as they had. James Blood could point out to her that aside from its victorious sound Victoria actually meant "born to triumph." He could tell her that her birthday in 1838 fell within the year of Queen Victoria's coronation in 1839 and that might be an omen too.

But James Blood's story was unfolding also with its own revelations for Victoria, introducing her to the world which had always lain just beyond her. His title of Colonel had been won in the war that passed her by, the war in which he had served as commander of the 6th Missouri Regiment and suffered five bullet wounds as testimony to the action he had seen. His position as City Auditor, to which post he had been appointed after his return to St. Louis, showed him to be a man acquainted with the respectable world of business and finance, very different from the world of coaxing dollars from rustics which Victoria knew.

It was when he talked of the causes that excited him, though, that the miracle began to happen for Victoria and the jumble of her past experiences gradually began to assume a kind of order. No subject about which he spoke was really strange to her. She was familiar in her own way with all of them. But he put them on a new level, investing them with dignity, meaning and an ordered framework of principle. A spiritualistic phenomenon had brought them together. Spiritualistic events had been part of her life since babyhood. James Blood, on the other hand, had been President of the St. Louis Society of Spiritualists when he and Victoria met, interested in its phenomena on a plane which Victoria barely knew existed. Blood, like thousands of men and women in the United States and Europe, was searching its manifestations for new religious horizons.

The objectives of the women's rights movement were hardly strange to her either. She, who had been forced into an unhappy marriage, known first dependency on an erratic husband and then the need to support him and her children, was aware emotionally of the need of women for more freedom, more opportunities and rights to match responsibilities. From James Blood, she heard for the first time the words and arguments that made it all reasoned, ordered and finally inevitable.

Most liberating of all, however, was his explanation of the doctrine of free love. How much that explained in her own past life and Tennessee's also. How it blew away the clouds that had hung over them in Cincinnati and Chicago and elsewhere. How it justified behavior that sprang really from free, natural impulses freely seeking natural gratification. But why then, Victoria asked, did most people behave as they did? Why had she and Tennie known such persecution and ostracism? What of the men who preached one set of rules by day and practiced another by night? What of that damning label "prostitute"?

And so James Blood talked to her of hypocrisy. Most people, he told her, were nurtured in hypocrisy from the cradle, trained to accept false standards and deny the most natural and obvious realities. Then, blinded by prejudice, fear and jealousy, they united to try to destroy those who lived by more honest standards than themselves.

Victoria's missionary zeal was kindled. For the first time she began to see a real way in which she might become a leader. She could be the one to rise up and tear away the veils of hypocrisy that were blinding so many. She could reveal the truth.

Principles! Principles that explained everything. She had found them at last.

The wagon trip came to a sudden end. The abandoned Mrs. Blood finally succeeded in tracing her husband, and James Harvey and Madame Harvey were forced to return to St. Louis and their true identities. Victoria turned over the proceeds of the trip to Colonel Blood and in due time he managed to make provisions for Mrs. Blood and his daughter and to obtain a divorce. Canning Woodhull did not present a problem. He still loved Victoria and, difficult as it was to reconcile with his usual behavior, he loved his children, caring for them tenderly when he was sober. But he bowed to Victoria's ultimatum and soon she had her divorce from him.

A marriage license was issued to James H. Blood and Victoria C. Woodhull in July, 1866. No record of a marriage was ever found later, which may or may not have meant that they were not legally married. Neither did Victoria take Colonel Blood's name. He may have told her by this time of Lucy Stone and her brave stand for individual identity, or perhaps Victoria felt some hesitation at the sound of the Colonel's surname, a premonition that Victoria Blood was nowhere near so euphonious a name with which to meet destiny as Victoria Woodhull. Colonel Blood made no objection to her keeping the name she preferred.

One of Victoria's sisters, Margaret Ann or Polly, visited the Claflins in St. Louis about this time. She saw Canning Woodhull hovering in the background and asked him about the handsome stranger at Victoria's side.

"That's Colonel Blood," replied Woodhull. "Victoria's new husband."

"Where do you come in?"

"We don't live together anymore," said Woodhull. And soon after that he departed quietly from the lodgings that housed Victoria, her new husband and the Claflins.

St. Louis, home of the first Mrs. Blood and the scene of James Blood's earlier, more conventional life, hardly seemed the most comfortable place for Victoria and James to linger much longer, either. Within a few weeks, they, the children,

Buck and Roxanna, Tennessee, Hebern and Utica were on
the road again.

Where they went, how they traveled and what they did were
not recorded. In the world at large, there was a ferment of
activity as the country began rebuilding after the war. Construction on the Union Pacific Railroad to link the Middle
West with the West and so create a railroad line spanning the
continent was resumed. Railroad lines were being extended
and branching out everywhere in the East and the Middle West.
Manufacturers, businessmen and entrepreneurs in the North,
rich with war profits, were expanding, building new factories,
new office buildings, mansions that reflected their owners'
wealth and prestige, if not their cultivated taste. In New York
City, speculators thronged the Stock Exchange, vying for
fortune as stocks, manipulated by such unhampered individual-
ists as Cornelius Vanderbilt and Daniel Drew, went up and
down with the breathtaking rapidity of a weight-testing machine
at a county fair.

Making enough money to get along on was presumably no
problem to Victoria and the Claflins during these months. Men
and women with a desire for spiritualistic advice, comfort or
healing, had, in general, more money to spend in gratifying
their desire than ever before. Still, it was a curious time for no
dramatic event to star Victoria's life. She had found and married
a man who gave her direction and purpose, and then for two
years she did nothing about it.

But the very absence of any documentation suggests that
something had changed. Tennessee was no longer getting into
trouble wherever she went. No complaints or police charges
were recorded against her or any of the Claflins during this
time. Tennie liked Colonel Blood from the beginning, following Victoria's lead in this as in almost everything. Seeing
Vicky so bemused by his conversation, Tennie too, began listening to him, picking up a glimmering of the ideas that were
transforming life for her sister.

Probably, also, this was the period during which Victoria
began to slant her spiritualist consultations along the lines of

free-love doctrine advocated by Colonel Blood. "Hundreds, aye thousands, of desolate, heartbroken men as well as women have come to me for advice," she would say in later years. "I came to recommend the granting of entire freedom to those who were complained of as inconstant; and the frank asking for it by those who desired it. My invariable advice was: 'Withdraw lovingly, but completely, all claim and all complaint as an injured or deserted husband or wife. . . . Be kind to and sympathize with the new attraction, rather than waspish or indignant.' "

The one person who did not like the new addition to the Claflin entourage was Roxanna Claflin. She begrudged Colonel Blood's power over Victoria and she hated his influence on Tennessee, who had always been her favorite child. From the beginning, she shrilled curses at him, berating him for infatuating her daughters. But James Blood, part of a strange, new gypsy life, caught up in emotional tempests the like of which he had never known, bore himself with such tact and forbearance that sometimes Roxanna flung herself in his lap and called him the best son-in-law she had ever had.

Still, somewhat improved as her life had become, Victoria's restlessness must have been growing. Evidence of that came out some years later. In the course of some legal proceedings at that later date, Colonel Blood testified that he and Victoria had been divorced in Chicago in 1868. However, when asked how long they had been separated, he said, "We were never separated. We continued to live together and were afterwards remarried."

A man who brought her pleasure in love, a man who had given her principles as a backbone to her life, but perhaps not a man to initiate action—if that was what Victoria finally realized her husband to be, she must also have realized that she had other sources for counsel.

Victoria's account of her life picks up the record in 1868, the same year in which she and Blood were divorced but continued to live together. From Chicago, they and the rest of the Claflins traveled on to Pittsburgh. And it was in Pittsburgh that

Victoria was visited once again by the spirit-guide who had first prophesied wealth, fame and leadership for her so long before.

She was alone in a boardinghouse sitting room when he appeared, as noble-looking as ever in his white toga.

"Go," he said, "to New York City. To 17 Great Jones Street. There you will find a house ready and waiting for you and yours."

A vision of a house, and then of its interior, its hall, stairway and parlor, floated momentarily beside the figure of her ghostly visitor.

Victoria stared. Never before had he been so explicit in his advice and instructions.

"Who are you?" she whispered. "All these years, you have never said. Tell me now. Who are you?"

The apparition stretched forth a hand. With one finger he began to write letters on the marble-topped table beside her. It was impossible to decipher what he was writing at first. Then the letters began to glow, brighter and brighter, until the whole room was illuminated. They spelled the name *Demosthenes.*

Perhaps Victoria might not have recognized the name two years before, in the days before Colonel Blood had begun to introduce her to classical learning. It did not matter. She knew it now. The greatest orator of ancient Greece, the champion of its liberties against the Macedonians, was her spirit-guide.

Slowly, the glow of the letters on the tabletop faded. She looked up. Demosthenes had vanished also. She rose and made ready to carry out his instructions.

Victoria always liked to tell of how she went to New York City, hurried to the address given her by Demosthenes and found there a house exactly like the one in her vision. She entered and found the hall, stairway and parlor just as she had previsioned them also. Then, on a table in the parlor, she saw a book. Stamped in gold on its cover was the title, *The Orations of Demosthenes.*

She felt, she said, "a blood-chilling astonishment" at this confirmation of her spirit-guide's identity.

Soon the whole clan had moved from Pittsburgh to take up residence in the house at 17 Great Jones Street. If the house was not exactly a mansion, it was a solid, respectable brownstone in a respectable and stimulating section of the city. Great Jones Street, with its curious name, was actually the segment of 3rd Street that ran between the Bowery and Broadway. Since the end of the war the city no longer straggled out into country roads at 42nd Street but had been built up with streets, homes, apartments and mansions as far north as 57th Street and the margin of the newly laid-out and landscaped acres of Central Park. The Murray Hill area in the East 30s was now the site of rich homes. The Fifth Avenue Hotel on Madison Square at 28th Street was a glittering, gaslit center of fashionable activities. But Great Jones Street, suddenly so much farther downtown in the city's push northward, was still in no stagnant backwater. The Bowery, to the east, was not nearly as elegant and respectable as Broadway, to the west, but it was the second principal street of the city, all the same, throbbing with life on Sundays as well as weekdays, lined with saloons, "free and easies," immense German beer gardens, dance cellars and theaters as well as shops, stores, warehouses and dwellings of every description. Broadway, running parallel, had richer fare and was a promenade for wealthier New Yorkers who could at least afford to look at the jewels, silks and other fine goods displayed in the windows of its shops. A few blocks north of Great Jones Street where the Bowery ran into Fourth Avenue was the brick pile of Cooper Union, where Lincoln had accepted the Republican Presidential nomination in 1860. And just around the corner on Lafayette Street was the building that had been established as Astor Library under John Jacob Astor's will in 1854, an institution that made the area something of a literary center. Also on Lafayette were those connected houses, fronted by marble columns, called Colonnade Row, which had

been an architectural triumph of the 1830s and the Greek revival home of John Jacob's son, William Backhouse Astor.

East and west, New York was also a city surrounded by ships,
and if Victoria had been there before, in 1861, without finding
her destiny, she was sure that this time it would be different.

Tennessee, lighthearted and loving, was the one who made it
different, opening the door to destiny for herself and Victoria
both. Just how it all came about in the beginning was never
elaborated. Victoria simply said, "We met Commodore Vanderbilt."

4 § You Will Know Wealth ...

"ADVENTURESSES!" The charge would be flung at both
Victoria and Tennessee all their lives and would pigeonhole
them even more completely afterwards. And yet of all the many
and varied events of their lives, their meeting with Cornelius
Vanderbilt was one of the most logical.

Vanderbilt—the richest man in America according to various
contemporary reporters who spent a good deal of time totting
up his millions as compared to those of A. T. Stewart, the
merchant prince, or William Astor, the tenement-building heir
of John Jacob Astor's fur-trading fortune—had been addicted to
spiritualism and faith healing for some years before meeting the
sisters. A man of rough, unpolished speech and manners, impatient of furbelow and swank, a man generally considered a
ruthless, hard-bitten "pirate" in business affairs, Vanderbilt
still would have been welcome in any church that he chose to
honor with his presence. But Cornelius Vanderbilt despised
the fashionable, rustling, perfumed social life that centered on
New York's churches and scoffed at the organized piety and

sentimentality of its ministers. For years, he had been finding whatever spiritual solace he needed in visits to a medium who lived on Staten Island and regularly brought him messages from his dead mother. As suspicious of accredited doctors as of ministers, he consulted spiritualist physicians and faith healers for any aches or illnesses.

These facts being generally known, it would have been surprising if Buck Claflin had *not* taken his onetime wonder child, Tennessee, to call on the Commodore. Probably they went to his home. Vanderbilt lived at 10 Washington Place, just off Washington Square, not far from Great Jones Street. The area was no longer quite as fashionable as it once had been, and the house itself, a large but classically severe residence of red brick, was considered frugal by millionaires of the new school who were building florid palaces uptown. But whether they went there, or to his office downtown, Vanderbilt would not have been difficult to see. He saw everyone, merely demanding that business be stated and dispatched promptly. Buck had only to introduce Tennessee as a magnetic healer of extraordinary talent and suggest that the Commodore test her ability at his convenience. He may have taken Victoria with him on the first visit also, to present her as a medium of great power, or Victoria may have accompanied Tennessee on a later visit. However the first meetings were accomplished, it took no deep-laid planning or scheming to continue the association.

Vanderbilt was seventy-six years old that year of 1868. Erect and spare, a fringe of white hair forming a frosty aureole around his hawk-nosed face, he did not look his age. Driving his fast trotters up Broadway to Central Park and racing them on the Harlem Road, he did not act it either. But for the first time in his life he was knowing pangs of loneliness and boredom. His son, William, who, by middle age, had finally managed to win some of his father's confidence, handled most of the details of the Vanderbilt shipping and railroad empires. Only when grand strategy was required was it necessary for the Commodore to step in. In August, his wife had died. He and she had not been close for years but her passing was a shock, re-

minding him that life was short. There was little he had to
do to take his mind from his melancholy and few things that
amused him except his horses, his annual visits to Saratoga
and the races, and his regular whist games with a few cronies.

Into this void stepped Victoria and Tennessee, Victoria to
gesture mysteriously and bring him messages from the other
world, and Tennessee, laughing and ebullient, to push and
press away his pains with the magnetic positive force of her
right hand and the magnetic negative of her left.

Tennessee was the one who captivated the Commodore most
completely. She liked to talk with the same colloquial vul-
garity that he did. She knew how to liven her magnetic treat-
ments with unexpected tickles, squeezes or slaps. Before long,
Vanderbilt was feeling youthful excitement running again in
his veins. He was reaching for the magnetic hands of his healer
to draw her into bed with him.

Naturally obliging, Tennessee did not protest unduly. Her
visits to the house at 10 Washington Place grew more frequent
and longer in duration. The servants grew used to finding her,
rosy and tousled, in the Commodore's bed in the morning.

"My little sparrow," the Commodore called the young
woman. And he chuckled when Tennesse called him "old boy."
As a young boy he had known little pleasure or laughter. As
an old one he was discovering how enjoyable they were.

But Vanderbilt admired Victoria also. Her beauty, her gravity
and grace made her unique among the mediums he had known.
Sometimes he asked her for spirit-advice about the stock market.
If the answers Victoria brought him conflicted sometimes with
his own considered judgments, he was untroubled. It was likely
that even the spirits were not so informed about financial matters as he.

Victoria felt no need to worry that principle might be com-
promised by her own and Tennessee's relationship with Vanderbilt. Natural urges, honestly expressed and gratified, were part
of the code Colonel Blood had taught her. The Commodore
was admirable for his lack of hypocrisy in this matter and

showed the same bluntness in other fields as well. He scorned
to pose as a public benefactor with his shipping and railroad
lines. If these enterprises offered people safer and more reliable
transportation than they had known hitherto, it was merely
because he had learned that providing these considerations
helped to confuse competition and insure profits. He was impatient of appeals to his charity, feeling that his own success
laid him under no obligation to those who had striven less
tirelessly than he. All in all, there was no "humbug" about him,
a word that Victoria was beginning to find almost as satisfactory
as hypocrisy.

As the friendship grew, so did the material rewards. The
Commodore was generous in his emoluments for services rendered and gradually he began following up spiritual counsel on
the stock market with advice of his own, giving Victoria and
Tennessee tips on various stocks which he thought they would
do well to buy with some of their earnings. Victoria relayed
these tips to Colonel Blood, who took care of the necessary
transactions with brokers. When the stocks rose or fell, as
predicted, the Commodore was glad to give further counsel,
hold or sell, or buy more. Soon, the profits from these transactions were mounting and so was the general level of satisfaction
among all the residents at 17 Great Jones Street.

The only people not particularly pleased by Vanderbilt's new
friends were his children. There seemed little that they could
do about the situation, however. Their father had never concerned himself with their opinions. And so they were briefly
relieved when two relatives of the Commodore's who lived in
Alabama made a visit to New York. Tennessee's regular visits
were interrupted as the Commodore played host to Mrs. Crawford and her gentle daughter, who bore the manly name of
Frank.

All the Vanderbilt sons and daughters and their respective
spouses noted with interest that Mrs. Crawford was a widow,
very near to their father in age. With Sophie Vanderbilt's
death still so recent, it might be too soon to talk openly about

their father's remarriage, but they could not help feeling that when the time was right Mrs. Crawford would be a very suitable match and solve the problem of the Claflin sisters. They did what they could to encourage their father's attentions to the two Crawfords.

But as soon as the Crawfords left the city, Vanderbilt summoned Tennessee back to him. Undoubtedly it was soon after their reunion that he proposed marriage to her, asking how she would like to be Mrs. Vanderbilt.

"To be Mrs. Vanderbilt . . ." It was, one might have thought, the dearest goal of any adventuress.

But Tennessee shook her head and said no to the proposal, thus winning for herself a little of the aura of mystery that so often surrounded Victoria.

Years later, after Vanderbilt's death, his biographers would puzzle over why Tennessee Claflin did not accept the golden opportunity. The Commodore had indeed made her a bona fide offer, affirming the fact himself on various later occasions. Some biographers suggested that his children stepped in to prevent the marriage. But their father being the man he was, the children would have done so at their peril and the price would have had to be very high. Besides, nothing that followed seems to allow such an explanation.

The ties between Vanderbilt and the two sisters became even stronger after Tennessee's refusal. The tips on the stock market flowed more freely. Colonel Blood was busier than ever, buying and selling on the Exchange. And the standard of living at 17 Great Jones Street began improving out of all recognition.

There were maids there now, and a cook, and a governess for helpless Byron and young Zulu Maud. Word of the general good fortune reached Margaret Ann and Polly in the Middle West and they came to New York with their families. Both of them were divorced from their first husbands by this time, but Polly had remarried. With Buck and Roxanna already in residence as a matter of course, and Hebern and Utica regarding it as home however they might sally forth on their own from time to time, accommodations must have been strained. But commitment to any family demand had long since been drilled into Victoria and Tennessee. Room was made somehow for all comers.

Meanwhile, very little of her time being required for the periodic seances with Vanderbilt, Victoria was getting acquainted with New York in ways other than financial, and with other than the richest of its citizens. It was inevitable that, going about the city with Colonel Blood, she should see New York as one of the grandest monuments to hypocrisy ever created.

The city was full of churches. There was one every few blocks, and newer, more lavish ones had been going up between the downtown and uptown area every year since the war. The jangling of their bells filled the air on a Sunday morning and streams of fashionable and middle-class New Yorkers flowed smoothly to their doors. It was easy to believe that never since Puritan days in New England had there been such a public show of religion as the ruling force of life. Ministers were the elite of the city, competing with its millionaires for fame, and not doing too badly financially themselves. Henry Ward Beecher, across the river in New York's sister city Brooklyn, was the brightest star, casting a spell so potent that special ferries were run on Sunday mornings to carry worshippers to Plymouth Church—Beecher's ferries, they were called. A stocky man with a full, mobile face and a mane of gray hair that hung to his shoulders, he had such eloquence and dramatic power that he made his listeners laugh, weep, and in general run a gamut of emotions that no theater could provide. He was the best known —adding to his fame as a lecturer, a writer and an editor, so that his words and personality swept the nation—but he was by no means the only famous minister in New York. And these were the men who seemed to shed a glow of holiness and righteousness over their surroundings by their very passage down a street.

Victoria saw it and sensed it and marveled, for surely never had there been such a show of religion in such open, blatant contrast with vice and degradation. Just as ubiquitous as the city's churches and just as plain to see were its streets and houses of shame. No attempt was made to conceal houses of prostitution. Their keepers sought custom and made them as obvious as possible. Colonel Blood, who liked statistics, could have told Victoria that as of two years before the police commissioner had reported over six hundred such houses, another hundred houses of assignation and seventy-five "concert saloons of ill repute." By police count there were almost three thousand public prostitutes and some seven hundred "waiter girls" in music saloons. This number, in a city of almost a million, seemed quite reasonable to the commissioner. But an eminent Methodist minister, unconvinced by the commissioner's figures, had made his own estimate of twenty thousand prostitutes. And to Victoria, no figures made any difference when she could see on every hand the outcast women who were the subject of the statistics. Some, still young and fortunate, might be well-dressed and walk with defensive pride, but she saw the older ones, haggard, painted, openly soliciting and she saw the way the so-called respectable men and women detoured around them, avoiding even a contaminating glance.

Victoria, so lately escaped from the fringes of such a life herself, was roused to a passion of empathy. The honored ministers of the city harangued periodically against these "lewd women" as though the fault for their fate were their own. The "good people" closed their eyes, shuddered, and to them, also, one "fall" condemned a girl or woman forever. No quarter would be given her, no opportunity to find some other way of living. She had branded herself a moral leper.

To Victoria, the opposite truth was so plain that it seemed it must shout itself into the consciousness of everyone, however he willed himself deaf or blind. Society itself had doomed these women. False standards of morality, and false ideas about sexuality had created a world where respectable women refused to admit there was such a thing as sex and respectable men gave lip service to the same lie. Then, gratifying themselves furtively, they publicly despised those whom they had made the instruments of their pleasure. All the words and arguments she had learned from Colonel Blood boiled and churned within Vic-

toria. If the truth did not proclaim itself, then someone had to
shout for it.

Fortunately, little by little, she was beginning to find an
audience to whom she could unburden herself. Colonel Blood
was striking up acquaintances around the city with radicals and
reformers who thought as he and Victoria did. He was bringing them home to meet Victoria. They talked and she talked,
and soon she was talking more and more, while her visitors
listened entranced. Most of them were sincere and thoughtful
people and some were truly talented and accomplished. But few
of them could speak of their convictions with such dramatic
effect as Victoria could. And not one of them was beautiful and
clairvoyant as well, able to converse with geniuses of ages past
in the spirit world and reveal some of their suggestions for an
ideal society. Summer came, and Victoria was on her way to
establishing a salon of sorts at 17 Great Jones Street.

The need for a new sexual morality was not the only problem
she and her friends discussed. Visionaries and idealists had much
to distress them in these years after the war when business and
politics both were corrupted by men seeking nothing but
personal gain. And so they could talk of the machinations of
some of the unprincipled men on Wall Street who bought
legislators to do their bidding in lawmaking just as they bought
women to go to bed with them. Victoria had first-hand comments on some of these men from the Commodore, who had
tangled with them all—Daniel Drew, old Dan'l, the nearly
illiterate power behind the Erie Railroad for years, a predatory
pessimist, forever selling his stocks short and then arranging
for the legislation that would make their value drop and his
take increase; Jay Gould, a foxlike, silent, scheming man,
and James Fisk, Jr., fair, plump and flamboyant, both of
whom had joined with Drew in the Erie operations to prevent the Commodore from getting control of that railroad
and ruin him too, if they could. They had won in the Erie
battle, but they had not ruined the Commodore by any means,
and he had worsted them in their struggle to keep him from
bringing the tracks of his Harlem Railroad as far into the city

as 42nd Street. Talking of how legislators were bribed as a matter of course brought on discussion of New York's own city government, firmly under the control of the Tammany organization and William Marcy Tweed, chief sachem of that all-powerful political club. "Boss" Tweed and his ring of cohorts might indeed sell services and favors to the railroad manipulators but that was only a sideline. They had their own ways of making a fortune out of the city. Visitors to Victoria's salon were the kind of people who knew or could guess at some of the facts behind the construction of the new County Courthouse, for instance. The building had been begun a year before and the estimated cost for it had been $250,000, but already millions had been poured into it and the foundation was barely laid. Victoria and her friends agreed that the veils of hypocrisy that hid this kind of corruption should be torn away also. Nor did Victoria seem to tremble lest all this tearing and rending might expose some unattractive financial behavior on Vanderbilt's part. Principle was everything.

As always in the summer, Commodore Vanderbilt left New York for Saratoga and the races. But he did not forget Tennessee and Victoria. Advice and counsel about their holdings in the stock market continued to arrive from time to time, and there were hints about some new railroad activities about to be undertaken which would affect the market. If Victoria and Tennessee also heard that Mrs. Crawford and her daughter were visiting the Commodore, the news did not seem to trouble them.

Word of Vanderbilt's marriage came in late August. He had eloped with his bride to Canada and was married, not to Mrs. Crawford, as his children had hoped, but to her daughter, Frank. Youth, which he had tasted with Tennessee, had won over maturity. If Tennessee felt any regrets for the opportunity so irretrievably lost, she did not voice them, nor would she ever do so in the years to come.

Various railroad stocks began behaving just as Vanderbilt had suggested they might. Well prepared, Victoria and Ten-

nessee counted more profits and went on about other concerns.
Then, in late September, there came a development for which
Vanderbilt had not prepared them and for which he was un-
prepared himself. His old enemies, Jay Gould and Jim Fisk, had
been busy with a new scheme for cornering the gold market.
President Grant, deluded as to their good faith, had allowed
them to go on and on buying gold until suddenly it appeared
that the whole financial structure of the country was threatened.
Alarmed, the government had acted, the corner collapsed and
the consequences shook the market like an earthquake.

The Vanderbilt honeymoon was quickly interrupted. Vanderbilt hurried to New York to appear personally in Wall Street
and bolster the sagging market. But busy as he was with large
affairs and despite his recent marriage, he kept his "little sparrow" and her sister safely under his wing. They were to buy
as he bought, adding to their holdings in his own railroads,
or roads that would soon be his at these depressed prices, or
they were to pick up other specified stocks selling at remarkable
lows, which would soon rise again.

Investors in general recovered slowly from the day known as
Black Friday. Commodore Vanderbilt and his cohorts recovered
more quickly. As for his protégées, Victoria and Tennessee, one
way or another they were soon really rich.

A brighter affluence than ever shone about 17 Great Jones
Street. Buck Claflin, his beard trimmed, his boots polished,
walked out flashily to visit his favorite haunts. Hebern, too,
could dress and spend like a swell. Margaret Ann, Polly and
Utica could have elegant walking suits, rich décolletages and
bonnets. Victoria, always restrained in her taste, encouraged
Tennessee to the same lack of ostentation, but the broadcloth
of their walking suits was of the finest quality. Victoria could
keep vases of roses everywhere about the house and wear a
fresh tea rose at her throat or in her hair every day. Wealth—
Demosthenes had promised it to her.

But he had prophesied more—"you shall know fame."

Roxanna Claflin, a relentless hater, always blamed what happened next on Colonel Blood. "Blood has suthin about him that

infaturates and he infaturated my da'athers," she shouted to some reporters several years later. "This Hell-hound Blood," she went on, ". . . he said, 'Let's start a bank an' all the brokers on Broad and Wall Street will deal with you an' take off their hats when your carriage drives up.'"

Perhaps James Blood did make the original suggestion but it was an idea sure to delight Victoria and Tennessee and one likely to be encouraged by their radical friends.

Sometime in the fall of 1869, Victoria and Tennessee spoke to Commodore Vanderbilt about it. He must have been astonished at first, but his response when he recovered was gratifying. He was married now, to a sweet but very proper young lady. Still, he did not consider that sufficient reason to give up the prospect of future entertainment from two young women who had already given him many hours of happiness.

He agreed to give them aid, advice and a certain amount of financial backing in opening a brokerage office. Not a platform of some sort, from which Victoria could air her views and launch her career as a leader—not a newspaper, a forum or an institute. But a leap for fame, all the same, for it would be the first brokerage office to be managed by women brokers in the history of Wall Street.

5 } . . . and Fame!

At the start of the year 1870, Victoria and Tennessee rented a suite in the Hoffman House, a stylish hotel in the downtown area near Wall Street. On January 19, they opened their doors for business. And it became clear at once that whether by design, intuition or just plain luck, they had chosen the one sure way to attract not just attention, but respectful attention. The next day James Gordon Bennett's gossipy newspaper, the New York *Herald,* noticed the event:

> The general routine of business in Wall Street was somewhat varied today by the mingling in its scenes of two fashionably dressed ladies as speculators. Who they were few seemed to know, except that they were from the Hoffman House. Where they obtained their knowledge of stocks was a puzzling conjecture with those whom they met. After investing to the extent of several thousand shares in some of our principal stocks and selling others, and announcing their intention to become regular habitues of Wall Street, they departed, the observed of all observers.

To be "observed of all observers" was always stimulating to Victoria but she bore herself with quiet dignity, affording the observers no hint of the pleasure they gave her. And the note which she, or more probably Colonel Blood as amanuensis, sent off to the *Herald* in response to its notice was just right in its tone, cool and unexcited:

> We were not a little surprised at seeing our appearance in Wall Street noticed in your columns of today. As we intend operating as mentioned, we should be glad to make your personal acquaintance when convenient. Woodhull, Claflin & Co.

Two neatly engraved cards were enclosed with the letter. One bore the name of Mrs. Victoria C. Woodhull and the address "Hoffman House, Parlors 25 and 26." The other was Tennessee's card, but she had recently decided on a new spelling for her name so it read "Mrs. Tennie C. Claflin."

A reporter from the *Herald* lost no time in accepting the invitation to visit. Two days later the newspaper ran a long story reporting on his impressions and describing the offices:

> The parlor is a small comfortable room fronting on the avenue and is profusely decorated with oil paintings and statuary, and is furnished with sofa, chairs, a piano and the various other articles, useful and ornamental, which go into the makeup of a ladies' drawing room.

Neither Victoria or Tennessee had any intention of hiding the identity of their sponsor in this new venture and so the story mentioned that a picture of Commodore Vanderbilt was hung on the wall of the parlor. Enemy of hypocrisy that she was, Victoria had also allowed a small, framed religious motto to be hung—"Simply to Thy Cross I Cling." Bennett's reporters were encouraged in a certain irreverence. Few other newspapers presented the obligatory résumés of Sunday sermons around the city with such tongue-in-cheek spirit as did the *Herald*. So the *Herald* reporter at the Hoffman House did not fail to mention the juxtaposition of the pious sentiment and Vanderbilt's picture.

The news story went on to describe the sisters. Victoria had "a sanguine, nervous temperament." Her plain, tasteful costume and the single rose in her hair were noted. Tennie C.'s "features are full," the reporter wrote, "and a continuous smile plays upon her countenance. She is ... a firm foe of the 'girl of the period' creation, whom she describes as a sickly, squeaming nondescript ..." Tennie herself, "to all appearances," was "the photograph of a business woman—keen, shrewd, wholesouled."

The same issue of the *Herald* also carried a long editorial on "Women in Wall Street." The obvious aspects of the situation were reviewed, the uniqueness of women invading the masculine stronghold, the way it reflected women's growing interest in the world outside the home, and their concern for achievement in fields hitherto closed to them. Unprecedented as it all was, however, the editorial writer wished "the fair brokers" every success and concluded gallantly, *"vive la frou frou."*

Their appearance on Wall Street having been duly noted, Victoria and Tennie C. promptly moved their headquarters to more businesslike offices at 44 Broad Street. It was a well-timed maneuver. Interest in the two "she-brokers" had been aroused. Other papers sent reporters to the opening. Every financial house in the Wall Street area sent a representative. Curious businessmen from all over the district hurried to the suite at 44 Broad Street to see for themselves what was going on. All told, "a miscellaneous throng of 4,000" called during the course of the day. No wonder that the New York *Sun* of February 6 headlined "New Furor in the 'Street'—First Levee and Business Reception of Victoria and Tennie C."

The New York *Herald* now hailed the sisters as "The Queens of Finance," and went into detail about "the Palace of the Female Sovereigns of Wall Street," "offices . . . magnificently fitted up. . . . The best 'Marvin safes' . . . walnut desks, finely finished and covered with green baize." Nor was it overlooked that the "inspiration for the new undertaking" was "Commodore Vanderbilt as Prime Minister."

"The steady stream" of people making their way down Broad Street to No. 44 was noted by the *Evening Express,* and its reporter found the two brokers "in the prime of life . . . and very affable and agreeable in their manner." The *Evening Post* merely commented that "for the first time . . . in the history of the street, a firm has been formed both of whose active members belong to what is styled the fair sex."

The "eventful Saturday" was chronicled in an even longer article in the *Sun* the next day, which listed in paragraph after paragraph the names of the financial giants who had put in an appearance at No. 44, with Commodore Vanderbilt's name featured. Daniel Drew, who gave evidence of being "deeply impressed," was also among the callers. In the *World,* a long story about the new firm noted "a clarence that remained in front of the door the greater part of the day," to serve the ladies as they had occasion to drive here and there, and also a sign that had been hung inside the offices to discourage the crowds of idle curiosity seekers, "All Gentlemen will state their business and then retire at once." By the 19th, the *Herald* had a new tag for the sisters, "The Bewitching Brokers," and a *Herald* reporter was writing that "their extraordinary coolness and self-possession, and evident knowledge of the difficult role they have undertaken, is far more remarkable than their personal beauty and graces of manner, and these are considerable."

A quiet admission by the sisters that in their private financial operations of the preceding year they had "turned $750,000" was mentioned by almost all the papers. It was a dazzling sum by any standards, but Victoria brushed it aside.

"What do present profits amount to when it costs us over twenty-five thousand dollars a month to live?" she said. Even taking into account the numerous Claflins at 17 Great Jones Street—Buck, Roxanna, Hebern, Utica, Margaret Ann and Polly, their families, and Victoria's husband and children— twenty-five thousand dollars a month "just to live" might have seemed a little startling. The reporters seem not to have blinked. Nor was the large, demanding family even mentioned in any of the stories. Except for their financial connection with Commodore Vanderbilt, "the bewitching brokers" appeared to have sprung from nowhere to amaze and entertain the city.

Gossip of a more intimate nature was soon spreading, however. Hardly a paper had failed to report the almost daily visits of Vanderbilt to the sisters' offices and the reporters had seen for themselves the cheerful familiarity that existed between him and Tennie. And so there was a good deal of talk about what Tennie's previous relationship with him had been. Many people must have reflected that the young new Mrs. Vanderbilt showed great forbearance as her husband displayed such public interest in an old flame.

Buck Claflin liked to visit his daughters' offices. Lounging about, glaring malevolently, he was a figure to invite speculation. The whole Claflin family invited it, for that matter.

No time was lost in bruiting about the fact that Victoria was a divorced woman, a scandalous item in itself, but shock waves really began to ring out across the city with the whispers that she, her husband and the friends who gathered at their home were believers in free love. After that, it was almost tame for gossip to move on to Victoria's clairvoyance, and her reliance on one particular spirit-guide, Demosthenes, for otherworldly advice.

The talk drifted from ear to ear and within a few months there were few people in New York who could not raise their eyebrows knowingly when the Claflin sisters were mentioned.

"Adventuresses!" Still, they were making money and for most people this fact enabled them to blink their eyes at some irregularities.

And still the newspapers fawned on them. They were such good copy, even better when played straight-faced against the gossip. Their manners, according to the New York *Courier,* were "those of duchesses, or better—of straightforward, well-bred American women, and [they] chatted as freely and decidedly as if they had been on the 'street' a dozen years."

"Yes," Victoria and Tennie said to the reporters, "we like newspapers and newspaper men, they are the salt of the earth just now—keep everything from spoiling. We hope they will not spoil us by flattery. We do not want flattery.... We want fair play—nothing more. We are business women. Give us a fair show as you give business men. We like all the newspapers, they have been very kind to us."

All their lives after this, Victoria and Tennie would like newspapers. They would have an equally enduring conviction that being mentioned favorably in the press, being cited for "courtesy, urbanity and tact," and "intelligent, business-like manners" created a reality that could not be denied.

Tennie's effervescent personality broke through in story after story. She obviously flounced and exclaimed as she spoke to reporters. She was asked if she did not find it awkward to go out on the "Street" where a woman was such a novel sight and she flung out her hands in a dismissing gesture.

"Were I to notice what is said by what they call society," Tennie said, "I could not leave my apartment except in fantastic walking-dress and ball-room costume. But I despise what squeamy, crying girls or powdered, counter-jumping dandies say of me."

Victoria's earnestness and dedication to principle were also evident. "All the talk about women's rights is moonshine," she told a reporter. "Women have every right. All they need to do is exercise them. That's what we're doing. We are doing daily more for women's rights, by practically exercising the right to carry on our own business than the diatribes of papers and platform speeches will do in ten years."

One question remained. A reporter heard it muttered over and over again at the first great "levee" of the new firm. "What does Vanderbilt mean?" And the nervous corollary was often, "Where will this end?"

Day after day, Wall Street regulars kept themselves alert, waiting for some hint of a Vanderbilt masterstroke in the making at 44 Broad Street. Smiling painfully, Henry Clews, of the dignified firm that bore his name, accepted for deposit a check in the amount of $7,500, made out by Cornelius Vanderbilt to the firm of Woodhull, Claflin & Co. However, when Tennie C. returned to Mr. Clews a few days later with a tip to buy New York Central stocks, Mr. Clews refused to have anything to do with a purchase that seemed so directly linked to Vanderbilt interests. He preferred to close out the Woodhull, Claflin account.

But no manipulation of New York Central stock ensued. The days passed and business at 44 Broad Street began to settle into a routine. Lady customers were ushered into a private office at the rear to conduct their business. Gentlemen were received in the front office. If Colonel Blood, unobtrusive in the background, was handling most of the actual work of the firm, no mention was made of it. Victoria and Tennie always appeared brisk and businesslike.

There were intervals of relaxation, as in any office. During these Victoria and Tennie were generally occupied by cutting out stories about themselves from newspapers and magazines and pasting them into scrapbooks. There were pictures as well as stories to clip by now. The New York *Telegraph* had immortalized them in a cartoon depicting "The Lady Brokers driving the bulls and bears of Wall Street, Tennie C. holding the reins, Victoria, the whip." *Frank Leslie's Illustrated Weekly* had noticed their arrival on the metropolitan scene with one of its darkly meticulous lithographs.

And still no scheme on Vanderbilt's part developed. In March, the sisters were instrumental in discovering a check forgery. "Attempt to Victimize the Female Brokers," head-lined the New York *World*. "They Prove Too Smart for the Forgers." A gentlemanly-looking stranger had appeared at the offices one day, purporting to be an agent for the grocer's firm of Park & Tilford. Presenting a large check, signed by the firm, he had asked that gold be purchased with part of the sum and the remainder given to him in cash. Victoria had noticed that the check was not certified and sent it around to the bank on which it was drawn for verification. There it was discovered that while the signature was genuine, the amount on the check had been skillfully altered from $66 to $6,600. "The ladies of the firm have come out of the affair with flying colors," the *World* story concluded. "Their shrewd management and business tact were equal to the emergency, and the precautions they took in regard to certification guarded them from all loss."

On the domestic front there was activity also. Sometime in February, Victoria moved her whole family from the fateful address on Great Jones Street to a more fashionable house on Murray Hill, at 15 East 38th Street, just off Fifth Avenue. Now she was indeed "in a mansion in a city surrounded by ships," and she furnished the house beautifully, with many little gilt chairs and tables and gilt-framed mirrors that extended from floor to ceiling. A full household staff kept the house spotless and glittering in spite of its many and generally disorderly inhabitants.

About this time, a sick and shivering figure appeared at the door one day. It was Canning Woodhull. Addicted to morphine as well as alcohol by now, he had no one to turn to in his desperation, it seemed, but his onetime wife, Victoria. Victoria might well have hesitated to offer him sanctuary, considering her current prominence and the talk already circulating about her and her family. But that would have been hypocrisy, which she scorned. She took Canning Woodhull in.

A new bit of gossip was flashing about the city almost at once. Not only was Mrs. Woodhull a divorced woman. Not only did she subscribe to free-love doctrines. Now, in the house on 38th Street, she was living with both of her husbands.

Victoria ignored the whispers. The arrangement worked out very well. Canning Woodhull, grateful to be part of a group so noisily self-centered that one more aberration was scarcely noticeable, took his place in the household with humble good grace. When he was not dazed by alcohol or otherwise incapacitated, he helped in the care of poor Byron, a lad of sixteen by now, but still with a child's mentality. Sober, Woodhull could find pleasure in exchanging views with Colonel Blood. There were even times when Woodhull, who had been so little able to help Victoria in earlier years, could soothe and comfort her in times of distress as no one else could. James Blood never objected to these evidences of lingering emotional ties between them. Committed to the principle that everyone should know perfect freedom in personal relationships, he lived by the commitment absolutely.

James Blood loved Victoria, and whatever made her happy made him happy also. And so, when still another man entered her life during these weeks, James Blood was only delighted. "Wealth, fame . . . and the ruler of your people." That had been the prophecy, and he believed it now as firmly as Victoria did. Anyone who could help her toward the goal was welcomed as a friend and ally.

6 § *I Place Myself Before the People . . .*

No trance overcame Victoria when she first saw Stephen Pearl Andrews, or none of which she ever spoke. Roxanna, who took the same instant dislike to Andrews that she had taken to

Blood, always bracketed him contemptuously with that "gang of free-lovers" that hung around Victoria, but there were no other hints that his destiny was linked to Victoria's through passion.

He was, rather, the great intellect of her life. Almost sixty years old when they met, tall, pale and bearded, he was another radical brought along to Great Jones Street, or 38th Street, by someone who had already discovered Victoria's open house for advanced thinkers. Another radical, but more than that, a man so prodigiously learned that lesser minds boggled before his knowledge, Stephen Pearl Andrews knew thirty languages and had written an admired textbook on Chinese. He had studied history, government, politics and science. His wife, Esther, had been one of the first women in the United States to study medicine and he followed the course with her. He had lectured and written in the cause of abolition before the war and had traveled to England in an attempt to raise funds for the cause. While there he had learned about Isaac Pitman's new system for shorthand writing. Revising and improving the Pitman version, Andrews introduced shorthand in the United States with a book that went through many editions. His scope was universal and his plans were universal also. Out of his study of languages, he had evolved a universal language which he called Alwato. Out of his study of government and history, he had synthesized what he considered the finest elements of every age to create a blueprint for a new world government— a Pantarchy, he called it, or together-government.

Followed by his disciples, who reverentially called him The Pantarch, Andrews made his way into Victoria's parlor. Cool and analytical, he observed her and saw how easy it was for her to spellbind almost any listener with her beauty and earnestness. His own disciples gathered around her entranced as she elaborated on topics that had long been almost too obvious for discussion among them. Andrews talked to her himself about some of his plans and projects and saw her eyes light with excitement as she followed his ideas, grasped them and gave them back to him enriched by her own sense of drama.

He talked with Colonel Blood, soldier, man of business, scholar, and now a man more than content to devote his talents to Victoria's glory and Victoria's goals. Andrews and Blood talked well together and Andrews had only admiration for the quiet integrity with which Blood practiced the doctrines in which he believed, the grace with which he granted Victoria the right to follow her own desires in love or sex, just as he claimed the same right for himself. For years, Andrews had been tilting for this kind of reform in people's ideas about love and marriage. In the 1850s he had been engaged for months in a three-sided argument with Henry James, another student of religion and history, and Horace Greeley. Greeley had printed letters from first one, then another, of the trio, in the *Tribune* columns until Andrews' arguments in favor of radically relaxed divorce laws had offended Greeley's sense of propriety in that direction and he stopped printing letters from Andrews. Nothing daunted, Andrews had collected the whole correspondence, including his censored letters, and had it published as a pamphlet, which was widely distributed.

"Mr. Greeley," Stephen Pearl Andrews liked to say, "has no conception, and never had, of the entirety of the Social Revolution, which is actually, if not obviously, impending."

Colonel Blood, on the other hand, was committed to the social revolution and had a conception of it almost as sweeping as Andrews'. So did Victoria Woodhull, who was beautiful, convincing, and sure that one day she would become ruler of her people. Pondering her, and what she had already achieved, Stephen Pearl Andrews could not have overlooked the fact that she had money, money that was her own, earned by her, a well-nigh unique situation in the 1870s. He had no thought of personal gain. His thoughts, his heart and soul were in the revolution—and how Victoria might help him advance it.

Esther Andrews had occasion to be out of the city. Victoria suggested that Stephen Pearl Andrews stay with her and her family in the house on 38th Street while his wife was away. But for once it seemed that even the elasticity of a Claflin residence might be strained. Polly and her husband, Benjamin Sparr, were asked to take lodgings elsewhere to make room for Stephen Pearl.

Scenes of protest and bitterness ensued. Roxanna loathed the idea of Andrews as a permanent fixture in the household. She wondered what was wrong with Vicky that she kept taking up with such men, and got Tennie involved with them too. She was sure that if it were not for Victoria, she and Tennie might still be junketing happily around the Middle West, telling fortunes and selling elixirs, instead of condemned to a weird, incomprehensible life in the city. Never one to be bound by consistency, Roxanna also blamed Victoria's fancy ideas for the fact that both the girls were not the spoiled darlings of some rich men, "driving about in their own carriages." Polly and Benjamin Sparr, the ones chiefly affected by Victoria's invitation to Andrews, sided with Roxanna in all her complaints and had a good many of their own to make. But in spite of tantrums and fits of screaming, the change was effected. Stephen Pearl Andrews joined the household on 38th Street.

A new project, one that had probably helped lure Andrews, was under discussion at once. Victoria, fated by prophecy, was to be the focal figure in this move, but all those who loved and admired her felt themselves personally involved. Tennessee, who never knew such satisfaction as in following Victoria, was excited. Colonel Blood saw all his causes advancing with her. Stephen Pearl Andrews had found a new outlet for his views. All the members of his Pantarchy and all Victoria's radical friends and free-thinkers formed an enthusiastic "cabinet of advisors."

Not three months after Victoria and Tennessee had surprised the city with their brokerage office, the group on 38th Street was ready with the new bombshell. On April 2, 1870, a long letter to the editor of the New York *Herald* was published in that paper. The letter was headed "First Pronunciamento." It was probably the joint composition of Andrews and Blood, with perhaps a few revisions by Victoria. It was signed Victoria C. Woodhull.

The writer presented herself in the opening paragraphs as "the most prominent representative of the only unrepresented class in the Republic." This claim did not ignore such battling representatives of the class as Susan B. Anthony, Elizabeth Cady Stanton, Julia Ward Howe, Lucy Stone and dozens of others who had been moving to prominence in the women's rights movement when Victoria was still a child in Homer, Ohio. It simply relegated them to second place.

"While others argued the equality of women with men, I proved it by successfully engaging in business; while others sought to show that there was no valid reason why women should be treated, socially and politically, as being inferior to men, I boldly entered the arena. . . ." But all that was just a restatement of Victoria's claim earlier that "women have every right. All they have to do is exercise them."

She had more to say this time and soon after the prelude she said it. "I now announce myself candidate for the Presidency."

The announcement was followed by examples to show that this was "an epoch of sudden changes and startling surprises. . . ." Events to which Victoria had paid little heed in years past were now brought in as evidence. "The blacks were cattle in 1860; a negro now sits in Jeff Davis' seat in the United States Senate."

"I anticipate criticism," the letter concluded, "but however unfavorable the comment this letter may evoke, I trust that my sincerity will not be called into question. I have deliberately and of my own accord placed myself before the people as a candidate for the Presidency of the United States, and having the means, courage, energy and strength necessary for the race, intend to contest it to the close."

For most people, the announcement was too preposterous to warrant serious criticsm. What Victoria had offered the newspapers was more magnificent copy, copy that was sure to lure almost every kind of reader, all who had heard titillating gossip about the "bewitching brokers" and were eager for more.

Gravely refraining from questioning Victoria's sincerity, the *Herald* ran an editorial on her candidacy. "Mrs. Woodhull, the lady broker of Broad Street, independent of all suffrage tea parties and Grundy associations, proclaims herself as a candidate. . . . Now there can certainly be no objection to such a competition as this; it possesses the merits of novelty, enterprise, courage and determination. . . . Now for Victory for Victoria in 1872!"

The New York *Dispatch* on April 3 noted that the lady brokers had "received many calls yesterday from their friends on 'Change,' all desirous of offering congratulations on the advent of the ladies into the political field."

Making the most of the item, the *Herald* returned to it on the third with another editorial, commenting on Mrs. Woodhull's presumed financial resources among the brokers, both bulls and bears, and adding, "A woman, and a smart and handsome woman, she is the proper person to stand forth against the field as the woman's right candidate for the White House."

It all made for pleasant reading at the house on 38th Street, or in the handsome offices at 44 Broad. The scissors snipped, Tennie giggled and exclaimed, and the scrapbooks became thicker and thicker.

But none of the interested parties had any intention of leaving the matter at a mere announcement. Starting a good two years before the next national campaign, Stephen Pearl Andrews, Colonel Blood and Victoria were determined to make the whole country aware of its newest and most unusual candidate.

For Stephen Pearl Andrews, it was a wonderful opportunity to delve into his learning for the instruction of the public. He began writing, or collecting from previous writings, a series of papers on "The Tendencies of Government." Long, discursive essays, tracing men's systems of government from primitive times on through the civilizations of Egypt, Assyria, Greece and Rome to modern Europe and finally the United States, these articles were dispatched to the *Herald,* which obligingly printed them at intervals of a week or so. Signed, of course, by Victoria's name. Boring as they must have been to many readers, they could not help casting an aura of learning around Victoria's head, a pleasantly somber counterpoint to the golden glow of money already surrounding her.

A few weeks later, the *Herald* was commenting on its busy contributor. "It is evident that Mrs. Woodhull is imbued with at least one very sensible idea ... that fitness is the first perquisite of qualifications entitling the seeker to enjoy the position sought for. This is it, doubtless, which has led her to ... study and perfect herself in the nature of the functions that she seeks to exercise."

But for that particular commentator, a feeling was growing that the game had gone on long enough. He went on to say, "The public mind is not yet educated to the pitch of universal woman's rights. At present man, in his affection for and kindness toward the weaker sex, is disposed to accord her any reasonable number of privileges. Beyond that stage, he pauses because there seems to him to be a something which is unnatural in permitting her to share the turmoil, the excitement, the risks of competition for the glory of governing."

Troubled by "a something which is unnatural," the *Herald* may have wished to pause. Victoria and her supporters had no such desire.

Some hints had been dropped soon after the "First Pronunciamento" as to what Victoria, Blood and Andrews were planning next. The *Dispatch* had warned on April 3 that "Mrs. Woodhull announces her intention to spend a fortune in advocating her views ... and will soon begin the publication of a campaign sheet." And just as the news of the female brokerage house had made its way across the country to be noted in one local paper and another, so this further information was picked up about the lady who had announced for the Presidency. In St. Louis, Colonel Blood's hometown, the first Mrs. Blood could read of the exploits of her successor. "The Wall Street female brokers, Woodhull, Claflin & Co., are about

starting a weekly to support Mrs. Woodhull for the Presidency,
advocate women's rights and suffrage."

Now, at last, when there was no chance for it to be lost in
the obscurity that shadowed so many reform sheets, it was time
for the platform, the forum, the newspaper that would preach
all the causes that Victoria had made her own.

The first issue of the new paper came out early in May, 1870,
and was mailed broadcast across the country and distributed
widely in New York City. Titled *Woodhull & Claflin's Weekly*,
it was ambitious both in appearance and content for a mere
campaign sheet. A good-sized, sixteen-page paper, well printed
on excellent stock, it had every appearance of being a strongly
financed, respectable weekly, designed for more than a tem-
porary stay.

"Upward and Onward" was the motto emblazoned under its
masthead.

7 *Upward and Onward!*

BURSTING in among the ladies as self-proclaimed champions
of the cause for which so many others had labored so long,
Victoria and Tennessee might well have met more hostility than
had been shown them by the men on Wall Street. The true
leaders of the women's suffrage movement did not even know
Victoria and Tennie except as sensational lady brokers who
were the subject of much gossip. They might well have offered
some resistance.

But as it happened, the true leaders were too busy to take
much note of Victoria and Tennie's appearance. They were
quarreling among themselves over how much of their effort
should be directed toward the cause of Negro suffrage. One

faction, led by Lucy Stone and Julia Ward Howe, felt that the women should put aside their claims in this, "The Negro's hour," and wait until the freed Negroes had been assured of their votes before again pressing the women's claims. The other group, led by Susan B. Anthony and Elizabeth Cady Stanton, thought the two suffrage fights should be waged together. The conflict on this issue had brought dozens of other differences into the open. Charges and countercharges between the conservatives, who were for concentrating on the Negro fight, and the liberals, who refused to abandon the women's struggle even temporarily, filled most of the public utterances of both groups.

Out over this scene fluttered the new paper, *Woodhull & Claflin's Weekly*. It was supporting a woman as candidate for the Presidency, which was more extreme than anything either the conservatives or the liberals had dreamed of daring. It was supporting women's rights in general and various other causes linked to progress, but it ignored the dissension that was splitting the organized suffragists. And aside from its radical editorial stand, the *Weekly* was filled with lively articles and features of general interest.

Victoria's concern with sex and the doctrines of free love was not manifest in the first issue, unless one could count the first installment of a novel by George Sand, the Frenchwoman who demanded the same freedom for women that men knew, as an oblique gesture in that direction. Articles on legal tender and Egypt's role in history showed Stephen Pearl Andrews' pen at work, but the more extreme of his ideas were also missing. Instead there were items about the achievements of women in various fields. There were book and theater reviews, a chatty fashion column, sports scores, a competent financial column, and a fair number of advertisements.

"Editors receiving this number of the WEEKLY, who, in any manner, notice its contents, will greatly oblige us by sending the paper containing the notices," read a request at the head of the editorial column. Clippings had become an obsession with Victoria and Tennie.

Fifty thousand copies of the first issue were distributed, ac-

cording to report, and soon editors from all over the country
were obliging with notes that must have caused rejoicing among
all who were connected with the enterprise.

"Interesting and agreeable," commented the New York
Herald, which then went on to point a moral for the battling
suffragists. "While the two hostile divisions of women's righters
are passing their time in refusing to coalesce with each other
and in flooding the country with resolutions and chatter, there
are at least two advocates of the woman movement that en-
deavor to show by example and precept that their sex, with
ordinary fair play and industry, can take care of itself. . . . The
example of Woodhull and Claflin is a highly commendable one,
as they do more and talk less than any two divisions of female
agitators put together."

Staying clear of such issues, the New York *Standard* found
the new *Weekly* "a handsome and readable paper." From the
Day, in Philadelphia, came extravagant praise. "It is undoubtedly the ablest journal of its class and can hardly fail of success."
The *Inquirer* of the same city felt women's rights a delicate subject but wrote, "We must confess that the new weekly of Mes-
dames Woodhull & Claflin is one possessing more than ordinary
merits." From Ohio, Illinois, Indiana, Missouri, and all across
the country, came similar comments.

Two small weeklies had been rather feebly representing the
organized women's suffrage movement for several years. *The
Woman's Journal,* published in Boston by the conservative
wing, ignored the new weekly. *The Revolution,* which had
been started by Susan B. Anthony and Elizabeth Cady Stanton,
was the other suffragist paper, but it had fallen on evil days and
was no longer attempting to live up to its fiery title. A small
advertisement for the Woodhull, Claflin brokerage firm had
been running in *The Revolution* for some weeks prior to the
launching of *Woodhull & Claflin's Weekly.* But even this
generous gesture did not cause the editor of the magazine,
Laura Curtis Bullard, to take any notice of the sisters' latest
venture.

Victoria and Tennie were untroubled by this neglect. The

newspapers that counted had saluted them handsomely and life was fuller than it had been so far. The clarence that carried them about the city was kept busy, rattling from 38th Street to the brokerage office on Broad, or the *Weekly* offices at 21 Park Row, and back again.

Fortunately, as with the brokerage office, the sisters had enough help in the background so that they could spend most of their time in a supervisory role, moving about with a "keen, quiet air," and looking businesslike and thoughtful.

Stephen Pearl Andrews was the mainstay of the *Weekly* as one issue followed another and the presses constantly demanded new material. He had boxes and barrels of papers, reams and reams of essays, and if many of the articles already written were too learned for a popular magazine, he was glad to revise them or write new pieces. He did not push unduly for a public airing of his plans for the Pantarchy. Not until the last of July, after the *Weekly* had been building up goodwill for several months, did the Andrews' plan for the human race become part of the *Weekly*'s platform.

Even then, a tasteful column at the head of the editorial page simply listed the "Fundamental Propositions" for which *Woodhull & Claflin's Weekly* stood: "A United States of the World—the Pantarchy; the Universal Church; Universal Home; Universal Science, based on the Nature of Things and the Philosophy of Integration; The Universal Language, Alwato; A Universal Canon of Art;" and finally, "Reconciliation— Harmony of the Race through the Cooperation of the Spirit World, and the Inauguration of the Millennium." Vast as the program was, there was still no attempt to enlarge on it through the rest of the paper, which continued bright and interesting.

Colonel Blood, busy at the brokerage office, was not too busy to write articles from time to time and to help with the proof- reading and editing. There were also Victoria's radical friends and Andrews' disciples, members of the Pantarchy, to provide contributions. There were, in fact, almost too many helpers, too many who were eager to have their voices heard. Thanks to them, the *Weekly* would gradually come to be less crisply focused than it had been in the beginning—a grab bag that included a great amount of nonsense as well as sober philosophizing, reporting and crusading.

Subscriptions arrived in heartening numbers, taking advantage of the yearly rate of $3.00 instead of the single issue price of 10 cents a copy. If there were never enough subscriptions, or advertisements either, to totally finance the paper, that did not trouble Victoria or Tennie. They had their Wall Street earnings to pour into the *Weekly* and it was their joy to do so. Week after week, there they were in print—"We noticed with some amusement the other day . . ." "Looking out of our office windows onto the scene of the 'Change . . ." "As we have always felt and argued . . ." "A mother herself, knowing a mother's cares and hopes . . ."

Wherever they went in the city, they could see copies of their paper on the newsstands, or better yet, people carrying or reading copies. What happier proof could they have had of the importance of all that they noticed, felt, saw and advocated?

Did Victoria and Tennie ever look at each other and wordlessly remember days and years when things had been far different? Did scenes flicker across their memories, scenes of police calling in Cincinnati, or Chicago, suggesting that the Claflins move on? Did Tennessee remember Ottawa, Illinois, and an indictment for manslaughter against her there? Did Victoria remember even farther back, to a night in Homer, Ohio, when her father quietly left town after the mill burned, and then later, the relief of the townspeople when the rest of the family was also on its way out of town? Probably not. Victoria and Tennie both had a great facility for pushing anything they did not want to think about deep into their unconsciousness and for rearranging memories to match whatever was the current reality. And the current reality was the house on Murray Hill, the offices on Broad Street, the ink-smelling rooms on Park Row, and over it all, that printed masthead, week after week, *Woodhull & Claflin's Weekly*, "Upward and Onward!"

Tennessee liked to create little dramas now and then, sometimes with Victoria's help. One night they decided to have a light supper at Delmonico's. The famous restaurant near Wall Street that had brought French cuisine to New Yorkers in the 1830s was so popular with the wealthy and the illustrious that an uptown branch had been opened at Fourteenth Street and Fifth Avenue in the 1860s, with an outdoor cafe, Parisian-style. Victoria and Tennie had dined often at both establishments by this time, but always with male escorts, and both were quite familiar with the rule in most respectable restaurants that ladies without such escorts were not welcomed or served after six o'clock in the evening. They walked into the Fourteenth Street Delmonico's by themselves, even so, and seated themselves at a table. A flustered waiter reminded them of the ruling. They asked to see their friend, the owner. But he too, though he admired the sisters and valued their patronage, was firm. Ladies alone could not be served at this hour. Brushing aside his apologies, Tennie arose, went to the door, opened it and waved to the cabman who was waiting for them in the carriage outside.

"Come down off your box and come in here," she called.

When the red-faced and embarrassed cabman was finally pushed in with his knees under the snowy tablecloth, Tennie ordered. "Tomato soup for three," she said.

Such charades, enacted before the rich and respectable in the name of principle, charmed Tennie. She never lacked an escort when she wanted one, nor was there any limit to the fun, gaiety and sex she could enjoy when those suited her mood. She had her own special gentlemen friends by now among the brokers on Wall Street and among the reporters also. Victoria might admonish her sometimes, that free love as a doctrine kept its dignity only as those who practiced it did, but Tennie found such counsel difficult to follow.

Victoria's dignity was always manifest. She took it to court with her when she was summoned there during the summer by the self-styled Princess Editha Gilbert Montez, who claimed to be the daughter of Lola Montez and the King of Bavaria. The Princess also claimed that she had deposited a ring with three diamonds in it with the lady brokers and had been unable to effect its return when she asked for it.

"I am a broker," Victoria testified, quietly fluttering a Japanese fan. "I know the lady. She came to my office, I think about the time mentioned. She never gave me any jewels or money. I gave her five dollars to pay her board bill, to keep her, as she said, from a house of prostitution. . . . I think the girl never had a diamond or knew what a diamond was."

Buck Claflin had always liked courtroom dramas also, but Victoria's manner of conducting them was far quieter than his.

A note from Elizabeth Cady Stanton arrived that summer of 1870. Mrs. Stanton, an outgoing and friendly woman, seemed not to mind acknowledging the presence on the woman's scene of a new advocate. She had heard the gossip that was general about Victoria's large and irregular household and about Victoria's connections with the spirit-world, particularly Demosthenes. But it was plain from her note that she had also read the *Weekly* and discovered that the paper held views similar in many respects to those of the liberal suffragists, especially their view that the Fourteenth and Fifteenth Amendments to the Constitution, currently being enacted to ensure the Negro franchise, could be interpreted to grant the same right to women.

"Dear Mrs. Woodhull," Mrs. Stanton wrote. "Will you ask Demosthenes if there is any new argument not yet made on the 14th and 15th Amendments that he will bring out through some of us at the coming convention?"

If there was any friendly teasing in the request, Victoria was not the one to catch it. Sensitive as she was to the emotions and feelings of others, she was too serious about herself to recognize any kind of gentle mockery. She considered Mrs. Stanton's question quite gravely, the more so since she, Colonel Blood and Stephen Andrews had already been thinking along somewhat similar lines themselves.

"Upward and Onward"—what could lie upward and onward from the brokerage office, the candidacy for President, the *Weekly?* Victoria and her "cabinet" had been pondering the

matter. They were aware of the efforts that the suffragists had
been making for the past two years to set their views before
Congress. A customary procedure for groups protesting what
was deemed an injustice in legislation was the presentation of
a "Memorial" to Congress. In this, the grievance was outlined
and the petitioner prayed for relief. Just the year before, the
suffragists, meeting for their annual convention in Washington, D.C., had sent such a Memorial to Congress.

"New arguments—not yet made on the 14th and 15th Amendments—that Demosthenes will bring out—through some of us—?"
One can imagine Victoria pondering Mrs. Stanton's note and
wondering why any new argument should be brought out by
"some of them." One can imagine how completely James Blood,
Stephen Andrews and Tennessee agreed. Why should the quarreling, disorganized ladies of the regular association be given
any new arguments? Why should not Victoria, candidate for
President, present a Memorial to Congress herself?

Not long after that, with the good fortune that seemed to
follow her every step these days, Victoria met a member of
Congress. Nor was he just any Congressman, but the very one
she needed—a powerful member of the House Judiciary Committee to which all Memorials were referred—the Honorable
Benjamin F. Butler.

8 *A Startling Annunciation*

VICTORIA, or at least her advisors, kept up with the news.
They were aware that the difficulties of the organized suffragists
had split these ladies into two separate societies by this time,

the conservatives forming the American Woman's Suffrage Association, the liberals organizing as the National Woman's Suffrage Association. Tradition had established that a man should be the titular head of any ladies' organization, so the conservatives had invited the Reverend Henry Ward Beecher to fill that honorific role for them. The liberals had countered by choosing as their titular president Theodore Tilton, who was still an idolator of Beecher but by this time had become a protégé of the great man and his best friend as well. American—National, Beecher—Tilton, the differences seemed of academic interest only in the house on 38th Street.

Beecher—Tilton. The story that would bracket those two names in scandal more firmly than they had ever been united in friendship was still known only to a few people. It was just a few weeks since Tilton himself had heard from his distracted and contrite wife, Elizabeth, the confession that for the past two years she and the Reverend Mr. Beecher had been lovers.

Elizabeth Richards Tilton—often called Lib—was a small, birdlike woman with great, dark eyes, and she had been an admirer of Beecher even longer than Theodore, a member of the Plymouth Church Sunday School when she was ten and a friend of one of Beecher's daughters. The Reverend Mr. Beecher had officiated at the wedding of tall, golden-haired Tilton and tiny, dark-haired Elizabeth in 1855 and declared them "one of the finest pairs I ever married."

Beecher had become the household angel of the young couple after that, guiding and guarding them like a father or older brother. He had obtained for the talented Theodore an editorial position on the popular religious magazine of which he was editor, the *Independent*. He had beamed, sympathized and counseled as the children were born, officiated at their christenings and gamboled with them in their playtimes. There was, it seemed, as much that the Tiltons, in their rambling, comfortable, cozy-nooked house at 174 Livingstone Street in Brooklyn, could offer Beecher as he could offer them. An emotional man, with seeking eyes and a full, sensual mouth, Beecher found little response to his passionate enthusiasms and love of life at home. His wife, Eunice, known to most Plymouth Church parishioners as "The Griffin," was a cool, discouraging woman, rigidly devoted to duty and appearances. In the Tilton home, Beecher could relax, play, shine and be adored.

Tilton's career had advanced. He had doubled and tripled the circulation of the *Independent*. He took on lecturing engagements as well, touring the country from fall to spring, and as he left Lib lonely at home while he traveled, he begged Beecher, his pastor and friend, not to forget Elizabeth in his pastoral visitations. "There is one little woman down at my house who loves you more than you have an idea of," he told Beecher. So Beecher made a point of visiting frequently at the Tilton house.

That emotions were rising that might soon get out of hand might have been obvious to Theodore from some of the letters that Elizabeth wrote to him. Both had a habit of examining and analyzing their feelings and actions from a soulful point of view in the same way that later generations would examine and analyze using Freudian theories as a guideline. "My beloved," Lib wrote to Theodore in one letter. "I have been thinking of my love for Mr. B. considerably of late, and those thoughts you shall have. . . . Now, I think I have lived a richer, happier life since I have known him. And have you not loved me more ardently since you saw another high nature appreciated me?" In another letter she wrote, "Mr. B. called Saturday. He came tired and gloomy, but he said I had the most calming and peaceful influence over him. I believe he loves you. We talked of you. He . . . said as he went out, 'What a pretty house this is.' " And again, later, "Oh, how my soul yearns over you two dear men! I commit you both to God's love. . . . I do love him dearly, and I love you supremely, utterly, believe it."

She wrote a great deal more in the same vein in 1867 and 1868, and Theodore should not have been stunned with incredulity when, on the sultry night of July 3, 1870, Lib came home from a visit to the country expressly to make her confession. But he had fought against guessing what had happened for so long, he had analyzed and struggled against jealousy so fervently that perhaps he felt that he had finally triumphed over the situation and could dismiss it. Then Lib brought it all out into the open. Quiet and tragic as the figure of Grief on a monument, Lib told Theodore how the greater intimacy had come about. Mr. Beecher had assured her over and over that he and she shared a divine and valid love, and that a full expression of it was as proper as a handshake or a kiss. How could she help succumbing to the authority of such a "great and holy man" as she considered Mr. Beecher to be? But the "necessary deceit of concealment" had preyed on her mind. That very spring she had definitely and finally ended their intimacies. Now that every illicit aspect of the relationship was over, she begged Theodore to forgive her. She begged him also to forgive Mr. Beecher, and to say nothing to anybody about what had happened—to forget it as though it had never been.

Rising to the occasion, Theodore had promised what she wished. He would do his best to condone what she had done and try to restore her "wounded spirit." But soon he had found the promise impossible to keep.

Jealousy tortured him as he brooded on the double betrayal by his delicate, romantic wife and the preacher who had been "man of all men" to him, a man he had "loved as well as I ever loved a woman." At last he told the whole story to his employer, Henry Bowen, the owner and publisher of the *Independent.* Bowen was hardly the best confidant Tilton could have chosen, for Bowen had heard a confession from his wife, ten years before, when she lay on her deathbed, that was remarkably similar to the one Lib had made to Theodore. But Bowen, being one of the founders of Plymouth Church, with a large financial investment in it, had swallowed his outrage and taken no action against Beecher, on whom the whole success of the church rested. Bowen advised Tilton to pursue a similar course.

Tilton found the advice as impossible as the promise. One night in August he had dinner in New York with Elizabeth Cady Stanton, an old friend whose views on the women's movement he had long publicized in the *Independent.* Before the

meal was over, he was pouring out the whole story and expressing some of his bitterness against Beecher. "Oh, that the damned
lecherous scoundrel should have defiled my bed ... and at the
same time professed to be my best friend."

Returning home to Brooklyn, overkeyed from that recital,
Tilton found Susan Anthony, another longtime friend, spending
the night at his house with Lib. Again the whole story came
out, this time amid scenes of domestic hysteria, with Lib accusing him of infidelities while on his travels, and then locking
herself in her room with Susan Anthony guarding the door.

Mrs. Stanton and Miss Anthony, meeting together later,
compared the stories they had heard. Somehow, neither seemed
inclined to doubt Lib Tilton's story. All that they knew of
Beecher made it easy enough for them to believe that he had
seduced Lib as she claimed. Still, both were very much aware of
the damage that would be done should the story gain any general circulation. Both had counseled Theodore to forswear any
more confidences. Now both promised each other that the
story would not go any further through either of them.

But for all the good advice he received, Tilton could not
keep silent. Beecher-Tilton, Beecher-Tilton, the bracketing of
the names in whispered scandal was beginning, as the story
slowly, fatefully, uncoiled.

No word of it had reached the house on 38th Street, however.
When the decision was made that it was time for the *Weekly*
to become more forthright about sexual hypocrisy, the target
that was chosen was prostitution, or "The Social Evil."

Prostitution was, of course, a popular subject with all the
city's ministers, including Beecher, who loved to decry the
"painted women, whores and Jezebels" of the city, implying
that all evil would end if they simply went away. The editors
of the *Weekly* were, naturally, flinging themselves against this
conventional approach, defending the women whom the clergy-
men attacked and showing them as victims.

The discussion of prostitution in the *Weekly* asked who
benefited from conditions as they existed, who owned the

houses that were leased for prostitution, and what highly placed citizens, even what churches, owed much of their income to such holdings. A wealth of homely and precise detail showed how little the women within the houses profited from the trade in pleasure. There were approximate figures as to how much the women had to pay for board in the houses where they worked, how much for wine, how much for freedom from police interference, and how much more, in comparison, they had to pay in police fines when their houses were "pulled" as disorderly, than the men who were found with them.

A few recommendations concluded the survey: that prostitutes and houses of prostitution be licensed to make them independent of the police and that there be "weekly visits from medical men to each girl, as in Europe." It was emphasized that the *Weekly* did not mean to suggest authorizing sin by statute with these recommendations, but "prostitution exists and will exist so long as society maintains its present ideas and organization. As it cannot be extinguished, its evils should be palliated."

Crisp and factual, the article pleased the radicals who made up most of the *Weekly*'s readership and held gratifying information for those who read the paper from curiosity. Victoria felt a new sense of power and decided to supplant the moderate inspiration of the motto "Upward and Onward" with a more dramatic billboard. By September, the masthead read, "Don't Fail to Read the Lady Brokers' Paper! The Organ of the Most Advanced Thought and Purpose in the World!"

The Honorable Benjamin F. Butler, Representative to Congress from Massachusetts, was a man quite in sympathy with "advanced thought." Short, stocky, almost gnomelike, Butler had won several distinctions during the war, in which he had served as a general, due to his free thinking and impetuosity. In New Orleans, where he was military commander of the city after the Union occupation, he did not like the way the ladies of the city showed their contempt for the Federal troops. He ordered that any woman guilty of insulting a soldier be treated forthwith as a "woman of the streets." For this, the New Orleans ladies nicknamed him "Beast" Butler and knew how right they had been when another story was told. Some Southern women had turned their backs as he passed and he had remarked, "They know which end of them looks best."

"Contraband" was another word associated with Butler, and that one dated from the early years of the war when he took it on himself to declare that all the Negroes in territories he captured were free because they were "contraband of war." Lincoln had censured Butler for exceeding his authority in this order, but abolitionists across the North had cheered and never forgotten his bold stand.

Sympathetic with the women's rights movement, an advocate, like Colonel Blood, of paper money, as ready for a scrap in Congress as he had been in the army, Benjamin Butler wound up quite logically one evening, on one of his visits to New York, among the free-thinkers who gathered nightly around Victoria, Tennessee, Colonel Blood and Stephen Pearl Andrews.

He must have been pleased by Victoria. Beautiful, pale and cool to look upon, she was as slashing and dashing in her pursuit of what she wanted as he—lady broker, lady editor, self-proclaimed candidate for President, all within less than a year. To help her in yet another unprecedented move was just the sort of challenge to appeal to him.

"... ask Demosthenes if there is not any new argument on the 14th and 15th Amendments," Mrs. Stanton had written.

Later, Victoria would always say that it had been Demosthenes who inspired her. Ben Butler, who saw no need to mention Victoria in his autobiography, would never dispute the story. But he was a lawyer by profession, shrewd in argument as even the learned Stephen Pearl Andrews was not. All the gossip of the day credited Butler with drafting what Victoria wanted to say to Congress. And all of Butler's reactions later showed more than an idle interest in "a new argument" on women's right to vote.

The *Weekly* continued to emphasize "advanced thought." Sex was again being featured in September, but this time, with

Stephen Pearl Andrews explaining one of his pet theories, "stirpiculture," or the scientific propagation of human beings, the subject was more tedious than inflammatory.

More excitingly, the veils of hypocrisy that shrouded the business and political worlds were being threatened at last. "We entered upon the 'walks of money,' 'change,' to do a legitimate business. . . . We discovered . . . frauds. . . . We have employed the ablest detective talent . . . and we are prepared with the names of each party . . . the amounts of bonds and shares in many cases which gratuitously and dishonestly went to each banker, congressman and state legislator. . . . We shall not hesitate to give names, acts, transactions. . . ." Colonel Blood was probably the writer of this article, which was duly followed by other articles which did indeed give "names, acts, transactions"—perhaps not of the most famous or well-known bankers and legislators but certainly of real people.

Another new motto was blazoned on the masthead of the *Weekly* in October: "Progress! Free Thought! Untrammelled Lives! Breaking the Ground for Future Generations!"

A clear hint of how some new ground was about to be broken came in November. In an article headed "Startling Annunciation," Victoria presented to her readers a résumé of the legal arguments designed to prove that the 14th and 15th Amendments, written to enfranchise the Negro, gave the vote to women also. The language of the amendments, the article pointed out, directed that all "persons" born or naturalized in the United States were citizens with all of a citizen's rights. Surely women were persons, the article declared, and could claim all the rights pertaining to persons.

Note was taken of the "Annunciation" by the *Commercial Advertiser,* which blasted it with heavy sarcasm. However, if any of the ladies of the organized suffrage groups, either conservative or liberal, read the article, they seem to have drawn no conclusions about Victoria's next step.

Unnoticed by the suffragists, Victoria traveled to Washington, D.C., in December, to proffer to Congress her Memorial—the Memorial inspired by Demosthenes, encouraged by Stephen

Pearl Andrews and Colonel Blood and almost certainly written by Benjamin Butler. The same Benjamin Butler made everything easy once Victoria arrived in the capital. "The Memorial of Victoria C. Woodhull," duly printed, was presented to the Senate on December 22, 1870 by Senator John Spafford Harris of Louisiana, and to the House of Representatives by Representative George Washington Julian of Indiana, who asked that the petition be referred to the Committee of the Judiciary. "No objection was made and it was so ordered."

And still the ladies of the organized societies paid no attention. The liberals of the National Woman's Suffrage Association were planning their usual January convention in Washington. Susan Anthony, who generally organized such meetings, was off on a lecture tour. Mrs. Stanton was apathetic about such executive chores and so the responsibility was passed on to Isabella Beecher Hooker. (Isabella, half sister of the Reverend Henry Ward Beecher, who sponsored the American group, could almost always be found in an opposite camp from him.) Mrs. Hooker was aware of the need to focus on the 14th and 15th Amendments and began planning a convention that would study and discuss their bearing on the women's cause. She sent out invitations to various distinguished men and women to come and address the gathering.

Then, to Isabella Hooker's dismay, regrets and refusals began to come in. Some of the refusals were understandable but some were not. Isabella, knowing nothing of the ever-more-complicated hells which Theodore Tilton and his wife were building for themselves because of Lib's confession, was baffled when Theodore, titular head of the association, sent regrets. Finally, in a panic, she wrote to Susan Anthony. Soon Miss Anthony had traveled across half a dozen states to come to Isabella's rescue and with her at the helm plans were whipped into shape. Speakers were found and the convention was scheduled to begin on the morning of January 11.

Not until January 10, the day before the scheduled opening, did the absorbed ladies have a hint of the surprise Victoria had in store for them. They read of it in the Washington papers, their eyes blinking, their faces sagging.

Victoria C. Woodhull, famed lady broker and editor of *Woodhull & Claflin's Weekly,* was going to address the House Judiciary Committee *personally* on the subject of her Memorial on the morning of January 11.

A personal appearance before a Congressional Committee was an official recognition by Congress that no woman had ever received before. If the Honorable B. F. Butler, of the Judiciary Committee, had made it possible—if the mordant humor of the same Representative from Massachusetts had found it amusing to schedule this unprecedented appearance for the very time of the opening of the National Woman's Suffrage Association Convention—no word of that found its way into print.

Distracted, the convention planners ran about crying out to each other. How had Victoria Woodhull, of all people, achieved such an honor? How had she connived to have the hearing set for the very time when their convention was to open? All the gossip they had ever heard about her and Tennie C. came bubbling out. Victoria and Tennie inspired none of the protective sympathy which the ladies were wont to offer "erring sisters," for they flaunted their disdain for any standards that would find them "erring." Everyone had heard whispers about Tennie's relations with Commodore Vanderbilt, and of Victoria's living in the same house with two husbands. Everyone had heard that she believed in free love and the corollary gossip that the house on 38th Street was the scene of all sorts of orgies.

Susan Anthony's voice cut across the clamor. She suggested that they all attend the committee hearing to find out for themselves what Victoria Woodhull was going to say.

Isabella Hooker, her handsome face flushed with emotion, rejected the idea. Other ladies joined her. To associate in any manner with such women as Victoria C. Woodhull and Tennessee Claflin was unthinkable.

However, Isabella was a house guest while in Washington of Senator Samuel Clarke Pomeroy of Kansas. The Senator, apprised of the situation, reasoned with the overwrought woman.

"This is not politics," he told her. "Men could never work in a political party if they stopped to investigate each member's antecedents and associates. If you are going into a fight, you must accept every help that offers."

The Senator's advice combined with that of Susan Anthony finally prevailed. The ladies decided to postpone the opening of their convention until the afternoon and to attend the hearing in the morning.

Susan Anthony, Isabella Hooker and Pauline Wright Davis, another NWSA leader, had an acquaintance of their own on the Judiciary Committee, the Honorable A. G. Riddle. Mr. Riddle escorted the ladies to the Capitol the next morning and through its marble corridors to the antechamber of the hearing room. There, amid the Congressmen assembling for the hearing, the ladies had their first sight of the notorious sisters, Victoria Woodhull and Tennie C. Claflin.

The sight was a shock to them all. The sisters were not distinguishable from ladies. Both wore plain, dark street costumes. Victoria's brown hair, cut short, curled out from under a neat Alpine hat. Her only ornament was a rose. She was pale and looked frightened.

Still, the reluctant ladies of the delegation murmured among themselves. And later, Victoria would remember that it was here, in the antechamber, that she had her first hint of a scandal involving the Reverend Henry Ward Beecher.

Someone near Victoria spoke of having overheard Isabella Beecher Hooker say that she intended to snub Victoria Woodhull. "Instantly," according to Victoria's later account, "a gentleman . . . stepped forward and said: 'It would ill become these women, and especially a Beecher, to talk of antecedents or to cast any smirch on Mrs. Woodhull, for I am reliably assured that Henry Ward Beecher preaches to at least twenty of his mistresses every Sunday.'" Victoria would remember that this remark seemed to have "a subduing effect" on the ladies.

At the time, however, her mind was on the impending ordeal of her speech and she paid little heed. Victoria and Tennie C. were ushered into the hearing room. The ladies of the delegation and the committee members also entered and took seats. The hearing began. The visiting petitioner was introduced. Victoria rose to speak.

9 ❦ *Your Memorialist* ...

HER voice was so low it could hardly be heard as she began to read her "Further Argument in Support of Victoria C. Woodhull's Memorial." She had shown no timidity when confronting the giants of Wall Street as the nation's first lady broker. In the *Weekly,* she had boldly threatened to expose the frauds of "banker, congressman, legislator." But perhaps there was something awe-inspiring even for Victoria in standing before a committee of the highest law-making body in the land. Perhaps the presence of the ladies whom she had bypassed in her rush toward leadership added to her confusion.

Almost inaudibly, she worked through the preliminaries to her argument. Then, gradually, her thesis became clearer and more dramatic. "Women, white and black, belong to races; although to different races. A race of people comprises all the people, male and female. The right to vote cannot be denied on account of race. . . . With the right to vote sex has nothing to do."

Her voice strengthened. She began to be caught up by the sense of what she was saying and as always in such a case, her cheeks flushed, her eyes began to shine. The Honorable Benjamin Butler, sitting at the head of the table, must have relaxed. Glancing around him, he could see the committee members looking more attentive. The ladies had lost their grudging attitudes and were listening carefully. The argument was sharp and precise and Victoria was presenting it perfectly, neither hurrying nor hesitating, but speaking with just enough suppressed passion to emphasize the intensity of her conviction.

She concluded with a plea to the committee that it recommend to Congress that the existing laws be clarified in women's favor. If there was no applause when she finished, there was instead that beat before a general rustling that spoke of an audience even more surely held. Susan Anthony, forthright as always, turned toward Butler.

"Now I wish, General Butler, that you would say 'contraband' for us."

There was laughter. Then the Honorable A. G. Riddle rose to assure the Memorialist, Mrs. Woodhull, that the committee would take her petition under close consideration and make a report on it as soon as possible. The meeting was adjourned.

The committee members clustered around Victoria to compliment and congratulate her. But the behavior of the ladies was more remarkable. They pushed their way to her side, their faces aglow with enthusiasm and admiration. They babbled their praise, their gratitude, their excitement. Out in the antechamber, more women waited—delegates to the postponed convention. The ladies coming out of the hearing room informed those who were waiting of what had happened. The greatest step forward in the history of the women's movement had just been made, they declared, and Mrs. Woodhull had made it. The newcomers rushed to surround Victoria, exclaiming, wondering and admiring in their turn.

In a wave of excitement, the ladies swept Victoria, and Tennie with her, along to a hurried lunch and then to the opening of the convention at Lincoln Hall. There was no dissension among them and no doubt.

The hall was crowded. On the platform sat the notables who had finally gathered for the occasion: several Senators; the Negro leader, Frederick Douglass; various officers and leaders of the society. Susan Anthony and Isabella Hooker mounted the steps of the platform. Between them walked Victoria and Tennie C. The two sisters were seated among the foremost of the notables.

After the briefest preliminaries to open the meeting, Mrs. Hooker told the assemblage of the events of the morning, of Mrs. Woodhull's argument before the Congressional committee and of the impression she had made. Mrs. Woodhull, she said, had been prevailed upon to repeat her remarks for the convention and although it was her first attempt at public speaking, her heart was so completely in the movement that she had agreed to do her best. Isabella turned to beckon to Victoria.

Once again Victoria was pale. Her hesitation was such that Isabella had to take her arm to lead her forward on the platform. Once again her voice was low and trembled as she began to speak. Then, just as in the morning, it strengthened and became compelling.

There were few in the hall who had not heard some scandalized whispering about Mrs. Woodhull. But as she spoke on and on, her voice clear and ringing, the gossip seemed of less importance. It faded out of consciousness. Never before had there been an argument which seemed to prove so inexorably that women already had the right to vote and that all that was needed was implementation of the right.

Applause swept the hall as Victoria finished. Then, in a sort of mass enthusiasm that had rarely gripped the women before, the discussions, panels and resolutions that had been planned for the convention were canceled. That sort of study was no longer needed. Victoria had made it pointless. It was time for action.

Resolutions were hastily drawn up, proposed and adopted, to reinforce the Woodhull Memorial with a request to Congress from the association that the true meaning of the 14th and 15th Amendments be clarified. Even more aggressively, it was resolved to make it "the duty of American women ... to apply for registration ... and in all cases where they fail to secure it to see that suits be instituted."

When the convention was finally adjourned many delegates were startled to realize how far they had gone so quickly. But everyone was sure that the whole struggle had passed a milestone and was entering a new and triumphant phase.

Principles! It had taken Victoria years to find them, but once she had them it seemed there was no limit to what she could achieve.

The press in Washington, in New York, and then across the country, headlined Victoria's triumph before the Judiciary Committee. "Other speeches were made," reported the New York *Herald,* "but Mrs. Woodhull had captured the committee, and the others were not needed."

"This is the bravest and best movement that the women have yet made," declared the *Commercial Advertiser,* recently so cool to Victoria's "Annunciation." The *Star* wrote: "The National Woman's Suffrage Convention, sitting this time at Washington, has had the wind completely taken out of its sails by that lively little yacht, Mrs. Woodhull."

"A lively little yacht" she may have seemed to the *Star* correspondent, but a reporter for the Philadelphia *Press* painted another picture. "Mrs. Woodhull sat sphynx-like during the convention. General Grant himself might learn a lesson of silence from the pale, sad face of this unflinching woman. . . . She reminds one of the forces of nature behind the storm, or a small splinter of the indestructible."

Victoria probably preferred that description, "pale, sad . . . unflinching." To the "keen, quiet air" of a businesswoman, she was now adding the gravity of one who had suffered much in the pursuit of principle.

Woodhull & Claflin's Weekly reported the activities in Washington fulsomely, but there was no note of jubilation or boasting. The tone was earnest and firm, as of a determined leader addressing many people embarked on a high mission.

An extravagant new banner in tortuously ornamented type dominated the first page of the *Weekly.* "The Cosmo-Political Party," it read. "Nomination for President of the U.S.A. in 1872—Victoria C. Woodhull." But aware now that she could take the women with her, Victoria also added, "Subject to ratification of national convention."

There were some headlines for Tennie in the *Weekly* too. A Memorial had been prepared for her and duly submitted to the state legislature. The matter was fully chronicled although Tennie made no speech. But it was Victoria who was winning headlines now from the official paper of the National Woman's Suffrage Association, *The Revolution*. Its editor praised "The Woodhull Memorial," and urged women everywhere to follow the new line of action advocated by Mrs. Woodhull.

Repercussions were bound to follow. Many members of the NWSA across the country who had not been present at the convention read that the association was taking its direction from Mrs. Woodhull and were astounded. All they knew of Victoria Woodhull was that she was a notorious lady broker. Many men who had been irritated by the women's movement from its inception found in Victoria's elevation a perfect focus for their displeasure. They made their opinions known in articles, letters to the editors of various newspapers and letters to the association.

The conservative ladies of the American Woman's Suffrage Association naturally found the National's adoption of Victoria Woodhull the strongest evidence yet of the irresponsible, radical tendencies of the liberals. Vocally and in print, they decried the menace that women of Victoria's type were to the cause and they repeated and elaborated on the facts that were known about her life and Tennie's.

Against this storm of criticism, the spell that Victoria had woven over the leaders she had met in Washington held fast. Isabella Hooker was as emotional in her acceptance of Victoria once she knew her as she had previously been in her rejection. She defended her passionately against all attacks and wrote her letters pulsing with the sentimental hyperboles currently in vogue. "My Darling Queen," Isabella addressed Victoria, along with other equally extreme salutations.

Elizabeth Cady Stanton had not been present at the convention and still had not met Victoria. But she was willing to take

Susan Anthony's word for her, and as the attacks against Victoria continued, Mrs. Stanton was impelled to a public defense of her.

"When the men who make laws for us in Washington can stand forth and declare themselves pure and unspotted from all the sins mentioned in the Decalogue, then we will demand that every woman who makes a Constitutional argument on our platform shall be as chaste as Diana. . . .

"We have had enough women sacrificed to this sentimental, hypocritical prating about purity. . . . This is one of man's most effective engines for our division and subjugation. He creates the public sentiment, builds the gallows, and then makes us hangmen for our sex. We have crucified the Mary Wollstonecrafts, the Fanny Wrights, the George Sands, the Fanny Kembles, of all ages. . . . Let us end this ignoble record. . . . If Victoria Woodhull must be crucified, let men drive the spikes and plait the crown of thorns."

Susan B. Anthony spoke out firmly also, declaring that Victoria Woodhull had youth, beauty, money and an argument of which all women could be proud. Back on her lecture tour, Miss Anthony showed how highly she valued that argument by using the Woodhull Memorial as the basis for a brand-new lecture, "The New Situation."

The Judiciary Committee's report on the Woodhull Memorial came at the end of January. It was a blow to those who had hoped that Victoria had completely convinced the committee, for it was an adverse report, holding that Congress did not have the power to act in clarifying the 14th and 15th Amendments as the petitioner had prayed. The blow was softened, however, by the minority report that was published at the same time, signed by the two dissenting members of the committee, Benjamin Butler and William Loughridge of Iowa. The minority report, lengthily and carefully reasoned, was one of the strongest official arguments to date in favor of women's rights under the Constitution.

"Bravo, my dear Woodhull," wrote Susan Anthony from the

Middle West. "Your letter is here. . . . Glorious old Ben! He is surely going to pronounce the word that will settle the woman question, just as he did the word 'contraband' that so summarily settled the Negro question. . . . Go ahead, bright, glorious, young and strong spirit, and believe in the best love and hope and faith of S. B. Anthony."

Victoria did not need the encouragement. She was going ahead, as swiftly and steadily as possible. She made her first scheduled public address in February, in Washington, D.C. She and Isabella Beecher Hooker were presumably to present an argument which they had been refused permission to deliver to the entire House of Representatives. Actually, Victoria did most of the speaking and got all of the notice. On the platform were many notables, among them Victoria's private advisor, Ben Butler, "looking extremely happy," according to a newspaper report.

That Demosthenes, the orator, was Victoria's spirit-guide was beginning at last to assume its full prophetic proportions. After the same sort of nervous opening that had marked her previous speaking ventures, Victoria "became warmed to her subject, much of the fire of her ordinary conversation returned, her face flushed, and she was herself," wrote the Washington *Chronicle.* "The lecture was a triumph, and she demonstrated that, with a little experience, Mrs. Woodhull will be as strong upon the rostrum as she is with the pen."

"As strong?" Two weeks later, she was back in New York, giving the same address to an overflowing crowd at Cooper Union. "Loudly cheered as she left the stage," "literally covered with bouquets as she made her exit," and with a sheaf of clippings the next day all reporting the same sort of enthusiasm, Victoria was not only embarked on another phase of her career but had found the one in which her truest talents lay. Two weeks later, she was in Philadelphia, again giving her Constitution speech and again winning such applause that if "the audience did not endorse her sentiments, at least it demonstrated how doubly potent is genius when wielded by lovely woman."

The *Weekly*, appearing regularly, devoted more and more space to the woman's movement and to Victoria's speeches for the cause. Stephen Pearl Andrews was also beginning to enlarge on his plans for the Pantarchy, but curious as some of the details were, most readers seemed to take them in stride. "Read your journal with great pleasure," Mrs. Stanton wrote to Victoria. "It is the ablest woman's journal we have had yet."

The brokerage office carried on, thanks to Colonel Blood's devotion, and it was well for the other activities that it did, for it supported them all. Victoria found time to stop at the offices now and then. Once again she was summoned to court by a disgruntled investor. Once again she testified quietly. "I am a broker. . . . I know the lady. . . . I told her I would guard her money as my own, but I did not guarantee her against loss." The case was dismissed.

Further invitations to lecture began to arrive and it was clear that Victoria needed a new speech. Stephen Pearl Andrews welcomed the opportunity to branch out into other fields that interested him and chose the theme of capital and labor for the new address. Victoria delivered it first at the Mercantile Library and then at Cooper Union. If the crowds that were on hand for each appearance had not really expected a discourse on labor from Mrs. Woodhull, still they were won to enthusiasm by her increasingly magnetic platform presence.

But with each new increase in Victoria's fame, each new notice, article or report on her activities, the hostility of those who had not seen her or heard her in person was growing.

May was approaching, May, the month that was celebrated during the nineteenth century in both America and England as an "anniversary month," the occasion for the annual meetings of all kinds of church and reform organizations, missionary societies, temperance groups and women's rights groups. Both the conservative American association and the liberal National group were planning meetings in New York at the same time. Risking the disapproval of many members, the leaders of the National Association invited Victoria Woodhull to give one of the main addresses at their convention. Hearing this news, the ladies of the American group determined that some sort of protest had to be made. And everywhere, righteous, respectable women felt stirrings of alarm and asked themselves what the women's movement was all about if someone like Victoria Woodhull could lead even one wing of it.

At last Victoria's rush to fame, which had followed a charmed trajectory so far, was taking her into dangerous territory. One of those righteous, respectable women had a voice—and a pen— even more compelling than her own.

10 § *Rumors of an Awful Scandal...*

THERE must have been times during the later half of the nineteenth century when most Americans felt that there was a Beecher wherever one turned. Lyman Beecher, who had spread his gospel in the first half of the century, had sired eleven sons and daughters, of whom nine were still living in the 1870s. All but one of these were public figures one way or another. And they managed among them, except for the quiet one, to hold about as many different opinions within God-fearing limits, as were generally allowable among the respectable.

Isabella Beecher Hooker, one of the youngest of Lyman's children, and by now Victoria's ardent admirer, was the most extreme in the radicalism of her views. Catherine Beecher, the oldest child, was equally extreme in her conservatism. A spinster in her sixties, Catherine had fought some revolutionary battles in the past for such causes as female education and the right of females to teach boys in the primary grades, but she was angrily opposed to the woman suffrage movement and loathed such a representative of the "new woman" as Victoria Woodhull. Preacher sons Edward, William, James and Thomas held varying positions between those of Isabella and Catherine. One daughter, Mary Beecher Perkins, a contented wife and mother, eschewed public utterance and presided quietly over her household in Hartford, Connecticut.

Henry Ward Beecher and Harriet Beecher Stowe who were, of course, the best known of all, were the most middle-of-the-road, managing to stay just a little left of center most of the time, abreast of all that was new but never dangerously radical. Henry's sermons against slavery before the war had been passionate and sincere. He had aroused immense antislavery sympathy with his slave-auctions from the Plymouth Church pulpit and helped the antislavery cause in many ways. But he did not become an outright abolitionist until the last moment, and even then, not a radical, fire-eating one. Harriet, too, in spite of her book, which was such a potent antislavery weapon, was not really an abolitionist until war broke out. Their sentiments about the woman question were equally informed but moderate, Henry's perhaps more liberal than Harriet's. He was in favor of women having the vote but allied himself with the conservatives, who moved slowly. Now and then, when preaching on sin in the city, he had taken notice of the notorious sisters, Victoria Woodhull and Tennie Claflin, indicating he did not believe they helped the women's cause, but he had never launched any full-scale attack on them either.

Harriet was also in sympathy with the conservative suffragists (though she never officially joined them) but was much more vocal than Henry in her disapproval of Victoria and Tennessee, frequently making sharp comments about Victoria, in particular, in the column that she wrote for a new religious paper, the *Christian Union*.

It was an odd time for Harriet Beecher Stowe to start such an offensive against anybody, for she had just emerged from a nasty scandal herself, brought on by her own unexpected excursion into the field of sexual revelations. The success of

Victoria C. Woodhull, 1838-1927

Tennie C. (Tennessee) Claflin, wearing the mannish attire she sometimes affected.

Roxanna Hummel Claflin

Rubin Buckman Claflin

Commodore Vanderbilt
(Courtesy The New-York Historical Society)

Colonel James H. Blood
(Courtesy Emanie Sachs)

Stephen Pearl Andrews
(Courtesy The New-York Historical Society)

Theodore Tilton
(Courtesy
The New-York Historical Society)

Henry Ward Beecher
(Courtesy
The New-York Historical Society)

"GET THEE BEHIND ME, (MRS.) SATAN!"—[See Page 143.]
WIFE (with heavy burden). "I'D RATHER TRAVEL THE HARDEST PATH OF MATRIMONY THAN FOLLOW YOUR FOOTSTEPS."

The famous "Mrs. Satan" cartoon by Thomas Nast, which appeared in *Harper's Weekly,* February 17, 1872.

(Courtesy The New-York Historical Society)

Front page of the Weekly, announcing Victoria's candidacy for the Presidency. *(Courtesy The New-York Historical Society)*

The "Bewitching Brokers" transacting business in their office in Broad Street.

THE WALL STREET HIPPODROME.

HOW TO MANAGE A BALKY TEAM.

Victoria and Tennessee controlling the Bulls and Bears of Wall Street—a cartoon in the New York *Evening Telegraph,* February 18, 1870.

Victoria and Tennessee consulting with their lawyer in Ludlow Street Jail.

Victoria and Zulu Maud in the garden of their home at Bredon's Norton, England.

Victoria as Mrs. John Biddulph Martin

Tennessee as Lady Cook, Viscountess of Monserrat

Uncle Tom's Cabin had taken her to England in the 1850s. In England she had met and been wholly dazzled by Lady Byron, the widow of the poet. Lady Byron had confided in Harriet the reason why she and the poet had separated so soon after their marriage. The secret had lurked in Harriet's heart after that, until finally, after Lady Byron's death, she decided that it was her mission to vindicate Lady Byron's memory. She had not been a cold, hardhearted woman who could not understand the rebellious poet. She had left Byron because he had committed incest with his half sister. This was a revelation no one wanted to hear, either in America or England, where Mrs. Stowe's writing on the subject was also published. It was doubly horrifying to hear such an accusation from someone like Mrs. Stowe. The storm of criticism that had broken about the head of the once-beloved Harriet Beecher Stowe had been frightful.

Perhaps Mrs. Stowe was subconsciously trying to shore up her own reputation for unblemished morality with her attacks on Victoria Woodhull. Trying to recapture her popularity, she was also writing a new novel which was appearing serially in the *Christian Union*. A romantic comedy, titled *My Wife and I,* it reflected some of the fads and foibles of fashionable New York, but its main theme was the woman question. One character, the heroine's sister, was earnestly trying to prepare herself for a career, and this gave Mrs. Stowe an opportunity to express her views on the subject of women's rights. She approved of the character who hoped for a profession and made clear her belief that more avenues for self-support should be opened to women. Perhaps someday, when they were educated to it, they should have the vote as well. But there was no doubt that Mrs. Stowe believed women's finest roles would always lie in the home.

Mrs. Stowe refrained from criticizing those who held more radical views as she dramatized her own beliefs. She chose to laugh at them instead and presented as one of her dramatis personae, an extreme example of a "new woman," whom she called Audacia Dangyereyes. Laughing, slangy, impudent, apt to throw herself onto a man's lap and ask him up to her rooms "for a smoke," Audacia might well have been a caricature of Tennie in her livelier moments. Most readers, however, who had heard far more about Victoria's activities, quickly identified the character as a portrait of her.

The worst of it, so far as Victoria was concerned, was that Audacia Dangyereyes was a truly comic character. Mrs. Stowe was repairing her damaged reputation very nicely with this gay, mocking novel. The *Christian Union* doubled its circulation as the serial ran on, month after month. And readers everywhere were laughing at the absurd and dreadful Audacia.

Victoria could not escape knowing that it was she who was being laughed at. She hated it. Her own picture of herself was clear. Looking in the mirror, she would always see "the pale, sad face of this unflinching woman ... one of the forces of nature ... a splinter of the indestructible." She could bear the thought of being crucified, as the "Mary Wollstonecrafts, the Fanny Wrights, the George Sands ... of all ages" had been crucified. But to be caricatured as silly was not the kind of crucifixion she had in mind.

It was just then, while Victoria was feeling the sting of Harriet Beecher Stowe's mockery, that she first began to hear details that clarified the mysterious remarks made in Washington, in the antechamber of the Congressional hearing room. "It ill behooves a Beecher ... to cast a smirch on Mrs. Woodhull."

Pauline Wright Davis, Victoria's friend since that day of the hearing, had long been a friend of Elizabeth Tilton. She spent an afternoon with Lib about this time and afterwards visited Victoria. Mrs. Davis was full of what she had seen of Lib Tilton's unhappiness and told Victoria the whole Beecher-Tilton tale.

Just an ordinary story of adultery, really, except for two fatal elements. The accused adulterer was one of the most famous men in America, a hero in the country's noblest moments, a stainless knight of Christ in the public mind. And neither Theodore Tilton nor his wife could let what was past be bygone. Almost a year after Lib's confession, Theodore was still dwelling on the subject so obsessively that his life revolved around it. He had finally accused Beecher of adultery. Beecher had first denied the charge, then practically confessed in a "letter of contrition," then denied it again. Bowen had fired Theodore as editor of the *Independent* and Theodore had threatened reprisals. Mutual friends, chief among them a rational, civilized man named Frank Moulton, had hurried to mediate between Tilton and Beecher in an attempt to save the situation and everyone's reputation. A new weekly had been founded, with Beecher's help, for Tilton to edit. And meantime, caught in the spin of her husband's distraction, Lib Tilton was woebegone and frightened.

"I came away from that house," Mrs. Davis told Victoria, "my soul bowed down with grief at the heartbroken condition of that poor woman and I felt that I ought not to leave Brooklyn until I had stripped the mask from that infamous, hypocritical scoundrel, Beecher."

The hypocritical aspects of the situation must have been even more apparent to Victoria, smarting as she was under the attacks of the Reverend Mr. Beecher's sister. Talking it over with Mrs. Davis, she must have said that unmasking this kind of hypocrisy was the very mission she had undertaken when she entered public life. Certainly, a few days later, Mrs. Davis was writing to her, "I believe that you are raised up of God to do a wonderful work, and I believe that you will unmask the hypocrisy of a class that none others dare touch."

But however excited her remarks to Mrs. Davis may have been, Victoria did not really consider taking any action, or if she did, it was not for long. Retelling the story to Colonel Blood, Stephen Andrews, Tennessee and the rest of her cabinet of advisors, she could provoke the same outrage she felt. But from Colonel Blood and Andrews, at least, there were thoughtful words of caution. The magnitude and sanctity of Beecher's fame could make any exposure of him as damaging to the exposer as to him. There were the innocents who would be hurt to consider also—the Tilton children, Beecher's family.

Victoria had other concerns at the moment anyway, preparing the speech she was to make at the May convention of the National Suffrage Association.

Then, the May convention having brought Elizabeth Cady Stanton to New York from her home in Tenafly, New Jersey, Victoria at last met that leading suffragist.

Mrs. Stanton had, of course, promised Susan Anthony that what both of them knew about the Beecher-Tilton difficulties should go no further. But Elizabeth Stanton felt an immediate rapport with Victoria Woodhull, whom she had already defended as a martyr. And Mrs. Stanton was also feeling the bite of Harriet Beecher Stowe's sarcasm. Another character in Mrs. Stowe's novel, *My Wife and I,* was a large, lovely and impulsive reformer called Mrs. Cerulean, "who felt called to the modern work of society regeneration, and went into it with all the enthusiasm of her nature, and with all that certainty of success which comes from an utter want of practical experience." The readers who identified Audacia Dangyereyes as Victoria were equally quick to see Mrs. Cerulean as Mrs. Stanton. Mrs. Stanton could laugh at jokes on herself as Victoria could not but still it was irritating to have Mrs. Stowe parodying her defense of Victoria in a popular serial.

The talk between Mrs. Stanton and Victoria turned to those who presumed to "cast the first stone," and there it all was again—The Reverend Mr. Beecher's alleged habit of seducing many of his more attractive female parishioners, his alleged seduction of Elizabeth Tilton, her confession to Tilton, and all the troubles that ensued from that. But there was no suggestion from Mrs. Stanton that the Reverend Mr. Beecher be unmasked, nor did Victoria discuss with her the need for such an action.

At which point, still another Beecher entered Victoria's life. Catherine Beecher's criticisms of Victoria Woodhull had troubled Isabella Beecher Hooker but, infatuated as she was, she was sure that if Catherine met Victoria she would realize that in every way that mattered "Victoria was a pure woman holding a wrong social theory...." Isabella suggested that perhaps Catherine herself might be able to convince Victoria to modify her radical stands on free love and divorce. Catherine was making a trip from Hartford, Connecticut, where she lived, to New York. Isabella gave her a letter of introduction to Victoria and then wrote optimistically to a friend: "When she sees her she will be just as much in love with her as the rest of us are."

Catherine Beecher called at the house on East 38th Street. For some reason—perhaps the house was already crowded with family and friends—Victoria and Miss Beecher decided to get acquainted by going for a carriage ride in the park. Rattling along under the springtime green of the trees, Catherine embarked on her missionary project and told Victoria that to question the sanctity of marriage vows was to undermine the very foundations of Christianity. She said that advocating free love was the same as asking that civilized human beings return to the lustful instinctiveness of animals. If Victoria wanted decent people to listen to her, she must subscribe to the doctrines that had been proved right and holy through the ages.

Victoria listened patiently for a while. But Catherine had an imperious way about her. As she lectured on and on, repeating the tired homilies which Victoria had heard and forsworn years before, it was suddenly too much for the younger woman. Victoria told Catherine Beecher that such sentiments about marriage were especially unfortunate coming from her since her brother was well known for secretly practicing the very doctrines which Victoria preached.

Unlikely as it might have seemed, Catherine Beecher—and her sister, Harriet Beecher Stowe, as well—had not as yet heard any of the gossip about Henry. When Catherine regained her voice after the shock of Victoria's remark, she told Victoria that she would answer to the way her brother kept his marriage vows as though he were herself.

This pledge did not impress Victoria and she said so.

"I will strike you for this, Victoria Woodhull," cried Catherine Beecher, her eyes snapping, her gray side curls shaking. "I will strike you dead!"

With this threat hovering in the air between them, the carriage ride came to its conclusion, Isabella's hopes for a meeting of minds between the two women permanently dashed.

Complaints about the prominence being given Victoria Woodhull were made by many of the delegates assembling in New York for the convention of the NWSA. People were beginning to call her "The Woodhull," as though she were some unique creature like The Auk, embodying characteristics found in no other animal. The rank and file members had been disturbed ever since her triumph in Washington and many were outraged when they learned she was to make a key address to the convention. Even the gentle Quaker Lucretia Mott, leader emeritus of the movement, voiced a protest.

But Elizabeth Cady Stanton, even more Victoria's champion since their meeting, pleaded her cause with Mrs. Mott. When the convention opened, The Woodhull was sitting between Mrs. Stanton and Mrs. Mott on the platform. As before, facing such an assemblage, she sat very still, "a splinter of the indestructible," with every eye upon her.

The time came for her speech. She rose, moved forward and, as always, began in a low, almost inaudible voice. But then, as though the very hostility of her audience gave her strength, her voice grew louder and clearer and she was launched on her most astonishing speech to date. The speech was undoubtedly the composition of Stephen Pearl Andrews and bore all his marks of intransigent reform. But Victoria gave the words their passionate appeal. Victoria was the one able to capture her audience with them so completely that her listeners soared with her to her final challenge.

"If the very next Congress refuses women all the legitimate results of citizenship ... we shall proceed to call another convention expressly to frame a new constitution and to erect a new government. ... We mean treason; we mean secession, and on a thousand times grander scale than was that of the South. We are plotting a revolution; we will overthrow this bogus Republic and plant a government of righteousness in its stead. ..."

Not even Lucretia Mott could resist this call to revolution. To her, as to everyone in the hall, Victoria had managed to reveal a vision of a new heaven on earth that could be won if women only dared to act.

"The Great Secession Speech" was what the newspapers called Victoria's address the next day. And by common journalistic consent, the NWSA convention was "The Woodhull Convention."

Elsewhere in the city, in their own hall, the ladies of the conservative American Association agitated themselves with resolutions against Victoria Woodhull and everything for which they believed she stood. Scornfully, Susan Anthony noted in her diary: "AWS meeting passed resolutions saying that they were not Free Lovers. Why not one saying that men are not thieves and murderers?"

The members of the NWSA, still under Victoria's spell, began passing resolutions of their own the next day. The resolutions had been drafted by Stephen Pearl Andrews and were approved by Lucretia Mott and read to the assembly by Pauline Wright Davis. They demanded reforms in almost every aspect of government and life and most of them were so clearly beneficial that one resolution which was somewhat more questionable than the others was swept along in the general acclamation. The questionable resolution demanded that "all laws shall be repealed which are made use of by Government to interfere with the rights of adult individuals to pursue happiness as they may choose; or with the legitimate consequences of such pursuit; or with contracts between individuals, of whatever kind, or their consequences, which will place the intercourse of persons with each other upon their individual honor."

Not until the convention was over and it was much too late to do anything about it, did anyone seem to realize that this particular resolution wrapped up a very neat definition of what was generally called free love.

Returned to their homes, faced with the enormity of what

they had resolved, the delegates awoke to the fact that they had been carried away by the very person they had been most determined to resist. They felt a natural resentment.

Victoria might have ridden out that resentment had she been accompanied in the world only by such helpful partners as Colonel Blood, Stephen Andrews and Tennie C. She might have withstood the continuing attacks of Harriet Beecher Stowe and Catherine Beecher. But through all of her meteoric rise, Victoria had remained loyal to her family. She had housed mother, father, brother, sisters, supported them, borne with them.

Now her family did her in.

11 § Let Him Without Sin...

FOUR days after Victoria's triumph with the suffragists, Roxanna Claflin hailed Colonel Blood to court and with him, Victoria, Tennie and most of the rest of the clan. No sensible reason ever emerged for her action. Roxanna was living well, eating well, could have dressed well if she chose, thanks to the money earned at the brokerage office under Colonel Blood's supervision. But when Roxanna was aggravated by any aspect of life she liked to blame Blood.

She unburdened herself of her feelings about him in court. "Judge, my daughters were good daughters and affectionate children till they got in with this man Blood. He had threatened my life several times and one night last November he came into the house in Thirty-eight Street and said he would not go to bed until he had washed his hands in my blood." (Perhaps Roxanna, in simple association, had been put off by Blood's name all along.) "I'll tell you what that man Blood is," she went on, "he is one of those who have no bottom in their pockets; you can keep stuffing in all the money in New York; they never get full; if my daughters would just send this man away as I always told them, they might be millionairesses and riding around in their own carriages. I came here because I want to get my daughter out of this man's clutches; he has taken away Vicky's affection and Tennie's affection from their poor old mother. S'help me God, Judge. I say here and I call Heaven to witness that there was the worst gang of free lovers in that house on Thirty-eighth Street that ever lived. Stephen Pearl Andrews and Dr. Woodhull and lots more of such trash."

Her counsel tried to stop her but she managed lots more of such talk before customary court procedure took over. Polly Sparr, still annoyed by having had to move out in Stephen Pearl Andrews' favor, took the stand to corroborate Roxanna's testimony.

Colonel Blood was called and denied ever threatening Roxanna. He did admit that "one night last fall when she was very troublesome, I said, if she was not my mother-in-law I would turn her over my knee and spank her." Unfortunately, Blood was vague about the legalities of his relationship with Victoria. He was not sure if they had both been divorced when they were married. He testified about their divorce in 1868, "after which we continued to live together," and that was also confusing. Questioned about Canning Woodhull, he declined to say just where Dr. Woodhull slept in the house on 38th Street, but he was positive who supported him and all the others too. "The firm of Woodhull and Claflin supported the whole of them," he said.

The newspapers which, only a few days before, had been headlining "The Woodhull Convention," could hardly forbear printing every word of such testimony from The Woodhull's own family.

The next day, when Victoria and Tennie C. were called, Victoria did her best. With the quiet manner that had served her well before in courtroom dramas, she testified that "Colonel Blood never treated my mother otherwise than kind; sometimes when she became violent, he would utterly ignore her presence." But Victoria's very eagerness to defend Blood evoked squalid scenes. "The most I ever heard him say was when she would come up to the door and abuse him frightfully as if she were possessed by some fiend, 'If you don't let that door alone, I'll go out and push you from it!' "

She tried to explain the immediate rift with her mother. "She left my house on the first of April and went to the Washington Hotel to board. All bills for her maintenance were paid by Woodhull, Claflin and Company.... Sparr and his wife induced my mother to leave for their own protection and to excite public sympathy. I have always pitied my mother; she always seemed to have a desire to have her own way and seemed to know better what her children wanted than they did themselves.... The whole trouble was that mother wanted to get Tennie back to going around the country telling fortunes and Sparr and his wife were always telling mother that as long as Blood was around she could not get the girl back."

Tennie also testified that Colonel Blood had always treated Roxanna kindly. But Tennie, pleased to be in the limelight, did not know when to stop. "My mother and I always got on together until Sparr came to the house, Sparr has been trying to blackmail people through mother. I have been accused of being a blackmailer.... I have a lot of letters here supposed to be written by mother for the purpose of blackmailing different eminent persons in this city. My mother cannot read or write. They were written by this man Sparr...."

Talk of blackmailing, from the co-editor of a paper devoted to tearing away veils of hypocrisy from the rich and powerful, was ill-advised, to say the least. But Tennie had no sense of danger. She rushed on to tell of how she had told fortunes with her mother since the age of eleven, but "Vicky and Colonel Blood got me away from that life and they are the best friends I have ever had. Since I was fourteen years old, I have kept thirty or thirty-five deadheads.... I am a clairvoyant; I am a Spiritualist.... Commodore Vanderbilt knows my power. I have humbugged people, I know. But if I did it, it was to make money to keep these deadheads."

Then Tennie's mood changed. While a brief argument went on between counsel and the judge, Tennie leaped from the witness chair and ran to her mother to clasp her in her arms. Polly Sparr tugged at Roxanna from the other side. Colonel Blood hurried up to intervene.

"Retire, my dear, do retire," he whispered to Tennie. "You are only making yourself conspicuous."

The case was dismissed at last and decision withheld—by the court at any rate. Victoria did not need clairvoyance to sense what the public decision was, nor to imagine what the suffragists whom she had so lately impressed were thinking as they read the testimony. And there was no need at all to imagine what one of the Beechers was thinking, for Harriet Beecher Stowe quickly made use of the trial in her serial, keeping it up to date with the Claflin troubles by having Audacia Dangyereyes hauled into court amidst a stench of dirty linen.

Even Victoria and Tennie's relations with Commodore Vanderbilt, so long the rock on which everything else was built, were affected by the airing of the case in the press. Young Mrs. Vanderbilt was gradually winning more influence over her husband. She could not have enjoyed reading Tennie's testimony that "Commodore Vanderbilt knew her power." Vanderbilt ceased to be so available for advice about the market and soon after the court proceedings profits of the brokerage firm began to decline. Visitors to the house on 38th Street during the summer noted that the old lavish look was not quite as it had been. Valuable pieces of furniture and art objects vanished, one by one. A new austerity in food and entertainment prevailed.

But the *Weekly* went on. Victoria and Tennie would sell everything to maintain that. And in the *Weekly* Victoria's troubles with her family were reported just as painstakingly as her triumphs had been. Note was taken of some of the harsher newspaper comments across the country. The Cleveland *Leader* was quoted: "The unsavory piece of scandal tele-graphed from New York . . . could hardly have caused much surprise to anyone who had paid any attention to the record of Mrs. Victoria Woodhull. Her career as a trance-physician in Cincinnati, her brazen immodesty as a stock speculator on Wall Street, and the open, shameless effrontery with which she has paraded her name . . . as a candidate . . . for the Presidency . . . all this has proclaimed her as a vain, immodest, unsexed woman, with whom respectable people should have as little to do as possible. The one unfortunate fact . . . the only one which will justify a public newspaper in alluding to the vile story at all, is that Mrs. Woodhull has for the last six months made her-self a prominent figure in the Woman Suffrage Movement. . . . She is a Suffrage advocate because being so made her no-torious and her paper profitable."

The *Weekly* called the writer of this attack a "man-fiend," and told him that he was welcome "to all the reputation you have made from your experiment of villifying Mrs. Woodhull."

Henry C. Bowen, owner and publisher of the *Independent* (of which Tilton had been editor until his accusation of Beecher), printed a personal attack on Victoria in his paper. By now, Victoria knew a little about the role Henry Bowen was playing in the tangled Beecher-Tilton web. She had heard the story of his wife's deathbed confession. She had heard of how he first discouraged Tilton from confronting Beecher, then encouraged him, then, after the fact, withdrew his approval and fired him.

And now Henry Bowen was writing an article censuring Mrs. Stanton, Miss Anthony and Mrs. Hooker for having given "a prominent place to Mrs. Woodhull, about whose private affairs all gossip is needless. Woodhull & Claflin's Weekly with its coarse treatment of all the sacred things of human life is enough to condemn anyone whose name is associated with it."

The *Weekly* had a long defense of Victoria in answer to this. "People should withhold the shafts which they would hurl at her . . . lest they be found fighting against a courageous devo-tion to principle which it is impossible for a common mind to apprehend ... or is it that Mrs. Woodhull is so unfortunate as to have unprincipled relatives from whom she has suffered everything but death, that Mr. Bowen takes exception to her as a leader in the cause of women?"

The tone remained lofty for several more paragraphs. "Victoria C. Woodhull's personal and individual private life is something entirely distinct from her public position.... If Mrs. Woodhull has valuable ideas ... what has her past history to do with them?"

Then, suddenly, it was as though Victoria could bear this objective stand no longer. How did Bowen, Beecher's protector, dare to censure her?

"Three weeks ago we stated in good faith that we did not profess to deal in personalities and private histories. We meant what we said then, and we mean what we say now and we say now just the contrary. We are converts through the merciless treatment we are receiving to the necessity of carrying the war into Africa.... Civilization is festering to the bursting point in our great cities, and notably in New York and Brooklyn.... At this very moment, awful and herculean efforts are being made to suppress the most terrific scandal in a neighboring city which has ever astounded and convulsed any community.... We have the inventory of discarded husbands and wives and lovers, with dates, circumstances and establishments.... Bankers in Wall Street and great railroad men come early on the schedule. Confidences which are no confidences abound...."

The threat that she could do something if she chose and that she was on the verge of choosing to was clear but just how she was going to "carry the war into Africa" was only implied.

At this point, the two suffrage associations, in bitter disagreement over almost everything, found something on which they could agree. Soon after the Claflin family troubles were reported in the newspapers, representatives of both associations met in perfect harmony to censure Susan Anthony and the leaders of the National Association for their alliance with Victoria C. Woodhull. The representatives further demanded that Mrs.

Woodhull's name be stricken forthwith from any connection with the suffrage cause.

A year and more later, Victoria would reveal that there had been many long discussions between her and her cabinet of advisors as to whether she should actually make any of the revelations at which she had hinted in the letter to Bowen in the *Weekly.* Had she indeed, as Pauline Davis suggested, "been raised up by God to do so?" The revelations would have their cost in the "real, sentimental injury to thousands." Ought the "social revolution" to be served regardless? "Slowly, deliberately, reluctantly," she—and Blood and Andrews too, of course—came to the conclusion that "it would be cowardice ... to unearth the peccadillos of little men and leave untouched the derelictions and offenses of the magnates of social and intellectual power and position."

Still, at the end of May, 1871, she and her advisors "only saw clear in the matter to the limited extent of throwing out some feelers to the public on the subject."

The feelers consisted of two identical letters sent to the New York *Times* and the New York *World* and published in both.

"Because I am a woman," Victoria wrote, "and because I hold opinions somewhat different from the self-elected orthodoxy which men find their pride in supporting ... self-elected orthodoxy assails me, villifies me, and endeavors to cover my life with ridicule and dishonor. This has been particularly the case in reference to certain law proceedings in which I was recently drawn by the weakness of one very near, and provoked by other relatives."

She took the opportunity to defend herself against the charge of living in the same house with two husbands. "Dr. Woodhull, being sick, ailing and incapable of self-support, I felt it my duty to myself and to human nature that he should be cared for, and although his incapacity was in no way attributable to me. My present husband, Colonel Blood, not only approves of this charge, but cooperates in it. I esteem it one of the most virtuous acts of my life."

Self-justification was not the real theme of the letter, however. She had done what she thought right. "But let him who
is without sin cast his stone. I do not intend to be the scapegoat
of sacrifice ... offered up as a victim ... by those who cover
the foulness and feculence of their thought with hypocritical
mouthing of fair professions. ... I advocate free love, in the
highest and purest sense, as the only cure for immorality ...
by which men corrupt ... sexual relations. My judges preach
against 'free love' openly, practice it secretly. For example, I
know of one man, a public teacher of eminence, who lives in
concubinage with the wife of another teacher of almost equal
eminence. All three concur in denouncing offenses against
morality. ... So be it, but I decline to stand up as the 'frightful
example!'. ... I shall make it my business to analyze some of
these lives and will take my chance in the matter of libel suits."

Various stories were told later as to just what happened after
this letter appeared in print. Theodore Tilton said that Victoria summoned him to her office on Broad Street and confronted him with the published letter of which he had been
ignorant before. Victoria said that Tilton appeared in her
office unsummoned, holding a copy of a paper in which the
letter appeared.

However Tilton came, summoned or on his own, he and
Victoria met for the first time, and with their meeting a summer of delight was beginning for both of them.

12 } *I Ridiculed the Dreadful Suzz...*

SHE asked him to read the letter aloud. Or, he asked her to what "eminent teachers" she was referring in the letter. Theodore Tilton gave one version in the future, Victoria the other. But both agreed that the question about whom she meant in the letter was answered quickly enough.

"I am referring to you and to Mr. Beecher," Victoria told Tilton. She then went on to ask him why such efforts were being made to deny and hide a situation which was not only understandable and natural but a perfect illustration of the validity of free love.

A command of language, emotional and persuasive, had helped to make Tilton almost as successful a lecturer as he was a writer. Alarmed, even horrified, by the calm resolution of the woman confronting him, he burst into a torrent of speech, begging her to consider the innocents who would be hurt if the situation of which she spoke became general knowledge— his four children, his wife (innocent in spirit if not in fact), Beecher's wife and family. He reminded her of Beecher's devoted congregation, and of the multitudes across the country who revered him almost as a saint.

Victoria told Tilton she had already considered all these things. It was the very sweep of Beecher's influence that made her single him out. The social revolution was advanced very little when someone like herself preached a new code of sexual ethics. People could easily dismiss what she said and condemn her for saying it. But how swiftly the revolution could proceed

if a man of Beecher's stature spoke out for it instead of hypo-
critically practicing secretly what she preached openly.

Tilton beseeched her to realize that things were not that
simple, that there were many factors to consider. At last he
won a promise from Victoria that she would do nothing hastily
and that they would discuss the matter further. After that, he
hurried back to Brooklyn to consult with all of those currently
involved in keeping the story secret, including, so tangled was
the situation by now, the "lecherous scoundrel" who had betrayed him, Henry Ward Beecher.

Several years later, Tilton would testify that he became
friendly with Mrs. Woodhull at the advice of Beecher, who
thought that such a course would help insure her silence.
Beecher, denying later that there was anything on which he
wanted or needed Mrs. Woodhull's silence, would admit that
he had considered it "proper" for Tilton to establish friendly
relations with her. Victoria, more magnanimous than either
Beecher or Tilton, refused to justify anything in the name of
expediency.

"A woman who could not love Theodore Tilton, especially
in reciprocation of a generous, impulsive, overwhelming affection such as he was capable of bestowing, must indeed be dead
to all the sweeter impulses of nature," she said.

The friendship began with an invitation from Tilton to
Victoria to dine with him and his wife at their home in
Brooklyn. Victoria accepted and made her way one evening to
the house which the Reverend Mr. Beecher had found so pretty
and welcoming. Over the front door was inscribed the legend:
"And whatsoever house ye enter, ye shall first say, Peace to this
house." Ironic as the motto was at this juncture of the Tilton
marriage, Victoria seemed able to abide by the sentiment better
than most. Lib Tilton received her reluctantly, and only because Theodore had told her she must. Before the evening was
over, Lib had been both soothed and charmed by Victoria's
gracious ways. She gave Victoria a book of poems and inscribed

it, "To my friend, Victoria C. Woodhull, Elizabeth R. Tilton."

But as the intimacy between Victoria and Theodore grew, Lib Tilton's friendship cooled. It was summer in New York. Theodore took Victoria to Central Park one day, rowing on the Harlem River another day, and on still another afternoon they made an excursion to Coney Island. Theodore began spending his evenings at the house on 38th Street. The free-thinkers and radicals of Victoria's salon still gathered there along with the members of Andrews' Pantarchy. These regulars welcomed Theodore Tilton, delighted to argue their theories with him. He considered himself a liberal, enlightened in his views on almost every subject, but the advanced nature of some of their opinions shocked him. He flung himself into all sorts of discussions with them. Then, after the theorizing was over and the regulars had departed, there were the warm summer nights when Theodore did not go home to Brooklyn. Victoria remembered later how sometimes, when the night was very warm, the two of them went up to the roof of the house to seek cool breezes and look at the stars together.

"... he was my devoted lover for more than half a year," Victoria would say, "and I admit that during that time he was my accepted lover ... for three months we were hardly out of each other's sight. ... He slept every night for three months in my arms. ..."

James Blood remained true to his principles. He made no complaint, absented himself whenever possible and greeted Theodore pleasantly at the breakfast table or any other un-likely place that he might appear. His attitude should have been a perfect object lesson to Theodore Tilton of how free-love doctrine could work to the happiness of all, and at least for the duration of that summer, it was.

Alone with Victoria, her arms around him, Theodore wanted to pour out to her all the misery, jealousy and wounded pride that he had suffered in the last years. But then came more les-sons. Victoria listened to his outpourings and then she ridiculed them. She told him that he was exhibiting "maudlin sentiment and mock heroics and *dreadful suzz* ... over an event the most natural in the world, and the most intrinsically innocent." She guessed from what he told her that Lib's confession of infidelity had been inspired not so much by a guilty conscience as by a jealous fear that Mr. Beecher had found a new object for his affections. And she drew a lesson for Theodore from that. How illogical it was, she told him, for Lib, eager for freedom in love when it brought joy to her, to adopt the attitude of a "slave-holder" when Mr. Beecher continued on the same free course that had brought him to her in the beginning.

She pointed out to Theodore that he was showing this same "slave-holder's attitude" in his relation to Lib. He had confessed to knowing other women when he was away on one of his lecture tours. He was enjoying making love to her now. How then could he condemn Lib for following her impulses with the same freedom?

"Bogus sentimentality" had been pumped into him, she told him, by "sickly religious literature and Sunday School morality. ... Pulpit Pharaseeism had humbugged him all his life into the belief that he ought to feel and act in this harlequin and absurd way...."

This view of his behavior was an entirely new one to Theodore. "Harlequin and absurd...?" when he had been so sure of his injured righteousness? Intoxicated by Victoria's love and teachings alike, Theodore felt the first happiness he had known in years and was wild to share his joy with the world.

His magazine, *The Golden Age,* founded for him by Beecher and other sympathizers after Bowen had fired him, offered him a perfect opportunity. For it, he wrote a long celebration of the leading suffragists, titled "The Legend of Good Women." He praised his friends, Susan Anthony and Elizabeth Cady Stanton, and some of the other leaders. Then he came to Victoria.

"If the woman's movement has a Joan of Arc, it is this gentle but fiery genius. ... Little understood by the public, she is denounced in the most outrageous manner by people who do not appreciate her moral worth. ... Her bold social theories have startled many good souls, but anybody who on this account imagines her to stand below the whitest and purest of her sex will misplace a woman who in moral integrity rises to the full height of the highest." After this tribute, Tilton went on to admire Isabella Beecher Hooker, a worker in the cause who knew and loved Mrs. Woodhull, but to pause wonderingly at Mrs. Harriet Beecher Stowe, who did *not* know the lady but was "writing furiously and unwarrantably against her in *The Christian Union.*"

Still Theodore wanted to say and do more. He saw evidences of the financial difficulties that Victoria and her family were experiencing and asked if there were some way he could help. Victoria mentioned a biography of herself that Colonel Blood had written to use in her campaign for the Presidency. Victoria was not satisfied with it and felt that it lacked emotional appeal. Eagerly, Theodore volunteered to rewrite it and add the missing element and then have it published as a special tract by the Golden Age Press, which published his magazine.

James Blood relinquished the manuscript and Theodore threw himself at his task. The sordid reality of what Victoria's childhood had been in Homer, Ohio, was drenched in pathos as Tilton presented the young Victoria, drudging about in the "plain, simple frame dwelling of her parents," washing dishes, cooking, scrubbing, mending, until far into the night. He was not kind to her parents. They were cruel, demanding and selfish and had hurried her into marriage with that "gay rake, Dr. Canning Woodhull," whose hideous habits came out into the open as soon as he was "possessed of his treasure."

The mood of the narrative brightened with the advent of Colonel Blood. Tilton wrote of the felicitous relationship of the two who had been "united by the powers of the air." He told of the message from Demosthenes to go to New York, and then of the meeting with Commodore Vanderbilt. "Indomitable in their energy, the sisters won the good graces of Commodore Vanderbilt, a fine old gentleman of comfortable means, who of all the lower animals prefers the horse, and of all the higher virtues, admires pluck."

The triumph of the brokerage office led Theodore to punning. He envisioned the sisters: "a couple of fresh young dolphins, breasting the sea, they cleft gracefully every threatening wave. The breakers could not dash the brokers."

Some of Theodore's references to the *Weekly* were almost as arch: "a willow basket full of audacious manuscripts ... apparently picked up at random and thrown together pell mell ... a not ORDINARY journal, which is edited in one world and published in another...."

Humor vanished when he came to describing Victoria's personal appearance. He tried for objectivity. "One side of her face is perfect in outline ... the same view looking from the right is a little broken and irregular." Only a lover, finding no such studies tedious, could have joyed in being so exact.

He noted one idiosyncrasy of Victoria's that, surprisingly, had not been noted in any other writings about her. "For two years, as a talisman against any temptation to untruthfulness (which with her is the unpardonable sin), she wore, stitched into the sleeve of every one of her dresses, the 2nd verse of the 120th Psalm, namely: Deliver my soul, O Lord, from lying lips and from a deceitful tongue."

In a blaze of candor, he concluded, "She has some impetuous and headlong faults, but were she without the same traits which produce these she would not possess the mad and magnificent energies which (if she lives) will make her a heroine of history."

"Mad and magnificent...." Perhaps, in his flow of alliteration and rhetoric, Theodore had managed to catch two adjectives that came close to pertinence. But Victoria liked all of them. Her one objection to the finished manuscript was the omission of some of her clairvoyant triumphs. Theodore had to rewrite it sufficiently to include some of these, especially the account of the time when, according to Victoria, she had called her son, Byron, back to life after his nearly fatal accident.

When the manuscript was completed to Victoria's satisfaction it was read to the entire family and approved by all, presumably even the poor "rake," Canning Woodhull, and the "Mesphistophelian father," Buck Claflin. After that, Theodore hurried the manuscript into publication.

Tilton's reputation was not helped by its appearance as a published tract. As Victoria said later, "Mr. Tilton's warmest friends were shocked ... by his earnest and apparently conscientious" advocacy of her theories.

Neither did the tract modify the general public impression of Victoria. Magazines like *Harper's Weekly* reflected the respectable distaste for its extravagances. "If apples are wormy this year and grapes mildew and ducks' eggs addle, and bladed corn be lodged, it may all be ascribed to the unhallowed influence of Mr. Tilton's life of V.W."

One large and hitherto unnoticed group, however, welcomed the biography with acclaim. As a result of Victoria's insistence that Theodore make due note of her clairvoyant successes, the National Association of Spiritualists awoke to the fact that the well-known Mrs. Woodhull was one of them. They sent her an invitation to attend their annual convention in Troy, New York.

Years before, when Victoria first met Colonel Blood, he had been president of the St. Louis Society of Spiritualists and that was as close as Victoria had ever come to organized spiritualism. But she liked conventions and it had been four months since the last suffrage meeting. In September, she parted from Theodore for a while and, accompanied by Colonel Blood, went to Troy.

She was astonished by the sensation she created among the spiritualists. She had swept the suffragists off their feet in January but never seemed to dwell on that triumph. She would refer again and again to her success in Troy. Asked to speak to the assemblage, she did so with her usual felicity and was cheered. Then, to her further astonishment, she was nominated and elected president of the society in a wave of acclamation.

It was hardly the same as being elected President of the United States but it was being freely and unanimously elected president of something. Later, reporting the event in the *Weekly,* she enlarged on her emotions. "Her surprise at her reception, and her nomination to the Presidency of the Society was equaled only by the gratitude she felt, and will ever feel, at the unexpected and tumultuous kindness with which she was then and there honored beyond her desert." She called the election "the chief honor of her life."

Wealth, fame, leadership—Demosthenes had promised her those, and to a degree she had won them all. But the spiritualists gave her even more—a vast outpouring of public love that accepted her just as she was, free love, unspeakable family, spirit-voices and all. No one man, it seemed, could give her a love that brought her quite the same joy.

13   *Freedom! Freedom!*

TENNIE C., rejecting hypocrisy, could not compromise with her natural inclinations in any direction. When summer heat steamed in New York, Tennie liked to drift about the house in a loose mother hubbard and nothing else. If visitors arrived, she felt it would be only pretense to hurry off to don more conventional dress. As a result, there were occasions when conventional callers found themselves blinking and blushing. A suffragist friend of Victoria's, who had called along with her husband, remonstrated with him after they left, shocked by the furtive pats she had seen him giving Tennie. "But, my dear," he replied mildly, "when an attractive young lady who is nearly naked sits on the arm of one's chair and leans over one, what is one to do?"

Publicly, however, Tennie did her best to imitate Victoria. In the summer of 1871, Tennie proclaimed herself a candidate for public office, asking for a seat in the New York legislature. A post was vacant in the 8th Congressional District, a predominantly German ward. Flyers were sent out. A public meeting in Irving Hall was arranged. A speech was written. Stephen Pearl

Andrews, master of thirty languages, coached Tennie in a German translation.

Eager for a crowd, Tennie called on her Wall Street friends to attend. She still had some in spite of repercussions of the court case. And, according to the New York *Sun* of August 12, "The German American Progressive Association turned out in full number ... to listen to a speech in German by Miss Tennie C. Claflin, of the famous banking firm of Woodhull, Claflin & Co." Tennie's costume was reported: "A dress of black organdie with a small figure in colours, made *en train*, and very plainly trimmed. Her hair, which she wears short, hung loose and bushy about her forehead and temples. She wore no jewelry or ornaments." Excerpts, in English, from Tennie's speech in German were given. "At the conclusion of the speech, the hall rang again with cheers and applause, in the midst of which Miss Claflin was presented with an elegant basket of flowers.... On receiving this beautiful token ... which was understood to be the gift of her Wall Street friends, Miss Claflin retired from the stand."

Later that evening, Tennie was serenaded by some of her admirers "at her palatial residence in Murray Hill." And that, by and large, was the end of Tennie's campaigning.

Perhaps that was just as well. This summer, for the first time in years, New Yorkers were beginning to take their city politics seriously. Almost incredulously, they were learning just how happy a hunting ground the city was for the Tweed ring. The New York *Times* was not as susceptible to Tweed blandishments as most of the other newspapers were. Through a defection in the Tammany ranks, it had managed to obtain some extremely damning records and was printing the astonishing figures day after day—$1,826,278.35 paid for the plastering of one city building, for instance, and $170,000 for forty chairs and tables. Thomas Nast, a cartoonist for *Harper's Weekly*, whose graphic style of fantastic realism delighted contemporary taste, had begun a series of cartoons attacking "Boss" Tweed and the Tammany organization, which he depicted as a ferocious tiger. Roused by all of this, citizens were holding meetings and forming committees to work toward the formidable goal of wrenching New York free from Tammany clutches in the fall elections. Tweed himself, sure that he had everything under control, with the courts, the state legislature and even the governor on his side, was generally insouciant about the whole business and that attitude inflamed the newly awakened citizens even more. Nobody really had any time for a Tennie Claflin campaign in the midst of such excitements.

Exposé astonishments being currently in other hands, Tennie and Victoria turned their attention toward becoming known as serious thinkers and writers on long-term political problems. Stephen Pearl Andrews gathered up the papers that had been published in the *Herald* on "The Tendencies of Government," and was preparing them for Victoria to publish as a book. A publisher in Boston, D. W. Niles, asked Victoria for an introduction to a new edition of Goethe's *Elective Affinities*. A thoughtful little paragraph was supplied which mentioned how Victoria had read the book "with pleasure and profit in my early life." Another clutch of essays—there were always plenty of them available in the house on 38th Street—was bundled together so that Tennie could publish a book also. *Constitutional Equality, A Right of Women,* by Tennie C. Claflin, was published in the fall of 1871, just about the time that *The Origin, Tendencies and Principles of Government,* by Victoria C. Woodhull, was published.

Under the guidance of Stephen Pearl Andrews, Tennie shared with Victoria the distinction of being an enlightened friend of labor. Andrews had long since read and studied the writings of another radical and dreamer, currently resident in London, Karl Marx. Andrews was not only in sympathy with an international organization of labor such as Marx was organizing in England but felt that he had pioneered in this area with a League of Workmen which he had organized in the United States in the 1850s. Andrews encouraged Tennie, Victoria, the members of the Pantarchy and most of the radicals who gathered around them to organize themselves as Section Twelve of the International Workingmen's Association. And in the fall of 1871, *Woodhull & Claflin's Weekly* scored a beat which went unnoticed in the general hullabaloo over "Boss" Tweed and Tammany, by becoming the first American periodical to publish Karl Marx's *Communist Manifesto*.

More and more lecture invitations were keeping Victoria busy and traveling. President of the nation's spiritualists, she was asked to address local gatherings across the country. In New Jersey, she was acclaimed as the spiritualists' candidate for President of the United States. In Cleveland, she talked to three thousand spiritualists about women's rights. In Plymouth, Massachusetts, she talked about training children's souls and the need to inform them about sex. She was discovering that with the spiritualists, who loved her, she could talk freely about almost anything.

November came, and the off-year elections. Tennie's race for the legislature was forgotten, and small wonder. The citizens' Committee of Seventy, under the leadership of Samuel J. Tilden, had managed to obtain an indictment against "Boss" Tweed in October, another indictment against the mayor, A. Oakey Hall, and a series of indictments against lesser Tammany figures. Excitement was intense as New Yorkers went to the polls. Would the revelations about the Tweed Ring really bring out enough independent voters to wrest the election from the organization, with all its resources of stuffed ballot boxes, repeating voters and simple fraud? The city felt cleansed when the votes were finally counted. Tweed had retained enough loyalty in his own district to be reelected to the state senate but everywhere else the battle had gone against him, with judges, senators, assemblymen and aldermen who had been sponsored by Tammany falling as victims.

But Victoria and Tennie managed to make some news in spite of the general preoccupation with the major story. Both of them attempted to vote, as advocated by the NWSA. The *Herald* headlined the "Heartless Conduct of Tammany Inspectors—Vic and Tennie will invoke the law and make Rome Howl."

The *Herald* reporter had joined Victoria and Tennie "in the elegant drawing room of Mrs. Woodhull" at half-past two, preparatory to their march on voting headquarters. "A dozen intellectual ladies had there congregated, and to the accompaniment of rustling silks ... had listened to ... the irresistible Tennie" read the 14th and 15th Amendments. The group had marched out then and walked down the street, accompanied by several gentlemen "who have earned a wide notoriety by the interest taken in the women's rights movement." The scene at the polling headquarters attracted a crowd of two hundred or more spectators. Victoria and Tennie both took advantage of this audience to make speeches. Then, having been denied the right to vote, they led their followers back to 38th Street, planning a suit against the inspectors for illegally preventing legitimate voters from exercising their rights.

Indeed, on the very same day that the *Herald* was facetiously reporting the events at the polling place, Victoria had a long letter published in the New York *Times,* presenting once again in sober, reasonable terms, all the seemingly unanswerable arguments on the subject.

Theodore Tilton had not vanished from Victoria's life, nor was all passion spent between them, but the time when they could spend days and nights in each other's company was over. Victoria seemed not to mind. She had told Theodore at the beginning of their love that she foresaw six months of rapture for them and that then he would fall away. Theodore had protested the prediction, but as autumn came he was busy just as she was. He had his magazine to edit, articles and essays to write and lecture engagements to fill. At the same time, he was embarked on writing a novel which might almost have been a sublimation of the summer's particular enchantment. With his customary fondness for alliteration, Theodore called it *Tempest Tossed,* and its plot concerned a young man and his beautiful wife, left alone with their newborn child on a ship abandoned by everyone else during a storm. There were extravagantly romantic echoes of the *Swiss Family Robinson* situation as the couple, with their growing daughter, drifted for seventeen years on the South Atlantic currents, in the disabled but sea-worthy ship, living on the ship's stores and mutual love and understanding. Tempest-tossed, yes, but an idyll all the same.

The situation in Brooklyn, which Victoria had thought of "analyzing" and which had brought her Theodore instead, had not been forgotten by Victoria or anyone concerned with it. At various times during the summer, Victoria had urged Theodore to arrange a meeting for her with Mr. Beecher. She had been so successful in converting Theodore to her doctrines, at least for a while, that she was eager to try her persuasiveness on Mr. Beecher as well. She kept remembering what she had pointed out to Theodore at their first interview—how the social revolution would be advanced if a man like Beecher spoke out for its theories, and how she would be vindicated. A wild dream? Perhaps. But no wilder than many of her dreams that had come true.

During the summer, Theodore had done his best. One day he was able to send Victoria a note bearing good news. "My dear Victoria, I have arranged with Frank [Moulton] that you shall see Mr. Beecher at my house on Friday night. He will attend a meeting of the church at ten o'clock and will give you the rest of the evening as late as you desire. Meanwhile, on this sunshiny day I salute you, with a good morning. Peace with you. Yours. T.T."

They met, the most famous preacher in America, still hand-some in a stoutly ruddy way, and the most notorious woman in America, her beauty in full bloom. Each of them was anxious to win the other and they were both skilled at weaving emotional spells. They were really too much alike in this so that it became a case of two potent magics colliding and neutralizing each other. Each of them was most successful when dealing with characters who were easy to dominate. Theodore Tilton had proved a good subject for them both.

Still, according to what Victoria said later, Beecher freely confessed to her that he shared many of her ideas and told her that he considered "marriage the grave of love." But he was quick to add that he could not dream of saying such things publicly or he would preach to empty seats. He said that he gave his congregation the truth as fast as he felt that it was ready for it. Victoria chided him for this, calling on him to display the courage he had shown in so many other situations. But Beecher was adamant.

The meeting was not altogether a stalemate, however. Later, Victoria employed the terms of phrenology and said that she would rate Mr. Beecher 8 for Amativeness, which was a very high score.

They met again, and still again. Later, Beecher would insist that all the further meetings had been accidental and he would imply nothing but formality between them. Victoria gave a different impression. She spoke approvingly of the need of "every great man of Mr. Beecher's type" for "the loving mani-festations of many women," and she insisted that such a need was not a bad thing but intrinsically good, "one of God's best gifts to the world." A year and more later, she would tell a young lover that of course she had known Mr. Beecher sexually. But the most that she would ever admit publicly was that when together they had not spent all their time "talking about the weather."

However they may have tested each other's Amativeness, one thing soon became certain. Victoria could not move Beecher an inch toward any public avowals of his private attitude toward love. He did agree to try to stop his sisters, Catherine and Har-riet, from any more attacks on Victoria, but it soon appeared that even in this area he was able to accomplish little. Mrs. Stowe's comments in the *Christian Union* continued so in-temperate that Victoria reminded Theodore of what she could print about the Beechers if she chose. Whereupon it was Theo-dore's turn to reason with her, urging her to respond to Mrs. Stowe by way of "superior gracefulness and gentleness."

Beecher finally managed to convince Harriet by the end of summer that her attacks on Victoria Woodhull were actually harmful to him. Harriet could not understand why. She, and

Catherine also, had at last heard the story that gossip was repeating about Henry and Mr. Tilton's wife, but both of them rejected it as unbelievable, the fabrication of jealous, petty associates. To Harriet, The Woodhull was a snake that should be given "a good clip with a shovel" at every opportunity. But Henry was insistent and Harriet agreed to write no more about Victoria.

Catherine was more difficult to silence. Victoria was scheduled to deliver a lecture in Hartford, Connecticut, home of three Beecher sisters, Catherine, Isabella Hooker and Mary Perkins. A letter to the editor of the Hartford *Courant* expressed some of Catherine's feelings about Mrs. Woodhull and called upon the decent citizens of Hartford to prevent her appearance. There was an answer by a defender of Victoria (probably Colonel Blood), and then an even more outraged response from "A Lady of Hartford."

After this flurry, Victoria appeared on schedule. Seven hundred people were in the opera house to hear her. Whatever they may have expected, what they heard was her straightforward speech proving woman's constitutional right to vote. Only when she neared the end of her speech did Victoria interrupt her prepared remarks to read the letter from "A Lady of Hartford." She followed this by saying, "My friends, I had intended to say something in reply to Miss Catherine Beecher's article . . . but I remember that it is a purely personal attack. . . . Miss Beecher told me . . . she would strike me. She has done so, but now, instead of returning the blow, I will present her with my other cheek, with the hope that even her conscience will not smite her for speaking so unkindly of me as she has. . . ." If she had not responded with a gesture of superior gracefulness, which would have ignored the quarrel entirely, Victoria was at least "gentle."

But Victoria was wearying of gentility, wearying of attacks like Catherine Beecher's. Principles! What were they if they were not admitted as freely and openly as they were practiced privately?

Arrangements for a lecture in which she would tell the world exactly what she meant by her principles were under way soon after Victoria's Hartford engagement. Steinway Hall was rented for the evening of November 20 and Stephen Pearl Andrews went to work on a speech.

"FREEDOM! FREEDOM! FREEDOM!" proclaimed the banners that went up outside the hall. "If it is good in the Religious and Political Sphere, who shall deny that it is good in THE SOCIAL SPHERE?" The posters announced that the lecture was being given "for the express purpose of silencing the voices and stopping the pens of those who . . . persistently misrepresent, slander, abuse and vilify Mrs. Woodhull on account of her outspoken advocacy of, and supreme faith in, God's first, last and best law." Big capitals spelled out Victoria's name, the date, and the title of the lecture: "THE PRINCIPLES OF SOCIAL FREEDOM INVOLVING THE QUESTION OF FREE LOVE, MARRIAGE, DIVORCE AND PROSTITUTION." Horace Greeley, the conservative suffragists (or "Boston exclusives"), and other notables were invited to seats on the platform. "All her lesser defamers should secure front seats," the posters advised.

The banners up, the speech written, read, and probably sharpened and simplified by Victoria, a note was sent off to Henry Ward Beecher. It was a curious letter, guarded and threatening at the same time. Victoria wrote that she wanted to see Mr. Beecher before her lecture because she wanted justice and what she said or did would "depend largely on the result of the interview."

Beecher saw Victoria promptly and learned that what she wanted was for him to introduce her to the Steinway Hall audience. She did not ask him to agree publicly with what she planned to say. She offered him a copy of her speech so that he could see for himself that none of her remarks was outrageous or indecent. All she asked was his appearance on the platform and a brief introduction.

Beecher's horror was almost overwhelming. His emotionalism, considered a sign of his soulfulness by his admirers, was as great as Theodore's and he fell on his knees beside Victoria as she sat on a sofa and burst into tears. "Let me off, let me off," he begged. Then he left her and ran to consult with Frank Moulton, the patient friend who had been mediating between him and Tilton for more than a year now. Moulton summoned Tilton and then both Moulton and Tilton urged Beecher to make the introduction. He could deny sharing any of Victoria's views and still uphold her right to speak them. Finally Victoria was called to join this conclave. "A splinter of the indestructible," she watched and listened as the men argued, first with her, then with each other, then with Beecher.

But Beecher, the tears streaming down his face, was immovable. He pleaded for mercy. He threatened suicide. But he "could not, could not face it!"

Victoria rose to go. "Mr. Beecher," she said, "if I am compelled to go onto that platform alone, I shall begin by telling the audience why I am alone and why you are not with me."

14 ⸙ Yes, I Am a Free Lover!

THE night was wild, wet and windy but an hour before Victoria's lecture was scheduled to begin, Steinway Hall was jammed with people. Eager for sensation, respectable and not-so-respectable New Yorkers alike had turned out to see The Woodhull and to hear what she had to say about "Free Love, Marriage, Divorce and Prostitution."

A few members of Victoria's family were here and there among the three thousand in the auditorium. In one of the boxes, surrounded by friends, sat her younger sister, Utica. Utica was as beautiful as ever (some thought her lovelier than Victoria), but no miracle had ever occurred in her life to channel her emotions and energies. For a while she had tried to ape Victoria as Tennie did, but without Tennie's loving humility. Not long after Victoria's journey to California, as a very young woman, Utica had also journeyed to San Francisco to try her luck as an actress, but without success. After Victoria's move to New York and her emergence as a public figure, Utica also sought to win importance, but proud and impatient, and unwilling to take any direction, she had only created difficulties, for herself and others. She was married to her second husband by now, a Mr. Brooker of Brooklyn, and she burned with a sullen jealousy of her more famous sisters, especially Victoria, and waited for some disaster to overtake them. She waited now, as it grew nearer and nearer time for the lecture to start, and the more unruly members of the audience began to stamp, clap and call for The Woodhull.

In an anteroom of the hall, Victoria also waited, with Tennie beside her. Mr. Beecher had not appeared. Victoria and Tennie talked with the reporters who clustered around them. There were always many of those. Victoria was especially gracious to the *Herald* reporter. "That paper has never misrepresented me and I know it won't now," she told him.

It was almost eight o'clock and Mr. Beecher still had not arrived. Colonel Blood, watching from the fringes of the group, had no idea if Victoria was already planning what she would say to the audience about Beecher or what might be in her mind. Smiling, she was giving the *Herald* reporter the rose that had been pinned to her bosom and reaching for another for herself from the vase nearby. Tennie was coquettishly flicking up her skirt to amuse another reporter.

Stephen Pearl Andrews came in, holding a copy of Victoria's speech. Following him were various members of the Pantarchy. Victoria stood up. It was time to make her way to the platform.

Just then, in rushed Theodore Tilton and Frank Moulton. They hurried to Victoria. Victoria clutched at Theodore's hand and looked up at him sorrowfully.

"There isn't a brave man in the circle of two cities to preside at my meeting," she said. Then she walked out toward the corridor that led to the platform. Tennie hurried to follow. Stephen Pearl Andrews, Colonel Blood, the Pantarchy and the reporters trailed along. Suddenly, Frank Moulton, at the rear of the little procession, saw Theodore Tilton's blond head towering over the others at the front of the group. Theodore was beside Victoria.

"Are you going to introduce her, Tilton?" called Moulton. "Yes, by heaven," called back Theodore, "since no one else has the pluck to do it."

He may have been moving forward into the breach left by Beecher to protect his own name and his wife's reputation. On the other hand, he may have been acting on a generous, quixotic impulse, as he often did. He walked out onto the platform with Victoria, stepped to the front and raised his hands to quiet the crowd. His words, when he began to speak, sounded much more like the words of a man who had loved Victoria than of one who was paying blackmail.

He said that, having a free evening, he had come to hear what his friend was going to say in regard to "the great question" which had occupied her many years. He had discovered that various gentlemen had declined to introduce her because of "objections to the lady's character."

"I know it," said Tilton, "and believe in it, and vouch for it." There was applause then, and a few hisses. Tilton continued, speaking even more bravely of the lady's views.

"It may be she is a fanatic; it may be that I am a fool; but before high heaven, I would rather be both fanatic and fool in one than to be such a coward as would deny a woman the right of free speech." There was more applause.

He concluded ringingly. "Allow me the privilege of saying that with as much pride as ever prompted me to the performance of any act in fifteen or twenty years, I have the honor of introducing to you Victoria C. Woodhull, who will address you on the subject of social freedom."

Victoria moved forward on the stage and began to speak. Without hesitation, she followed the prepared opening. No one noticed whether Tilton, sitting on the platform behind her, sighed in relief or not. No one would ever know whether it had been his gallantry that prevented Victoria from mentioning the scandal or if she had only been juggling with the threats of revelation all along.

Her speech proceeded along the serenely logical lines drawn by Stephen Pearl Andrews, tracing the changing attitudes toward the freedom of the individual since the days of the sixteenth century. History was not what the crowd had come out on a stormy night to hear from The Woodhull. It was not all that Victoria had in mind to offer either. But at last the historical review brought her to the present day and she began to speak with more passion and emphasis. Stephen Pearl Andrews, at the side of the stage, looked up from the script he was holding, reassured. She was getting into the spirit of her message. "The court holds that if the law solemnly pronounces two married, they are married. There is no analogy in nature. . . . The law cannot compel two to love. . . . Two people are sexually united, married by nature, united by God. . . ."

Excitement began to tingle through the hall. Excitement was sweeping Victoria along now, flushing her cheeks as it always did.

"Suppose a separation is desired because one of the two loves and is loved elsewhere? If the union is maintained by force at least two of them, probably three, are unhappy. . . . All that is good and commendable now existing would continue to exist if all marriage laws were repealed tomorrow."

A wave of applause greeted this. There were cheers, then hisses also. The hisses grew louder, the clapping increased. Victoria cried out, "If any lady or gentleman in the audience— who is hissing—will come up on the platform with me—" But any further words were drowned out by the noise.

A slender figure stood up in the box to stage left. Utica Claflin Brooker, who had been waiting for an opportunity, had chosen her moment. The clamor in the hall quieted a little as people turned to stare at the young woman.

"May I speak to her?" Utica asked in a sweet, carrying voice.

Then, turning to Victoria on the stage, Utica said, "How would you like to come in to this world without knowing who your father or mother was?"

Tumult exploded. Obviously many in the hall were really frightened by Victoria's message and welcomed an answer to it. "Hurrah!" men shouted, flinging their hats in the air. "Yes, yes, answer that!" women cried, fluttering their handkerchiefs.

Victoria stretched out her arms. Her voice rose over the clamor. "There are thousands of noble men and women in the world today who never knew who their fathers were," she cried.

Cheers and hisses mingled again, but the pandemonium was checked. Utica sat down. Victoria rushed on with her speech, telling the men and women before her that they blamed free love for precisely the troubles and crimes that were the result of the slavery of marriage ties. She spoke of those who had consulted her through the years and of how she had advised the "granting of entire freedom to those who were complained of as inconstant. . . ."

Utica rose again in her box. There was applause for her. Victoria's friends and members of the Pantarchy began calling for the police to put Utica out of the hall. Soon an officer was seen entering Utica's box. "Shame!" cried many in the audience. Someone yelled, "Three cheers for Brooker! Brooker! Brooker!"

Victoria turned to Theodore behind her and motioned to him. He looked alarmed but rose and went to the front of the platform. Three times he tried to make himself heard. Victoria went to the edge of the stage and called to Tennie, sitting in the front row. "Tennie, can't you get Utie to go out?"

At last Theodore managed to gain some attention. He said that he believed in free speech and would gladly ask the lady in the box to come to the platform but that the meeting had been called so that Victoria could express her views. He would introduce Mrs. Woodhull again.

In the brief lull then, Victoria began speaking again. And now she was wholly caught up by passion. Free love was the religion of the future, she cried, the natural sequence of social freedom.

"Are you a free lover?" shouted someone.

"YES!" Victoria called back. "I AM A FREE LOVER!" Cheers, hisses, howls, hoots, erupted, but Victoria swept on regardless, her voice rising over the racket. "I HAVE AN INALIENABLE, CON-STITUTIONAL, AND NATURAL RIGHT TO LOVE WHOM I MAY, TO LOVE AS LONG OR AS SHORT A PERIOD AS I CAN, TO CHANGE THAT LOVE EVERY DAY IF I PLEASE! And with that right neither you nor any law you can frame have any right to interfere."

Stephen Pearl Andrews was looking at Victoria, ignoring the script even as she was. Not a word of all this had been prepared.

"I have the further right to demand a free and unrestricted exercise of that right, and it is your duty not only to accord it, but as a community, to see that I am protected in it. I trust that I am fully understood, for I mean just that and nothing less."

The crowd had what it had come for at last, a public proclamation of free sexual behavior that thrilled some listeners and horrified others. But Victoria was not finished. For ten minutes more she continued to talk. Some of the phrases, some of the logic, were Stephen Pearl Andrews'. The conviction and drama were all Victoria's. She cried out that she deemed it false modesty to shut off discussions of sex and the evils that attended its abuses. Sexual relations not founded in love were demoralizing. Promiscuity was not the end result of following free love, but simply an anarchical stage when the passions ruled supreme. When spirituality came in, promiscuity became impossible.

"I dearly prize the good opinion of my fellow beings," she cried. "I would so gladly have you think well of me. It is because I love you all ... that I tell you my vision of the future. ..."

Then she was restating her credo. "The love that I cannot command is not mine; let me not disturb myself about it, nor attempt to filch it from its rightful owners. ... Rather let me leave my doors and windows open, intent only on living so nobly that the best cannot fail to be drawn to me by irresistible attraction."

It was, in its own way, as honest and moving a statement as anyone was making publicly that year, but in 1871 it was at least fifty years in advance of a time when a woman could make such a statement without suffering fearsome consequences. In Victoria's case, these were not slow to arrive.

The "Free Love" speech was fully reported in the next day's *Herald,* which also noted all the disorders of the occasion and Victoria's spontaneous remarks. ("It was not the printed speech that did the damage," Theodore Tilton said sadly, departing on a lecture tour. "It was the interjected remarks in response to the audience; she said violent things.") People read those violent things and one after another, the axes fell.

Mrs. Woodhull was informed that she and her family were no longer welcome as tenants in the "palatial mansion on 38th Street." She, Colonel Blood and Tennie sought other lodgings, and finally moved everyone into a boardinghouse on 23rd Street. The move was probably made easier since so many of the fine furnishings at 38th Street had already gone to pay bills.

Business sagged to a new low in the brokerage office. Customers might have been able to ignore Victoria's beliefs when they knew about them only through gossip, but few were eager to associate themselves with her now that she had so publicly proclaimed them. Brokers on the Street who had previously been helpful and friendly in spite of everything withdrew their counsel and support just as Commodore Vanderbilt had already done.

One straw offered itself financially. Victoria was receiving more invitations to lecture than ever before. People across the country were just as curious as New Yorkers had been to see and hear for themselves how dreadful The Woodhull could be. Lecture fees could help to support the family, but the *Weekly* was a constant drain. And no one connected with it could bear to think of giving up the *Weekly*.

Still Victoria held her head high and espoused principles. In December, she and Tennie demonstrated their sympathy with the labor movement. The New York members of the International Workingmen's Association planned a memorial march for the martyred Frenchman, Rossel, who, with his companions, had been executed in France after the brief reign of the French Commune. Six hundred of New York's more radical thinkers joined the march up the Bowery, over to Broadway, then up Fifth Avenue to 34th Street. Among them were Victoria Woodhull, Stephen Pearl Andrews and Theodore Tilton. Colonel Blood and Tennie carried "a ponderous flag-staff" which bore the red banner of the Commune.

An unexpected, almost unhoped-for gesture of loyalty and friendship began the new year of 1872 for Victoria. The annual winter convention of the National Suffrage Association was being held, as was customary, in Washington, D.C. At the opening of the proceedings, Elizabeth Cady Stanton and Susan Anthony mounted the platform. Victoria C. Woodhull walked between them, pale, beautiful, and simply dressed, as always, in a "blue broadcloth suit with a double-breasted chinchilla cloth coat."

She had given the leaders of the National Association their argument and program and the leaders had not forgotten what they owed her. The year before, a large group of the membership had asked that Victoria's name be removed from the society's rolls, but Mrs. Stanton and Miss Anthony had asked Victoria to address the convention at both the daytime and evening sessions.

Remembering her triumph with the spiritualists in September, and leaning upon spiritual counsel more than ever before in these troubled days, Victoria's first speech dealt with plans for a better world that were already mapped out in the other-world. Such was the force of her platform personality that many in the audience who usually scoffed at spiritualism found themselves wavering toward belief as she spoke. Isabella Beecher

Hooker, enraptured by Victoria's clairvoyance, was so carried away by the speech that she declared that women could rule the world if they heeded Victoria's counsel.

Victoria's speech in the evening sounded a favorite Stephen Pearl Andrews' note as she pleaded for a United States of the World. After that address, Susan Anthony rose to pay tribute to the woman who had shocked New York two months before by declaring herself a "free lover."

"I have been asked by many, why did you drag her to the front? Now bless your souls, she was not dragged to the front; she came to Washington from Wall Street with a powerful argument and lots of cash behind her, and I can bet you cash is a big thing with Congress. . . ." Miss Anthony, just returned from another lecture tour in the West, admitted that she had been asked "all along the line of the Pacific Coast, what about Woodhull? You make her your leader?" Miss Anthony repeated her answer. "We don't make leaders, they make themselves. If any can accomplish a more brilliant effort than Victoria Woodhull, let him or her go ahead and they will be leaders."

Suddenly, it was triumph all over again for Victoria. The delegates forgot their hostility and applauded her wildly. There was more praise for her from Isabella Hooker and from a small and attractive delegate and new admirer of Victoria, Laura Cuppy Smith. When Stephen Pearl Andrews, also scheduled to address the convention, rose to speak, he was stopped by calls for "more Woodhull."

Before the convention adjourned, one delegate arose and asked that the NWSA nominate Victoria for the Presidency and support her campaign for that office just as the spiritualists were doing. But Susan Anthony demurred at that, just as she rejected any suggestion that women distract themselves from their chief goal by supporting labor reform, or any other cause, however worthy in itself.

Still, the general feeling of admiration and affection for Victoria remained so great that she had to rise one final time and stand before the delegates. She thanked the women from "a heart too full for utterance," and promised them to go home from the convention "more determined than ever to push the car of progress."

15 ⸄ *Always Faithful to My Principles...*

"BY a train of circumstances ... I found myself the inmate of a house of ill-repute in this city. ... I conceived an intense indignation ... for society ... and for men especially ... intimate with and caressing us in private, and coolly passing us without recognition before the world...."

Concerned about the financial difficulties facing her and Victoria, Tennie was taking steps of her own to try to improve matters, writing a letter for publication in the *Weekly*.

"I discovered in myself a shrewd business capacity," Tennie continued her composition, "and after a few years ... I found myself the successful mistress of a house of the kind of what I had been an inmate before. ... From the time that I opened my house ... I have kept a record of the men who have visited it ... the names and residences. ... My business has been successful but I am tired of it. I am arranging to go to Europe. ... If you, in the prosecution of your blessed mission as a social reformer, have any need to see more behind the scenes ... I will give you access to my two big books, or would even leave them with you in my absence. You will find in them ... doctors of divinity to counter-jumpers and runners for mercantile houses...."

Tennie signed the letter, "With love and admiration, Mary Bowles." Then she turned to writing an answer to the fictitious madam. She devoted most of the response to "cursing and denouncing" the slavery of women and then, in an almost offhand manner, brought up the subject of the "two big books," full of names and addresses.

"My sister and I have scrupulously adopted the policy of avoiding personalities when possible. But the time may come when that policy will have to be abandoned, for our enemies do not scruple to resort to them in the most scandalous manner. . . ."

The letter from "Mary Bowles" and Tennie's reply to it were both published in the *Weekly* soon after Victoria's "Free Love" speech. There was always the chance that some male readers of the *Weekly* might notice the letters, take alarm that their own names might be in one of the "two big books," and so do something to relieve the current financial distress.

Blackmail, of one sort or another, had been a fact of life in Tennie's experience since Cincinnati days, when her name had figured in a blackmail suit. It was an activity which a great many people took for granted in these years, as a hazardous possibility that might face them at any moment, or alternately, as a possible means for rescuing themselves from all sorts of difficulties. The stock market manipulators and railroad barons, Daniel Drew, Commodore Vanderbilt, Jay Gould and James Fisk and others of their stature, periodically seemed to face ruin unless they could obtain some quick concession from a competitor. Often the only way to get such a concession was to threaten revelations of past cupidities, nor did it ever seem to weaken the threat that there were cupidities on both sides. Timing and expediency forced the response.

Blackmail flourished on dozens of lesser levels as well, especially in New York, where the realities of prostitution, gambling and general vice were in even sharper contrast than elsewhere to the professed standards of morality. The most respectable man or woman was not proof against its menace. He, or she, only needed to be seen in some questionable place or with questionable company to become a target for someone with a grudge or someone who was simply hungry.

Blackmail could even bring pain in a kind of poignant reversal of its usual threats that misbehavior would be disclosed—as James Fisk was learning during the summer and fall of 1871. He had fallen in love several years before, to a degree he had never imagined possible, with a pretty, compliant young woman named Josie Mansfield. She had accepted his attentions, his gifts, his support, but she had never given him the devotion that he gave her. He was "Prince of the Erie," co-owner with Gould of the lavish Grand Opera House, where the Erie offices were located, and from the stage of which he had introduced New Yorkers to the delights of *opéra bouffe.* Self-styled "admiral" of the Providence Steamship Company, which he and Gould owned, he sometimes wore a natty naval uniform, but he also liked to appear in full regimental regalia as Colonel of New York's 9th Regiment of the National Guard, which he had transformed into a corps so ornamental that it dazzled natives and visitors alike. A man so extroverted and good-natured that the public had well-nigh forgotten his financial shenanigans and fondly called him "Jubilee Jim," he still had not been able to hold the woman he loved. In 1870, Josie Mansfield had left him for the more sophisticated charms of one of his friends, Edward A. Stokes. And in the summer and fall of 1871, Josie, directed by Stokes, was demanding more and more money from Fisk under threat of making public all his passionate, imploring, promising letters to her. And James Fisk, Jr., the extrovert, was quailing at the thought of a public disclosure of his deepest, most honest emotions.

The tragic consequences of this particular threat were still to come when the *Weekly,* soon after the publication of Tennie's letters, spoke out in defense of blackmail. The tone of Victoria's remarks about analyzing the "awful scandal in a neighboring city," as well as Tennie's letters, must have convinced Blood or Andrews that some sort of apologia would not be amiss. True to the *Weekly's* standard approach to moral matters, the editorial defended only women in the use of blackmail, it being their one weapon against "base treatment by the other sex." The *Weekly* compared the woman who "avenges the oppressions of her sex by what is called blackmailing," to Sir Walter Scott's hero Rob Roy, "the great Scottish blackmailer," and concluded that "as long as man is only a cunning animal . . . in his intercourse with such women as he dares to outrage, can it be expected that they will not meet cunning with cunning, fraud with fraud. . . ."

But however the logic of Colonel Blood and Stephen Pearl Andrews might justify the practice, however Tennie attempted it—and however Victoria might also have been attempting to "borrow" money from acquaintances whom she knew were vulnerable—no large sums of money eased life for Tennie, Victoria and the Claflins during the winter of 1872.

And early in January 1872, the suit that Edward Stokes and Josie Mansfield had brought against James Fisk on a trumped-up charge of libel had gone surprisingly awry. Instead of winning a judgment against Fisk, they were themselves indicted for attempted blackmail. Crazed by the unexpected collapse of all his schemes, Stokes went gunning for Fisk and shot him down in the stairway of the Grand Central Hotel.

The news of this murder quite eclipsed any news the Claflins might be making for a while. The newspapers were full of details about the mourners filing past Fisk's coffin, on display at the Grand Opera House, about the grief of the humble people whom he had befriended, and the leaderless state of the 9th Regiment. Thomas Nast took advantage of the event to draw several moral cartoons for *Harper's Weekly,* pointing out that the sins of the Erie "ring" were not all being buried with Fisk. At about the same time, Roxanna and Buck Claflin, restive under the financial pinch, grew so troublesome that Tennie rushed to court one day and swore out a warrant against them for disturbing the peace. She asked that they be removed from the family lodgings. But no arrest or removal was made, and even though the episode was duly reported in the papers, it was only a minor item in the Claflin saga, hardly noticeable amidst the press of larger events—Fisk's funeral, and at last, the beginning of court proceedings against the indicted "Boss" Tweed.

Then, in February, Thomas Nast turned from limning such familiar characters as Fisk and Tweed and catapulted Victoria to national attention again, making her the subject of one of his cartoons. He showed her as very beautiful but very menacing. Robed in black, with giant bat's wings, she held a tablet on which was inscribed "Be Saved by FREE LOVE." Beneath the drawing was the caption, "Get thee behind me, (Mrs.) Satan."

The cartoon undoubtedly served to remind thousands, whose memories it might have slipped, of Victoria's free-love speech three months before. And although it was certainly proof that she was still a figure to be reckoned with on a national scale, it was not a picture that Victoria appreciated. She did not save it among all the other cherished clippings, drawings and notices in the big scrapbooks.

In March, the poor, tired old "rake," Canning Woodhull grew ill. He had been living on alcohol and morphine for years but the doctor decided to withdraw the morphine from him now. In April, Woodhull died. His passing was marked by a long and loving obituary in the *Weekly*. The persecution that Victoria had suffered for having sheltered him was noted, but the character of the deceased was praised and the warm feeling between him and Colonel Blood was eulogized. "These two people were not rivals. They were brothers; and they remained friends to the last."

Utica Brooker, still hoping to confound her famous sister, informed the coroner that Woodhull had died "under suspicious circumstances." The coroner came to the boardinghouse on 23rd Street where the Claflins were in residence but a postmortem showed only that Woodhull had died of pneumonia. This episode was also reported in the press.

The *Weekly* did not flinch from reporting it, too. If Victoria asked that people admit publicly the lives that they lived privately, she was prepared to lead the way, confessing the sordid along with the splendid.

Perhaps it was this intransigent commitment to principle which kept her the friends that she had and even enabled her to persuade some of them to join her in a bold, new venture, that winter of 1872.

It was time, Victoria told Isabella Beecher Hooker, Pauline Wright Davis, and Elizabeth Stanton, that the suffragists do something to follow up their pronouncement of a year ago that the women "meant revolution, meant secession," if they were not granted their rights. The regular political parties, Republican and Democratic, were not even offering token recognition of those rights as they prepared for their nominating conventions and the fall Presidential election.

Victoria suggested that the women of the National Suffrage group form a political party of their own and name their own candidates for national office—male or female, it made no difference, so long as they were the best possible exponents of the reforms that were needed. With the Republicans committed to running President Ulysses S. Grant for another term, with the Democrats, whomever they nominated, unlikely to come up with any formidable resistance to him, such a gesture from the women could not fail to focus national attention on them and their demands.

Mrs. Hooker, Mrs. Davis, even Mrs. Stanton, were caught by the suggestion and grew even more persuaded as Victoria elaborated on the idea. Susan Anthony was away on another of her bone-breaking lecture tours in the West, so both Mrs. Hooker and Mrs. Stanton wrote to her, enthusiastically outlining the plan.

Miss Anthony read the letters, frowned and then replied to Mrs. Hooker and Mrs. Stanton, saying that she disapproved completely. For the first time Miss Anthony began to show some doubt of Victoria. "Mrs. Woodhull has the advantage of us because she has the newspaper," Susan Anthony wrote to Mrs. Stanton, "and she persistently means to run our craft into her port and none other. If she were influenced by women-spirits . . . I might consent to be a mere sail-hoister for her; but as it is, she is wholly owned and dominated by men spirits and I spurn the control of the whole lot of them. . . ."

Whether Miss Anthony was referring to Demosthenes, Victoria's spirit-guide, or to her more earthly counselors, Colonel Blood, Stephen Pearl Andrews or Benjamin Butler, was not clear. Perhaps she meant all of them. But Mrs. Stanton and Mrs. Hooker read her letter, remembered her unequivocal endorsement of Victoria as recently as January and decided not to take her objections too seriously.

Lucretia Mott, doubtful about Victoria in the beginning, also had some hesitations about her newest plan. Mrs. Stanton wrote to Mrs. Mott, trying to reassure her. "Since leaving you, I have thought much about Mrs. Woodhull, and of all the gossip about her past, and have come to the conclusion that it is a great impertinence in any of us to pry into her private affairs. To me there is a sacredness in individual experience. . . . This woman stands before us today as a speaker and writer. Her face, manners, and conversation, all indicate the triumph of the moral, intellectual and spiritual. The processes and localities of her education are little to us, but the result should be everything."

The plans for a new party to be organized by the suffragists went forward. A name was chosen—the People's Party—and it was decided that the party's first convention be held jointly with the anniversary meeting of the NWSA in New York in May. Signatures approving these decisions were collected. *Woodhull & Claflin's Weekly* published an announcement of the formation of the new party, the plans for the convention and issued a "call" to all who were interested to attend.

Miss Anthony was waiting for a train in an Illinois railway station one day. By chance, someone handed her a copy of the *Weekly*. She opened the paper, saw the announcement, and saw that it was signed not only by Mrs. Stanton, Mrs. Hooker, Mrs. Davis and others, but by herself. Astounded and indignant, she rushed off telegrams to all concerned, demanding that her name be removed from an announcement to which it had been appended without her consent or knowledge. Traveling on, she began to plan the scolding that she would give to her dear, but impulsive, friend, Mrs. Stanton, as soon as she returned to the East.

By the first of May, Miss Anthony was in New York, telling Mrs. Stanton and Mrs. Hooker in person that she refused to have anything to do with this new project instigated by Victoria Woodhull. Mrs. Stanton found it hard to believe that Susan could take such an attitude toward the woman she had once saluted as a "dear, bright, glorious spirit." She brushed aside Susan's objections to the kinds of people who might follow Victoria into the projected political party—spiritualists, members of the Pantarchy, communists, free lovers and cranks. She told Susan Anthony that she was "narrow." Isabella Hooker went further and called her a "bigot." Susan Anthony dropped the argument against Victoria's possible followers and spoke of the folly of trying to organize a political party at this time. Mrs. Stanton and Mrs. Hooker, who had been convinced by Victoria that this was the right time, argued a while longer. There was no doubt, however, that in the end loyalty to Miss Anthony, faithful servant to the cause for years, would have to override any commitment to Victoria Woodhull.

Steinway Hall, scene of Victoria's "free love" declaration, was the convention hall. A distressed Mrs. Stanton accompanied a determined Miss Anthony onto the platform to open the meeting. Victoria was not with them as she had been the year before. The proceedings were scarcely started, however, before Victoria walked up onto the platform. She announced that the People's Party was convening jointly with the Suffrage Association.

Miss Anthony immediately stepped forward and denied the announcement. She herself had rented the hall, she said, for the purpose of the suffrage convention and for no other purpose. Any members of the audience who had come in answer to Mrs. Woodhull's "call," and who were not members of the NWSA were requested to leave.

Victoria looked at Susan Anthony and realized that she meant exactly what she said. She turned and left the platform. At once there was a rustling through the hall as a number of Victoria's supporters, members of the association and nonmembers alike, rose to leave the building with her.

After their departure, the meeting limped along. Mrs. Stanton, angry and embarrassed, resigned as president. Miss Anthony was elected the new president. The usual sort of business was transacted in an atmosphere of awkwardness and restraint.

The evening session, also lacking the presence of Victoria and her friends, was drawing to a close when Victoria entered the hall through a side door and moved swiftly up onto the platform. Without waiting for any recognition from the chair, she announced that during the day she had managed to engage Apollo Hall for the next day and that the convention of the People's Party would be held there. She moved that this convention be adjourned to meet the next morning in Apollo Hall.

Someone in the audience seconded the motion. Miss Anthony refused to put the motion to the vote. Another ally of Victoria's rose to appeal Miss Anthony's decision. Victoria herself put the motion. There was a cry of "Aye." Miss Anthony rapped for order and declared the proceedings out of order. Then Victoria, caught by a sudden wave of inspiration, began to talk.

She called out a challenge for political action now and outlined the wonders that the women might achieve by such action. Miss Anthony rapped her gavel again and again—in vain. She began to speak simultaneously with Victoria, announcing the convention was adjourned, to meet the following morning in the same place. And still Victoria talked on, and still the delegates sat listening to her, heedless of Miss Anthony's adjournment.

Miss Anthony hesitated only a moment. Then she hurried from the platform, found the janitor of the building and ordered him to turn off the gas lights in the hall. Finally, as the lights went out, Victoria quit talking. In darkness, the delegates stumbled their way out of Steinway Hall.

Six hundred people appeared at Apollo Hall the next morning in answer to Victoria's invitation. Some were longtime radical friends, members of the Pantarchy, followers of Stephen Pearl Andrews, who was drawing up the resolutions for this political convention. Some were spiritualists, some communists, some merely curious, but a great many were suffragists who had deserted Miss Anthony to listen to Victoria.

No awkwardness or restraint marked this convention. Enthusiasm charged the air as business proceeded swiftly. The new party was organized. It was decided not to call it the People's Party but to adopt the name already chosen by the spiritualists —the Equal Rights Party. Victoria Woodhull was asked to address the evening session.

The hall was full in the evening and Victoria spoke with passion. "What is equality? . . . And what is justice? . . . Shall we be slaves to escape revolution? . . . Away with such weak stupidity! . . . A revolution shall sweep over the whole country, to purge it of political trickery, despotic assumption, and all industrial injustice." The crowd cheered and shouted.

"Who," she cried, in a final appeal, "will dare to attempt to unlock the luminous portals of the future with the rusty keys of the past?" As she finished, everyone in the hall was standing, applauding.

Judge Carter of Cincinnati leaped onto the platform to nominate Victoria C. Woodhull for President. "All those in favor of the nomination say Aye," he cried.

Men and women shouted their "Ayes." Hats were tossed in the customary gesture of approval and handkerchiefs waved. Some people were laughing and some women were sobbing excitedly. Passersby on the street outside heard the noise and came in to discover the cause. Many remained to join the hysterical shouts of "Victoria! Victoria!"

The selection of a Vice-Presidential running mate for Victoria was not quite so simple. Moses Hull, a radical from Kentucky, nominated the country's most famous Negro, Frederick Douglass. "We have had the oppressed sex represented by Woodhull, we must have the oppressed race represented by

Douglass." But in this assemblage of reformers, idealists and zealots, there were even some who remembered the Indians.

"I move the nomination of Spotted Tail," cried someone. "Indians ought to have a voice here before Negroes."

Even the faithful background figure, Colonel Blood, was remembered. A woman cried, "Let Colonel Blood go to Washington with Mrs. Woodhull. It is not well for man to be alone."

At last the choice was made. Frederick Douglass was nominated. Mr. Douglass was not present at the convention and perhaps did not know of its existence so the crowd had no reaction from him. But Victoria made her acceptance speech in earnest tones, thanking everyone from the bottom of her heart.

"I feel it all the more deeply," she said, "as I have stood by you so long, sometimes meriting your applause, and sometimes encountering your rebuffs, but I have been always faithful to my principles and without saying more, I again thank you for the great honor you have shown me."

Susan Anthony, alone in her room after the adjournment of the NWSA convention at Steinway Hall, wrote in her diary: "Small audience. The fiasco perfect, from calling People's Convention. Never did Mrs. Stanton do so foolish a thing. All came near being lost. . . ."

She did not mention Victoria's name in her diary. And although she would never join in any way with those who attacked Victoria Woodhull, she never spoke to her again.

16 ⸘ Victoria, We've Selected ...

THE post attracted Tennie and she did not see why she
was not as qualified to hold it, in her own way, as the murdered
James Fisk had been. Accordingly, she sent off an open letter to
the manager of the Grand Opera House, lately Jim's headquarters, applying for the colonelcy of the "gallant 9th Regiment." "Your connection with the Grand Opera House," she
wrote, "brings you in social contact with the committee having
the selection of the colonel in hand. See the gentlemen please,
and tell them I will accept the position and pledge myself, if
elected, to give such impetus to recruiting, that in thirty days
the 9th Regiment will be the foremost in the state."

The New York *Times,* which paid less attention to Victoria
and Tennie than any of the other newspapers, was jarred out
of its customary aloofness when this letter appeared in the
Herald. An editorial considered some of the activities of both
sisters and concluded: "It would be thought that one such
woman in a family was sufficient. That there should be two
such, jointly working at the same time, would surpass belief,
did not the fact stare one in the face."

Tennie's application to lead the 9th was ignored. She bethought herself of other military outfits in the city and then
offered her services as commander to two Negro regiments,
Company A of the Veteran Guard and Company C of the Spencer Grays. From these troops she received a response. They

would be pleased to have Miss Tennie C. Claflin as their commander.

Tennie assumed her honorary military duties just in time to have her troops on hand for the ratifying convention of the Equal Rights Party which was held in early June. They made a brave showing on the platform at Cooper Union Hall. But aside from their presence, and an even larger crowd than had been at Apollo Hall, this second convention was very like the one at which Victoria had been nominated. There were speeches by a number of people, including Captain Thomas Griffin of the Spencer Grays, who eulogized those "two noble women, Woodhull and Claflin." Victoria made another impassioned acceptance speech. The delegates cheered, applauded, and marched about waving banners and placards. There was also an especially written campaign song, sung to the tune of "Comin' Thru the Rye."

> If you nominate a woman
> In the month of May,
> Dare you face what Mrs. Grundy
> And her set will say?
> How they'll jeer and frown and slander
> Chattering night and day:
> Oh, did you dream of Mrs. Grundy
> In the month of May.

The second verse challenged Mr. Grundy:

> If you nominate a Negro
> In the month of May:
> Dare you face what Mr. Grundy
> And his chums will say?

The final verse sounded the note of triumph and it must have been pleasing to Victoria to hear a thousand voices singing:

> Yes, Victoria we've selected
> For our chosen head;
> With Fred Douglass on the ticket
> We will raise the dead.

> Then round them let us rally
> Without fear or dread,
> And next March we'll put the Grundys
> In their little bed.

As the song roared through the hall, Victoria could be up-lifted by the enthusiasm and optimism of the crowd around her. She could forget for a while, some of the reality outside the hall. But once the convention was over and her admirers had dispersed she had to face it again. The power of the Grundys was already closing in on her, and life was grimmer than it had been in years.

Soon after the convention in May, Victoria and her family had been requested to leave the boardinghouse on 23rd Street because of the doctrines she advocated. Victoria, Tennie and Colonel Blood embarked on a search for other lodgings and the real difficulties began. At boardinghouse after boardinghouse they met the same refusal. Their opinions made them unwelcome as boarders.

They looked for a house to rent. But no real-estate agent in the city would show them a dwelling. "We personally don't object to you," they said, "but you know there is such a prejudice against you that we really can't do it." Fortunately, Margaret Ann and her family, and Polly and hers, had found lodgings of their own some time previously and Buck and Roxanna Claflin could take shelter with them, but they seemingly had no place for Victoria, her children, Tennie and Colonel Blood.

They turned to the hotels. The Hoffman House, where Woodhull and Claflin had begun their career as brokers just two years before amid scenes of splendor, had its doors closed to them. It was the same at every other hotel where they applied. They came at last to an unpretentious family hotel called the Gilsey, and the manager of the hotel happened to be absent when they made their request for rooms. The room clerk was unable to resist the appeal of sad, beautiful Mrs. Woodhull and the group moved in. Then the manager returned and told Victoria and Colonel Blood that they, and all the rest of the group, would have to leave or he would lose his family trade.

Victoria and Colonel Blood claimed their rights as citizens and refused to leave unless some misdemeanor was proved against them. But the reprieve won by that stand did not last long. Four Negro lieutenants of the Spencer Grays called for Tennie in a carriage one day, to take her to inspect a drill of their company.

"Miss Tennie," said the manager, "if you go off with those men in that carriage, you need not come back here."

Tennie went off with them. When Victoria and Colonel Blood returned to the hotel in the evening from the brokerage office on Broad Street, they found all their belongings on the sidewalk. The doors to their rooms in the hotel were locked and guards were posted before them to prevent any attempt at an entrance.

The scene that followed cried out for someone like Theodore Tilton to describe it. Victoria's children, the handicapped youth, Byron, and good, pretty Zulu Maud, ran to her to cling to her skirts. Tennie returned, unrepentant, from her drill. Colonel Blood considered what they could do.

> Oh, it was pitiful,
> With this whole city full,
> Home she had none . . .

Victoria would quote the lines later when she remembered this night. Finally, she, Colonel Blood and Tennie, picked up some of the luggage on the street and, with the children, made their way back to 44 Broad Street. They went into the office and slept there as best they could upon the floor. For several weeks the office remained their only resting place, while Margaret Ann and Polly, hiding their connection with Victoria and Tennie, tried to find a house for them.

The office was still their shelter when the owner of the building at 44 Broad Street advanced the rent of the Woodhull, Claflin & Company's rooms by a thousand dollars a year, the whole sum demanded at once. Victoria and Colonel Blood went out to look for another office and found everywhere the same rejection that they had met in looking for lodgings.

Later, Victoria would insist that there was a planned program of persecution in all of this and that it was not merely a spontaneous manifestation of disapproval by the "Grundys" of the city. She would insist that the Beechers had organized it in some way. Harriet Beecher Stowe and Catherine Beecher, abjuring public attacks on Victoria, were still convinced that Victoria had something to do with the gossip about Henry Ward Beecher, and they could still talk and write letters to powerful friends. The Reverend Mr. Beecher, appealed to for help by Victoria when the housing crisis was at its height, said he was unable to do anything.

Sometime in June, Theodore Tilton came back from a lecture tour and made his way to Victoria to confront her with some proof sheets of an article presumably designed for the *Weekly*. Titled "Tit for Tat," the article made various allegations about the private lives of some of the women in the suffrage movement. Theodore asked Victoria if she had written the article or caused it to be written. She told him that she had a right to self-defense and that all of these women had united to try to make her life impossible, but finally she promised Tilton that she would not run the article in the *Weekly*.

Still, copies of the proof sheets circulated and Tilton heard that some of the women mentioned in the article had been offered the opportunity of having their names deleted for a price. Again Tilton sought out Victoria and told her that although he had defended her in the past he could do so no longer. He was through with her forever if she persisted in blackmailing others in this fashion.

Later, Victoria gave her own version of this meeting with Tilton. She said that most of their conversation had to do with Tilton's imminent departure for Cincinnati, Ohio, and the Progressive Republican Convention which was soon to be held there. She told him that she knew his political motives for going —he wanted to be the man who nominated Horace Greeley as the Presidential candidate for the Progressive Republicans and he had hopes of a political future for himself as a consequence. She warned him that such hopes were vain and told him that she could see something clairvoyantly—a coffin, with Greeley in it, following any such move as Tilton planned. By the time she related all of this to reporters, however, the election of 1872 was over and Greeley had died a few days later.

In Tilton's version of their meeting, he said that he and Victoria parted bitterly. Victoria said that they parted with sad tenderness. Whatever their emotions were, it was the last time they would speak to each other.

New office space was finally located almost next door to the old offices, at 48 Broad Street. A house was also leased on 34th Street by one of Victoria's sisters, so that there was no more need to sleep on the floor. But there was small comfort in any of this. "We were paralyzed in strength, health and purse," Victoria wrote later, "and reduced to a condition in which we were obliged to stop all business." The brokerage office had already ceased to function. The cessation that really spelled paralysis was something else.

With the issue of June 28, 1872, *Woodhull & Claflin's Weekly* suspended publication. It was like the stopping of a heartbeat to Victoria, Tennie, Colonel Blood, and to Stephen Pearl Andrews too. Andrews no longer lived with the group and had not shared the housing problems but he was still loyal. No more *Weeklys*—no more opportunities to instruct, convert, exhort and explain.

In August, Victoria Woodhull was sued for debt but testified that she owned nothing, not even the clothes on her back.

"Yes, Victoria we've selected," the delegates had sung not two months before. Not even an echo of those thousand voices seemed to linger now.

September came and the National Association of Spiritualists was having its annual convention in Boston. Victoria went to

Boston, "dragged by a sense of duty . . . tired, sick and discouraged . . . to surrender my charge as President."

She found nothing to cheer her among the assembled spiritualists. The men and women who had acclaimed her so spontaneously a year before in Troy and given her the "chief honor of her life" had been listening to rumors circulated by several of the delegates. Mrs. Woodhull had a habit of obtaining money under false pretenses, the rumors claimed. She was known to engage in blackmail. Not all the delegates believed the charges but the stories persisted and Victoria felt herself surrounded not so much by "positive hostility . . . but painful uncertainty and doubt."

A kind of rage must have been rising in her as she listened to the buzzing around her. What had she done? She had not only lived but honestly proclaimed her beliefs in social freedom. As a result, she had been condemned and persecuted—and not just by people who honestly disagreed with her theories but by people who secretly practiced them. Had she no right to defend herself against them? Had she no right to ask that the revered and powerful who persecuted her merely be as open and as honest as herself?

The convention began. She listened to the opening speeches and "tried to gather the sentiment of the great meeting." Then it was her turn to speak. Later, she described what happened next.

"Standing there before that audience I was seized by one of those overwhelming gusts of inspiration which sometimes come upon me, from I know not where; taken out of myself; hurried away from the immediate question of discussion, and made by some power stronger than I, to pour out into the ears of that assembly . . . the whole story of the Beecher and Tilton scandal in Plymouth Church."

Some months before, she and her advisors had spent long hours deliberating whether or not that story should be revealed "in the cause of the social revolution." The decision had gone no further than the sending out of some feelers. Now, pushed on by a "power stronger than herself," the need to vindicate herself as *right,* whatever she did, she was putting an end to cautious deliberation.

She had no clear memory of exactly what she said to the assembled spiritualists. Those who heard her told her afterward that she spoke "in a rhapsody of indignant eloquence." They said that she had "used some naughty words," but, "with tears streaming down their faces," they insisted that "she swore divinely." One listener, a Mrs. E. A. Meriwether, visiting the convention from Memphis, Tennessee, wrote an account of the speech a few months afterward. "Mrs. Woodhull's speech poured out like a stream of flame. . . . Editors, teachers, preachers, she spared not. . . . When she finished off Beecher she came back to Boston and lifted some of its editors high in the air and scorched them with accusations. . . ." And still "her fiery flame went on, until she suddenly stopped, and flashed from the platform and out at the side door just as swiftly as she had flashed in. . . ."

Astonished, thrilled, electrified, the delegates unanimously reelected her president of the Association. They had not been shocked by her speech but uplifted. To them, she was tearing aside the veils of hypocrisy that hid the rottenness of the world as it was, and she had filled them with a sense of moving forward to the time when all such corruption would be exposed and destroyed, and the plans of the spirit-world for a better society could come to fulfillment.

All was praise and acclamation among the spiritualists. The curtain fell outside the hall where they were convening. No Boston newspaper printed a word of Victoria's speech. One paper reported that she had slandered a clergyman. The others simply noted that Mrs. Woodhull's speech had been obnoxious.

After that, it seemed to Victoria that she "must either endure unjustly the imputations of being a slanderer, or . . . relate in formal terms, for the whole world, the simple facts of the case." She chose the latter course, deciding to "justify, in cool deliberation," the words that she had uttered "almost unintentionally, and by a sudden impulse," in Boston.

17 ⸨ To Mr. Beecher, My Humble Apology ...

"WAS I not, in withholding the facts, and conniving at a putrid mass of seething falsehood and hypocrisy, in some sense a partaker in those crimes ... ?" So ran part of Victoria's lengthy justification for publishing the full story of the Beecher-Tilton scandal in a special issue of *Woodhull & Claflin's Weekly*.

Where the money had come from to make possible the resumption of publication was never explained. Perhaps some of the reenchanted spiritualists had contributed, caught up as they were in Victoria's belief that "a series of rapid and astounding events" would lead "in a marvelously short time" to a changed face of the social world.

Wherever the funds came from, Victoria, Colonel Blood, Tennie and Stephen Pearl Andrews planned the issue with great care. Columns were devoted to the persecution Victoria and her family and associates had known after the May convention of the Equal Rights Party—persecution which had caused the suspension of the *Weekly*. Columns were devoted to the deliberations that had preceded any decision to make certain revelations in the interests of the social revolution.

"I went back to and studied the history of other reforms," Victoria declared in the lead editorial. "I found that Garrison not only denounced slavery in the abstract, but that he attacked it in the concrete. ... He bravely and persistently called things by their right names. ... A new public opinion had to be created, and he knew that people had to be shocked, and that individual personal feelings had to be hurt." The comparison with the particular reforms sought by the *Weekly* was made and the consequences accepted. "We enter upon our work, fraught, it may be, with repugnance to ourselves as it is necessarily with repugnance to others."

The "great Universal Washing Day," which the *Weekly* had predicted a year before, was then launched in the form of an interview allegedly held between a New York reporter and Victoria after her return from Boston. The interview had been suppressed, the *Weekly* declared and surmised that this had been made possible because "an impecunious reporter can be bought off with a few hundred dollars." Fortunately, the editors had a "verbatim copy of the report, as the reporter prepared it." All the details that Victoria had ever heard about the Brooklyn scandal were included in this report, as well as descriptions of her meetings and relationships with various principals of the affair.

Tennie was eager to make her own contribution to the Washing Day. She knew scandalous facts about a great many people by now, but she seemed particularly obsessed by an episode involving a Wall Street broker named Luther B. Challis. Challis, according to much later testimony, had been on very intimate terms with Tennie for a while, visiting her at the mansion on 38th Street, fondling her in the view of various witnesses, even going so far as to call Roxanna "mother," on occasion.

The story that Tennie wanted to tell concerned a visit that she and Victoria had made, "closely dominoed," to a French Ball, held at the Academy of Music. One of the newspapers had reported that the ball was attended by "three thousand of the best men and four thousand of the worst women" of the city. Tennie had been outraged by this classification according to a double standard and burned to show that the "worst women" had earned this classification only because of the activities of "the best men." Luther Challis and a male companion were acompanied at the ball by "two young girls, fifteen or sixteen years of age." Tennie had watched the men ply the girls with wine until she had begged the girls to stop drinking. Later, she had followed up her acquaintance with the girls and discovered the circumstances of their seduction by Challis and his friend. The most lurid detail of all, which Tennie was determined to include, was that "this scoundrel, Challis, to prove that he had *seduced a maiden, carried for days on his finger, exhibiting in triumph, the red trophy of her virginity.*"

Victoria, Colonel Blood and Stephen Pearl Andrews were not sure that this story had any bearing on the point at issue. Luther Challis, unlike the Reverend Mr. Beecher, was no towering figure blocking the road to social revolution. Challis surely was "a little man," among those whose "peccadilloes it would be cowardice to attack."

Buck Claflin listened with his ear against the closed door as the argument went on. Colonel Blood opened the door and found him there. Buck spoke up boldly. He was against printing anything against Challis—it would get the girls into trouble.

Colonel Blood told him, according to what Buck said later, to close his "venerable mouth." He said, "We believe it and we mean to publish it."

Victoria would say that Colonel Blood had advised against publishing the Challis story and that it was she who had upheld Tennie. However it came about, in the end Tennie had her way. The revelations about Challis were included in the special issue of the *Weekly,* and Stephen Pearl Andrews wrote an introduction to the Challis article decrying the manner in which women were always judged on the basis of their sexual morality while this criterion was ignored in the consideration of a man's character.

The chief burden of the issue was still a full "ventilating" of the Beecher-Tilton matter. And to show how completely this revelation was tied to the cause of social progress and how little it was inspired by personal animosity, Victoria concluded the expose with an apology.

"I believe," she said, "in the law of peace, *in the right of privacy,* in the sanctity of individual relations. It is nobody's business but their own, in the absolute view, what Mr. Beecher and Mrs. Tilton have done, or may choose at any time to do, as between themselves. And the world needs too, to be taught just that lesson. . . . It is not therefore, Mr. Beecher as the individual I pursue, but Mr. Beecher as the representative man: Mr. Beecher as a power in the world . . . or Mr. Beecher as a violent enemy and a powerful hindrance to all that I am bent on accomplishing. . . . To Mr. Beecher, as the individual citizen, I tender, therefore, my humble apology, meaning and deeply feeling what I say, for this or any interference on my part, with his private life. . . ."

The issue was dated November 2, 1872. In accordance with usual practice, however, it was printed and ready for distribution several days before that. Everyone connected with the project was aware that this particular *Weekly* was likely to cause a sensation and that attempts might be made to suppress it. By October 28, copies had been mailed to the *Weekly*'s list of subscribers. In line with its recent policy the first page carried advertisements. There were no sensational headlines anywhere in the paper to give a clue as to its contents but by afternoon of that day, New Yorkers were already beginning to ask at newsstands for the "*Weekly* with the Beecher scandal."

The usual number of copies had been sent to the American News Company for local distribution. A glance at one copy had convinced the management that it might be wiser to refuse to handle this November 2 edition. The copies were sent to the Woodhull, Claflin offices on Broad Street. But the news dealers of the city quickly learned that copies were obtainable there and a rush of dealers to Broad Street was soon under way. The throng of men hurrying into the offices, emerging with bundles of *Weeklys* and then trying to fight their way out of the area grew so great at one point that the police were called to direct the traffic.

That evening, Victoria, Tennie and Colonel Blood felt satisfaction, a certain amount of quiet jubilation and anticipation all combined. Margaret Ann and her two daughters visited them at their current quarters and friends stopped in to congratulate Victoria and Tennie and to tell them that *Weeklys* were already so much in demand that in some places they were selling for fifty cents a copy. Victoria found this proof of "the terrible eargerness of the people to learn the facts." Margaret Ann's older daughter, who had begun a stage career, sang and gave recitations.

The first reports of Mr. Beecher's reactions to the public exposé of his love life came the next day as the "great sale" continued. Friends told Victoria that Mr. Beecher and his friends were hurrying to every newsstand that had the *Weekly* and buying all the copies available. It was reported that Mr. Beecher himself had made several triumphant raids of this nature. But a large sale had been anticipated and a much larger run than usual had been ordered. Friends, helping to deliver copies to depleted newsstands, laughed as they contemplated the discomfiture of the Beecher forces when they found themselves unable to stem the tide. Victoria, Tennie and Colonel Blood also helped to deliver copies.

The rush went on throughout the week. Even with the large printing, the *Weekly* was sought so eagerly that the price for a single copy went up to five dollars, to ten, to twenty. One man was said to have paid forty dollars for a copy and some fortunate purchasers were renting their copies for a dollar a day.

Outrage was undoubtedly mingling with fascination and shock for many New Yorkers as they perused the scandal issue of the *Weekly,* but more even than outrage galvanized one young man when at last he saw a copy. His name was Anthony Comstock and he was a sturdy fellow with broad shoulders, big feet and luxuriant, ginger-colored, mutton-chop whiskers. Raised in the Puritan tradition, he was only a boy when he decided to devote all his considerable energies to fighting the "powers of evil" in the world. He had spent his years in the army during the Civil War earnestly examining not only his own mind and heart for "wicked imaginings," but pointing out the errors of their ways to his camp mates. Coming to New York after the war, he had obtained a job as a salesman with a dry goods firm but his chief concern was in pitting himself against

the unrighteousness he saw flourishing on every side. He began
to believe that the root of the evil lay in the obscene books and
pamphlets, so easily available everywhere, that first inflamed
young men's imaginations and then led them on to vice. He
crusaded alone, at first. Dressed always in somber black, he
stomped in and out of the bookshops of the city, seizing any
erotic material that he could find, then calling on the police to
arrest the guilty book dealers and confiscate their offending
merchandise. Then he decided to get some outside backing for
his efforts and managed to interest the Young Men's Christian
Association in his crusade. The YMCA set up a Committee for
the Suppression of Vice with the dedicated Comstock as its
head. When Congress passed a statute, in the summer of 1872,
making the transmission of obscene literature through the
mails a misdemeanor, Comstock was encouraged to further in-
tensify his efforts.

Comstock saw a copy of the sensational *Weekly* late one evening. The next morning he easily obtained evidence that it was
sent through the mails and went at once to the District Attorney's office, asking for a warrant for the arrest of Victoria Woodhull and Tennie C. Claflin. The District Attorney agreed to
prepare one but when it was not forthcoming by midafternoon
Comstock went to the Federal authorities.

The morning after that Victoria and Tennie were in a carriage driving down Broad Street, five hundred copies of the
Weekly on the floor at their feet. Suddenly, their carriage was
stopped by two United States marshals with a warrant for their
arrest. Later, the marshals would imply that the sisters had
been in flight when stopped. Victoria would say that she and
Tennie, anticipating a visit from the police, were on their way
to their office to meet them. One marshal climbed up on the
box to sit beside the driver. The other "politely disposed himself" across the laps of the two women as though he feared they
might try to leap from the vehicle. In this fashion, the sisters
were conducted to the United States Circuit Court and an
examination by Commissioner Osborn.

Word of the arrest began to spread as soon as they stepped

from the carriage before the courthouse. The usual loungers and idlers straightened at once and began to take a lively interest in what was going on. The sisters, escorted by the marshals, were led to the doors of a "star chamber," with a rapidly growing procession behind them. Bankers, brokers, clerks and tradespeople from all over the vicinity were hurrying to the courthouse by this time, so swiftly had the news traveled.

It had been planned to make the examination a private one by Commissioner Osborn, the District Attorney, Assistant District Attorney and two other officials. Victoria and Tennie had no desire for such a private examination. "Indeed, we wished the public to be made thoroughly acquainted with all that was connected with the case," Victoria said later. They also demanded counsel. As they remained resolute, a lawyer, Mr. J. D. Reymart, was finally summoned and they were conducted to a courtroom.

The courtroom was crowded and everyone stared at Victoria and Tennie, dressed alike in simple costumes of dark blue with purple bows. It was noticed that Victoria looked "grave and severe, never smiling," while Tennie C.'s "eyes sparkled with excitement. She smiled affably as something in the remarks of her counsel or the District Attorney struck her as funny."

The Assistant District Attorney, General Davies, explained the charge. The sisters had been arrested for having circulated through the United States mail an "obscene and indecent publication." The offense was punishable by imprisonment and a fine.

The sisters' attorney, Mr. Reymart, asked for an adjournment so that he would have time to consult with his clients and study the case. The following Monday or Tuesday was suggested as a possible time for continuing the hearing. It was noted that Tuesday was an election day (the very Presidential election in which Victoria had been slated to run as the candidate for the Equal Rights Party just six months previously). Monday was chosen. At which point General Davies asked that bail be fixed for the two sisters in the amount of $10,000 each.

"The circumstances of this case," he said, "are circumstances of peculiar aggravation. Not only have the defendants, by circulating an obscene publication through the mails, been guilty of an offense against the law, but they have been guilty of a most abominable and unjust charge against one of the purest and best citizens of this State, or in the United States, and they have ... aggravated the offense by a malicious and gross libel upon the character of this gentleman, whose character it is well worth the while of the Government of the United States to vindicate."

General Davies would ultimately have reason to regret being quite so carried away by his personal emotions in this request. Admired as the Reverend Mr. Beecher was, there were many who felt that it was going rather far to suggest that the Government of the United States should undertake a vindication of his reputation and that, in a democracy, there was no need to free him from the responsibility of defending himself when necessary, just as any other citizen would have to do.

Disregarding this aspect of Davies' remarks, Victoria and Tennie's lawyer was quick to remind the court that the Assistant District Attorney was exceeding his authority even so. The sisters were not being charged with any offense against the Reverend Mr. Beecher. They were not being charged with libel of him—or anyone. There was only one charge against them, that of sending obscene matter through the mails.

But the Commissioner's sympathies were with those of General Davies. "An example is needed," he said, "and we propose to make one of these women." He set their bail at $8,000 each and remanded them into the custody of the marshals until the Monday hearing.

Someone—"a stranger," according to Victoria—offered to post the bail required by both sisters. But word had already reached them that Luther Challis, unlike the Reverend Mr. Beecher, *was* preparing to sue them for libel and was obtaining warrants not only for their arrest but the arrest of Colonel Blood, Stephen Pearl Andrews, and a printer and an engraver connected with the *Weekly*'s publication. An arrest on the

Challis warrant would imprison them in the Jefferson Market Prison, known as New York's "Black Hole of Calcutta." Victoria and Tennie's lawyer advised them to go to the Ludlow Street Jail under their present indictment and remain there until all suits against them developed.

By Saturday evening, November 2, 1872, Victoria and Tennie were in Ludlow Street Jail and Colonel Blood, arrested under the Challis warrant, was in the Jefferson Market Prison.

The collision that Victoria had been asking for, between herself and the hypocrisy of society in general, and the Beechers in particular, had at last taken place.

18 § Conscious of the Right . . .

AT first it seemed that respectable society would have no trouble in slamming down the windows against the "ventilation" which Victoria and Tennie had tried to provide. For a great many people it was enough, after their initial shock, to follow the line laid down by the Reverend Henry Ward Beecher himself. His attitude was reported in the *Sunday Mercury* the day after the Woodhull-Claflin arrest.

"How is Brother Beecher taking this Woodhull affair?" a reporter asked a deacon of Plymouth Church.

"He ain't going to say anything about it," Deacon Hudson replied. "He's going to cut the whole thing and let it go."

"But Deacon Hudson," the reporter persisted, "will Mr. Beecher not take the trouble to refute those charges when they are made circumstantially?"

"No, I don't think Brother Beecher will take the trouble. You see we know him, and we don't propose to take anything that a woman like Woodhull says against him. . . . I think it is blackmail. She wanted him to preside at the free love meeting and he wouldn't, so she came down on this Tilton thing."

"Well, Brother Hudson, do the Plymouth flock intend to stand by Mr. Beecher?"

"Of course we do. We know him and we will support him. Take the case up? Not a bit of it."

Shock and outrage at the first blast of cold wind, then a slamming down of windows everywhere, and a refusal to admit that the wind had any reality—these were enough for Beecher's congregation and for millions across the country who revered him.

"Cut it and let it go." As nearly as possible most newspapers were taking that line, offering only the briefest of reports on the arrests of Victoria Woodhull and Tennie C. Claflin for slandering the Reverend Mr. Beecher. Later, it would be alleged that the Associated Press had wired a release to its subscribers across the country reporting that the confiscated *Weekly* had contained "immodest cartoons" as well as "testimony too filthy to publish." Certainly the belief was soon current among those who had not seen the *Weekly* personally that it did contain obscene pictures as well as text. The less said about such matters the better seemed to be the general attitude of most newspaper editors.

"Take the case up? Not a bit of it." After all, there was no need to. Society itself, as it was represented by the dogged Anthony Comstock, the YMCA, and the District Attorney and Court Commissioner, was taking care of the matter for Beecher. Later, there would be those who insisted that not all of Beecher's congregation were as detached from the problem as Deacon Hudson professed to be. They were sure that the speed with which the law proceeded against the sisters was secretly encouraged by men with powerful reasons to want Beecher's reputation kept unblemished. There were quite a few of these —stockholders in Plymouth Church, who knew its success depended on Beecher; the publisher who had advanced Beecher $25,000 to write a book on the life of Jesus; Henry Bowen, publisher of the *Christian Union* which also depended on

Beecher's name. All these had quickly applied pressure where it would do the most good, or so it would be claimed. And the swift action against Victoria and Tennie, once it was started, did give such claims a certain validity.

Arrested on Saturday afternoon, November 2, Victoria and Tennie were taken from the jail to a courtroom in the Federal Building on Monday afternoon, November 4, for an examination by Commissioner Osborn. The courtroom was packed with spectators, eager for spicy details, but it soon developed that there would be no examination after all. A Grand Jury, hastily summoned, had met that morning and found indictments against the sisters. Bench warrants for their formal arrest had already been issued by the Circuit Court. They would be given no hearing.

Victoria and Tennie had managed to engage another lawyer over the weekend, William P. Howe, of the celebrated legal team of Howe and Hummel. He was now their chief counsel. Noted for his sartorial brilliance as well as his oratory, Howe was a resplendent figure at the sisters' side, wearing plaid pantaloons, a purple vest and a blue satin cravat. And although the case was now out of the Commissioner's jurisdiction, Howe spoke briefly and dramatically. He and Mr. Reymart, the sisters' first counsel, had a perfect defense for the "persecuted ladies," he said. No word that had been printed in the *Weekly* could be called obscene, he declared, for if so held, then "the transmission through the mails of the Holy Bible, the works of Lord Byron, or any edition of the works of Shakespeare would be liable to the same penalty." Again he spoke of persecution, "instigated by private malice from a source which dare not come into court itself to expose its malignity."

After that, the sisters were formally arrested and escorted back to their cell in Ludlow Street Jail to await trial by the government at some future date.

Victoria and Tennie were not without some friends and supporters of their own to rally round them now—readers and

disciples of the *Weekly*, members of the Pantarchy, a conglom-
erate number of radicals and reformers who admired Victoria's
principles and her passionate insistence on pursuing them no
matter what the consequences. Their cell was crowded from
morning till night with visitors and they held court sitting on
the prison cots, gravely greeting their callers and expressing
their "willingness to suffer for what they conceive to be right."

New sympathizers, roused by their arrest, also appeared.
Among these was a tall, long-legged man muffled in a huge
sealskin coat. He was George Francis Train, a millionaire well
known for a variety of exploits, achievements and eccen-
tricities. Train's background, in fact, almost surpassed that of
Stephen Pearl Andrews' in its wide-ranging eclecticism. After
making a fortune in the shipping business as a young man,
Train had gone to Australia, where he pioneered in a supply
system for settlers in the outback; to England, where he had
introduced street railways; to France, where he hobnobbed
with Louis Napoleon and the Empress Eugenie; to Spain,
where he interested the queen in an American land venture.
Back in the United States, he had helped in the planning of
the Union Pacific Railway, helped to organize the Credit
Mobilier, a new sort of funding system by which the owners of
the railway sold stocks and financed its construction, and then
disassociated himself from the whole affair before the corruption which later discredited it was begun. In 1870, Train had
set out to see how fast he could travel around the world and
he had accomplished the journey in eighty days, thereby inspiring, or so he always claimed, the French author Jules Verne
to the writing of a famous novel. Train also found time to
interest himself in a number of causes. Violently against organized religion, he was violently in favor of women's suffrage.
Once he accompanied Susan Anthony and Elizabeth Stanton
on a lecture tour in the West, creating a sensation wherever
he went by his dandified manner, his lavender kid gloves and
his tousled mop of curly hair. He had always avoided Victoria
Woodhull and Tennie Claflin, however, because he disliked
their free-love doctrines.

But Train's past reservations about the sisters were forgotten when he heard of their arrest. He was making a speech against religion from the steps of a Wall Street bank when someone brought him a newspaper reporting the event. Immediately, he dispatched a note to them, telling them that he thought the language they had used in the *Weekly* was "grand" and "full of truths eternal." Then he sent off a second note, offering to pay their bail. "I am satisfied," he wrote, "the cowardly Christian community will destroy you, if possible, to cover up the rotten state of society."

Victoria and Tennie replied gratefully but declined his offer. "Conscious of the right," they wrote in answer, "we prefer to be independent and remain where we are at present. Having been the first to come to our aid, we shall be the last to forget it."

Train then hurried to visit them in jail, to encourage and help them in any other way that he could. It may have been his money that was making possible the expensive legal services of William Howe. If so, that was only the beginning of Train's devotion to Victoria and Tennie's cause. He visited them daily, composed epigrams and couplets for them, which he wrote on the walls of their cell, and he bombarded the newspapers with letters in their defense. Soon he was busy with a project to dramatize their plight. Putting together a little newspaper which he called the *Train Ligue*, he was reprinting in its columns all the more controversial sections of the *Weekly* of November 2. He planned to mail it widely and then to challenge Anthony Comstock to arrest him as the sisters had been arrested.

Meantime, there was another hearing to be faced, this one on the matter of the Luther Challis libel charge against Woodhull, Claflin, Blood, Andrews, et al. On November 8, Colonel Blood was brought from his cell in Jefferson Market Jail, and Victoria and Tennie were escorted from the Ludlow Street Jail to the Jefferson Market Court. Anthony Comstock was present, somberly accusative, and George Francis Train was on hand also, his gray curls arranged in "a distractingly talented manner," according to the *Herald*. William Howe wore a plaid vest, a glittering watch guard and a diamond tiepin. And at this hearing he and almost everyone else were given ample opportunity to speak.

Victoria and Tennie both testified that they assumed full responsibility for the Challis article and they denied that Colonel Blood had anything to do with it. Colonel Blood, on the other hand, insisted that if anyone were punishable because of it, he must be also. Buck Claflin testified in a cheerful fashion about his eavesdropping when the article was being planned and the way he had warned his daughters against its publication. Luther Challis was asked various pointed questions about his past relationship with Tennie to which he gave evasive answers. Laura Cuppy Smith testified that she had once seen Tennie on Challis' lap when she was visiting the house on 38th Street. A Mr. Maxwell, to whom Victoria said she had talked about the Challis article before its publication, testified that he had heard Mr. Challis use the words quoted in the *Weekly*.

Mr. Howe, as counsel, spoke at length, again calling attention to the Bible. He referred specifically to a passage in Deuteronomy XXII, in which the disputed words of the *Weekly* were used in almost exactly the same fashion. Then the hearing was concluded and the prisoners returned to their cells to await the Commissioner's decision in the matter.

"Sick in body, sick in mind, sick at heart," Victoria wrote in a public letter to the New York *Herald*, "I write these lines to ask if, because I am a woman, I am to have no justice, no fair play, no chance through the press to reach public opinion. . . ."

Writing from Cell 11, Ludlow Street Jail, it would have been impossible for Victoria to describe herself otherwise than "sick in body . . . mind . . . heart," for this was a cluster of phrases she found irresistible under almost any circumstances. Still, she and Tennie were not actually suffering physically. Later, Victoria would confess that Ludlow Street Jail was nothing like the dungeon she and Tennie had anticipated. "We admit we were somewhat surprised by our polite reception. . . . We not only found in Warden Tracy a true-hearted gentleman of philanthropic impulses and devoted to the alleviation of prison-life, but in the assistant and clerk, Mr. William L. Gardner, a person of refinement . . . a gifted author and poet." The jail, Victoria said, "had all the appointments of a regular hotel . . . opportunities for bathing, exercise in the open air, a generous table, and scrupulous cleanliness."

Nor was it altogether true any longer that she had "no chance through the press to reach public opinion." The ranks of the respectable, which had been almost solid against her and Tennie at the time of their arrest, were beginning to waver a little here and there.

Newspapers published by the spiritualists had, of course, been loyal to their national president from the beginning. "Victoria C. Woodhull in prison! And for what?" demanded the Syracuse *Morning Herald,* of Syracuse, New York. "*Ostensibly,* for mailing obscene literature; really for telling the truth about a famous divine who hasn't the consistence to preach two sermons on the same line of thought, nor the moral courage to defend his unpopular utterances."

But now a few papers without any previous bias in the sisters' favor, papers that had openly decried them, were beginning to express some uneasiness at the workings of the law as it had operated in their case. The Brooklyn *Eagle* commented: "The statute on which the proceeding independently and disinterestedly initiated by Mr. Comstock is based, reads larger than the astute mind of the Assistant Federal District Attorney at first suggested. . . . It shows that without having generally known it, the people of this country are living under a law more narrow and oppressive than any people with a written constitution ever lived before. . . . We can discover no intention on the part of the authorities to try these women at all. The seeming disposition indefinitely to incarcerate them . . . is discernible."

In Hartford, Connecticut, home of three Beecher sisters, the *Times* declared that "the United States Government is taking possession of the people and ruling them. The servants are becoming masters of the people." The writer of the editorial also asked why Victoria Woodhull and Tennie Claflin had been arrested by United States marshals instead of by representatives of the state of New York.

In Troy, New York, a young journalist named Edward H. G. Clark, writing for the Troy *Whig* and Troy *Daily Press*, was showing a concern for the issues involved that would deepen as time went on. Clark had been an abolitionist disciple of William Lloyd Garrison before the war, and as such, a friend of Theodore Tilton, who had also written and talked the Garrison line. He did not defend Victoria Woodhull personally in his articles in the *Whig* and the *Daily Press*. He had met her, he said, a year or so before, and "I instantly perceived her to be just what I say she is now, a woman thoroughly in earnest ... a strange combination of good and evil ... faithful only to her own ideas." Still, he declared flatly (just as William P. Howe was maintaining; just as George Francis Train was) that there was no obscenity in the disputed issue of the *Weekly*, and he was sharply critical of the way Victoria and Tennie had been arrested and imprisoned. It seemed to Clark an action engineered by those so concerned about the Reverend Mr. Beecher's reputation that they were ignoring all constitutional guarantees of the freedom of the press.

Those who found no fault with the way the law was proceeding took fresh comfort from further comments by the Reverend Mr. Beecher. A friend spoke to the minister about the "Woodhull outrage," and offered his sympathy.

"My friend," said Beecher, "I do not need any sympathy," and he went on to explain that he was troubled because his friends were troubled but that his life in Plymouth Church was his defense.

The friend suggested that Mrs. Woodhull must be insane to have made such charges. "I believe so too," said Beecher, smiling. "At any rate, I can only wish people had better minds."

The friend persisted. "Of course, Mr. Beecher, the whole thing is a fraud from beginning to end."

At this, Beecher nodded his head and said, "Entirely." And such was the force of the Beecher personality that the friend later said that he had never before realized the potency of the word "entirely."

But there were also those who were not impressed by Beecher's oblique disclaimer. Susan B. Anthony's feelings about Victoria had not changed since Victoria almost wrecked the National Woman's Suffrage Association Convention the summer before. She was credited generally as being one of those who knew the facts in the Beecher-Tilton affair and was questioned by reporters wherever she went after the appearance of the scandal issue of the *Weekly*. Miss Anthony steadfastly refused to make any comment. Still, after reading about the Reverend Mr. Beecher's resounding "Entirely," Miss Anthony wrote to Isabella Beecher Hooker that if the Lord ever did strike anyone dead for telling a lie, surely He should have struck then.

Elizabeth Cady Stanton, mentioned by name in the *Weekly* as one of the sources for the Beecher-Tilton story, was also pursued by reporters for comments. Not quite able to match Miss Anthony's restraint, Mrs. Stanton had deplored and denounced the publication of the story, but it was noted quickly that she had not denied it. And when Mrs. Stanton read of Henry Ward Beecher's "Entirely," she wrote to Miss Anthony that if her testimony could help Victoria in her difficulties she would give it.

As for Isabella Beecher Hooker, she positively approved of Victoria's revelations about her half brother. A year and more before, when Victoria was not yet sure of her mission in the matter, Isabella had been urging Henry to avow publicly his belief in social freedom. She had even threatened to mount his pulpit and make the avowal for him and had so frightened Henry that he had detailed his sister, Harriet, to sit in a front pew at every service to head off Isabella should she appear. Now, with the story published at last, Isabella wrote to another Beecher brother, Thomas, to tell him how troubled she was by the course of evasion Henry was following and her own sense of responsibility to the truth. "At present, of course, I shall keep silent; but truth is dearer than all things else, and if he will not speak it in some way, I cannot always stand as consenting to a lie."

The Reverend Thomas Beecher replied, "I respect, as at present advised, Mrs. Woodhull, while I abhor her philosophy. She only carries out Henry's philosophy against which I recorded my protest twenty years ago, and parted (lovingly and achingly) from him. . . . Of the two Woodhull is my hero, and Henry my coward. . . . You cannot help Henry. You must be true to Woodhull. . . . Follow the truth, and when you need me cry out. . . . I think you are all in the wrong, but I honor and love them who suffer for conviction's sake."

So, in spite of the slammed windows, the ventilating wind continued to blow, agitating more and more people as they pondered things long known but never admitted, things surmised but never faced. And for two weeks, three weeks, almost four, Victoria and Tennie remained in Ludlow Street Jail. They were waiting, they said later, for powerful friends to rally to their support. Just which powerful friends they never indicated. Not-so-powerful friends continued to mill around in their cell each day, expressing sympathy and stirring up minor alarms. "Cell No. 11, now well known as the residence of Woodhull and Claflin, was a perfect camp meeting yesterday," reported the New York *Mercury*, which went on to describe a typical little drama. "On a small table was an appetizing dinner served for Mrs. Woodhull, who had eaten no breakfast. Just as Mrs. Woodhull began her dinner a woman entered and whispered, 'Your food is being poisoned,' and her appetite fled."

Finally, at the end of November, it was decided that the sisters should seek their release on bail. Two admirers, Dr. Augustus Ruggles and a Mr. Kiernan of Brooklyn, offered to put up the $16,000 that was required. Mr. Howe accompanied Victoria and Tennie to the Federal Building to meet with their bondsmen and secure their release. Almost at once it was discovered that an officer of the Jefferson Market Court was waiting in the hall to arrest the sisters on another charge. Hysterical rumors were circulating—that Victoria and Tennie were to be forced to the Jefferson Market Jail, that while they were there the prison was to be set on fire and they left to perish, and that the judge had been spirited away to prevent the prisoners from being bailed.

Mr. Howe took charge and advised Victoria and Tennie to return to the Ludlow Street Jail until bail could be arranged in the matter of the new arrest. They managed the return without any special incident. Four days later, on December 5, bail for the new charge had been obtained and the sisters were again at the Federal Building.

And again Victoria and Tennie were arrested, on still another variation of the original charge.

This time Howe was able to arrange for satisfactory bail immediately. He also had obtained a writ of *habeas corpus* to release Colonel Blood from the Jefferson Market Prison. At last, a month after their imprisonment, Victoria, Tennie and Colonel Blood were free on bond.

Their long stay in prison, the lack of any public hearing on the obscenity charge, and then their repeated rearrests after obtaining bail, were causing further agitation among the ranks of the respectable. The widely read *Frank Leslie's Illustrated Newspaper* was commenting on the sisters now: "Mrs. Woodhull and Miss Claflin have been placed in a position to give them real consequence. They have been arrested by the United States Government, and thrust into jail.... Another thing which we dislike in the case is that it had assumed too much of the form of an 'Inquisition.' All the facts should have gone to the public. Woodhull and Claflin have a right to public opinion and public opinion depends on the press."

Edward H. G. Clark, in Troy, was less widely read but persistent, and he was doing his best to meet the obligations of the press by filling columns with all the facts that he could ascertain, along with his own conclusions. He reminded his readers that six different persons, all living and well known, had been cited by Mrs. Woodhull as having related or acknowledged to her the Beecher-Tilton scandal story. "Of these six persons, three at least—Mrs. Davis, Mrs. Stanton and Mr. Moulton—were bound by every tie of private friendship and every call of public justice to refute and confuse Mrs. Woodhull instantly, if such refutation and confusion were possible." No such refutation had taken place. He spoke of his own longtime respect for the Reverend Beecher and his willingness to "sacrifice a hecatomb of Woodhulls to save one Beecher," if that were possible. But the facts made it impossible to "hold Henry Ward Beecher as a true and pure man against the torrent of direct evidence and suspicious circumstances against him."

And yet, Mr. Clark went on, "to sustain a hollow *pretension* of his innocence, and a thin, trembling crust of Plymouth Church 'respectability' two women have been thrown into jail on a charge so contemptibly false that no court can be persuaded or kicked into trying them for it; the press of the nation has been confused and bullied into helping the fraud along; while Challis and Comstock—the Young Men's Christian Association and the Rake's Club—have joined hands to strangle liberty and law, honesty and truth...."

Out of jail, Victoria, Tennie, Colonel Blood and all their usual helpers, including Stephen Pearl Andrews (who had been cited in several of the warrants against the sisters, but against whom charges had been dropped), hurried to make ready another issue of the *Weekly*, which would relate all the events following the issue of November 2.

George Francis Train was busy also with another issue of his paper, the *Train Ligue*. Disappointed because his first effort had provoked no response from Anthony Comstock, Train was preparing a second issue in which he was printing excerpts from the Old Testament under sensational headlines. When this was published in mid-December Train at last won his objective. Comstock saw it and was outraged. For some reason, the Federal authorities declined to oblige him with a warrant against Train but the state authorities were more agreeable. Comstock got his warrant and Train was indicted for sending obscene matter through the mails.

Train refused to give bail. Embracing his martyrdom, he allowed himself to be hurried off to the Tombs. This prison offered none of the amenities that Victoria and Tennie had found at the Ludlow Street Jail, but George Francis Train took a reformer's relish in his miserable surroundings. Quartered in Murderers' Row, along with twenty-two convicted murderers, he determined to spend his time in exposing the conditions in this pesthole of society. He buckled down to composing long letters to the newspapers and lengthy bulletins headed "Hark! From the Tombs!," destined for publication in *Woodhull & Claflin's Weekly.*

The first issue of the *Weekly* after the sisters' arrest appeared shortly before Christmas, 1872. If facts on the proceedings against Victoria and Tennie had been sparse in most papers, the *Weekly* made up for the omissions, offering an accounting so detailed that the story was advanced only to the hearing of November 8 in the Challis case, at which point it was suspended, "to be continued in next number."

Victoria was eager also to tell the story in person. Efforts were made to hire a hall in Boston so that she could speak on "Moral Cowardice and Moral Hypocrisy, or Four Weeks in Ludlow Street Jail." But the governor of Massachusetts himself intervened. "She is no better than a panel thief or a common street walker," he declared, "and I will see that she don't open her vile mouth in the city which was so recently honored by Mr. Beecher's presence." An auditorium was found in Springfield, Massachusetts, instead, and Victoria delivered her speech there.

She spoke with a "singularly pathetic voice," according to a reporter for the Springfield *Republican,* and had a "rapid, eager magnetic manner," as she warned the YMCA, and its one man vice squad, Anthony Comstock, Plymouth Church and the

Government of the United States, that the *Weekly* would tear down the social system unless the press lost all its freedom. In that case, Victoria cried, the plaintiffs would go from state to state, sowing the seeds of social revolution. "Stop their presses they may, but their tongues, never!"

Firm in that resolve, Victoria planned to speak next in New York City. Arrangements were made for her to talk in Cooper Union on January 9, and her speech was now titled "The Naked Truth," after the title of a poem by William Cullen Bryant. Announcements of the event were sent to the newspapers and posters were printed for the hall.

But Anthony Comstock had marked the advent of 1873 with a resolution also, a vow "to do something every day for Jesus." He was sick in bed when he read of Victoria's scheduled speech but he rose at once and arranged for an order to be mailed from Connecticut to *Woodhull & Claflin's Weekly,* requesting copies of the issue of November 2. A few days later he was gratified to hear that the paper had been received in Connecticut along with a letter offering further copies at a reduced rate. Armed with this evidence that "obscene literature" was still being sent through the mails by the editors of the *Weekly,* Comstock went to the Federal authorities and again obtained an indictment against Woodhull, Claflin and Blood.

The timing was perfect. On the morning of January 9, the very day on which Victoria planned to speak, police officers set out with warrants for the arrest of Victoria Woodhull, Tennie Claflin and James Blood.

The officers found Colonel Blood on Broad Street near the brokerage office. Somehow, before he was driven away to Ludlow Street Jail, the Colonel managed to send a message uptown to Victoria and Tennie to warn them that the police were on their way.

Accordingly, when the officers arrived at the Woodhull-Claflin living quarters, they were unable to find the sisters. In the kitchen, they discovered the cook, busy at a washtub set on another overturned tub. The cook flourished a wringer at them, bidding them get out. They left, not knowing that Tennie was hiding underneath the overturned tub.

Victoria had fled the house entirely. Accompanied by her bondsmen, she hurried to the ferry and traveled to Jersey City, where she checked in at a hotel.

"Cut it and let it go," had been the Reverend Beecher's first response to Victoria's challenge, but the zealous defenders of the order he represented would not be so advised.

"Stop their presses they may, but their tongues, never!" had been Victoria's response. But now, on January 9, it seemed that she was wrong. Respectable society was stronger at slamming shut doors and windows than she was at prying them open.

19 } Truth Crushed to Earth . . .

THE posters advertising Victoria's lecture were up in front of Cooper Union just as posters had been up, a year and more before, at Steinway Hall, to herald her dramatic "free love" speech. A year and more before, the night had been wet and windy but Steinway Hall had been jammed with people eager to hear her. The night of January 9, 1873, was also unpropitious for it was bitterly cold. But once again crowds of New Yorkers were braving the weather to find out what The Woodhull had to say about the Beecher scandal and what had befallen her as a result of her revelations. Up the Bowery and down Fourth Avenue they came, to converge on the hall at the junction of the two streets. But at the doors they found United States marshals and policemen who were telling all comers, "There will be no lecture tonight. Mrs. Woodhull is being arrested and flung into prison."

Many turned away, disappointed. But a surprising number went on into the hall anyway and took seats. They stared at an empty platform. More policemen, fifty in all, were stationed around the auditorium. They too repeated, "There will be no lecture. Mrs. Woodhull is being arrested."

A little old lady, dressed in Quaker gray, her face hidden by a coal-scuttle bonnet, walked slowly down one of the aisles toward a front seat. The audience, in a mood for any distraction, stared at the old woman and smiled at her old-fashioned appearance. But impatience was growing. People began to clap in rhythm, to stamp, and then to shout, "The Woodhull! Woodhull!"

At last a slight figure walked out onto the platform. Laura Cuppy Smith, Victoria's friend, held up her hand to quiet the audience and then began apologizing for Victoria's absence. Mrs. Woodhull was being flung into an "American Bastille," for daring to speak and publish the truth.

As Mrs. Smith spoke, the old Quaker lady was seen to rise. With the hesitation of age, she made her way to the stairs leading to the platform and then slowly mounted the steps. Again there were smiles in the audience as the curious figure tottered halfway across the stage. Then the old lady disappeared behind one of the broad, square pillars that supported the roof of the hall.

Laura Cuppy Smith told the audience that at least it would hear the speech that Victoria had prepared, for Victoria had entrusted it to her to read. "The task, under the circumstances, is as painful to me as it is disappointing to you," she said, "but the custodians of the law guard the doors of the Institute, and neither Mrs. Woodhull nor Miss Claflin can, no matter how much they may desire it, appear upon this platform tonight."

There was a sudden flash of movement on the stage as she spoke. The old Quaker lady, moving with an energy quite unlike her previous hesitation, was dashing out from behind the pillar. She was flinging off her coal-scuttle bonnet. The gown of Quaker gray was torn off and was sliding down over the dark dress beneath it to lie coiled on the floor.

And there stood Victoria Woodhull, her hair disarranged, her cheeks flushed and her eyes blazing.

The audience gasped its astonishment and then screamed its joy.

"Comstock's euchred!" shrieked one voice above the uproar.

Victoria held out her arms to the crowd. Then, as the noise abated, she began to speak. It was a measure of the dramatic effect she had achieved that not one of the fifty policemen in the hall made a move to stop or to arrest her. Instead, they stood seemingly as transfixed as her audience while she talked on and on.

She told of how she, Tennie and Colonel Blood had been deprived of their rights as American citizens, of how the newspapers had not printed their side of the case, of the way law officers had broken into their printing office and seized their type, destroyed presses and taken private papers. She accused Comstock and the YMCA of being Beecher's agents, hired by him to silence her. Her voice rang out as she dwelt on the distinction between prosecution and persecution. And still the policemen stood at their posts.

She came at last, as she always did, to the "social question," and spoke of brothels crowding the streets and of "passional starvation, enforced by law and a factitious public opinion, that oppressed sick and weary wives and even husbands. . . ." She spoke of "ten thousand forms of domestic damnation, and everybody crying Peace! Peace! where there is no peace!"

For an hour and a half she talked, with her audience alternately spellbound or cheering. Then, suddenly, she was finished and moving swiftly off the stage.

A long account of the dramatic evening appeared some time later in the *Weekly*, written by one of the newspaper's contributors, Anthony Higgins. Mr. Higgins told of how, Victoria's spell finally broken, the audience began to stir, and the policemen, too, woke to their duty and hurried after Mrs. Woodhull to arrest her.

"Too late!" wrote Anthony Higgins. "The much-dreaded Naked Truth had reached the public ear through the silver-tongued Woodhull, the brave. She is the superior strategist. The terrible syren has defeated you and charmed your cohorts and battalions to silence and inaction."

Still, once their enchantment was ended, the police moved swiftly enough, soon caught up with Victoria, made their arrest, and then drove her off to Ludlow Street Jail, where Colonel Blood was already imprisoned.

This latest arrest, following such a spectacular public appeal, evoked more uneasy press comment.

"For the second, third, fourth and fifth time Mrs. Victoria C. Woodhull has been arrested," reported the New York *Mercury*. "If the charges against her can be maintained by proof, the proper way is to proceed to trial and convict her. But that 'this great Government of the mightiest Republic the world ever saw' should repeat from day to day its sledge-hammer attacks upon these women is, to say the least, unjust."

And the *Commercial Advertiser* asked: "Why do the United States Marshals continue to play with Woodhull and Claflin as a cat plays with a mouse?"

A hearing on the latest arrest was held the next morning before Commissioner Davenport. Once again William Howe pressed Anthony Comstock for his opinion of certain phrases in Deuteronomy XXII. Once again Comstock sat solidly and insisted on the sanctity of the Biblical language while holding that the same language used in the *Weekly* was obscene. Bail was set and bondsmen stepped forward. Some objections by the Commissioner to the bondsmen were overcome. Bail was accepted. Victoria and Colonel Blood were released.

Two days later there was still another hearing, this one in connection with the charge against Tennie, who had finally emerged from under the washtub and submitted to arrest. Again Mr. Howe quoted Deuteronomy XXII. Bail was set at

$5,000. Dr. Ruggles, already one of the bondsmen for the $16,000 surety, offered to provide it. Tennie was released.

Just eleven days later, on January 23, police officers appeared late in the afternoon at the Broad Street office with new warrants for the arrest of Woodhull, Claflin and Blood.

"What have we done now?" Victoria asked resignedly and the police were confused themselves. A study of the warrants showed that Luther Challis was making a second charge. Following Comstock's lead, he was complaining that the editors of the *Weekly* had sent an obscene article about him through the mails.

The police had appeared so late in the day that the District Attorney had left for home by the time they had escorted Victoria, Tennie and Colonel Blood to his office. There was nothing to do but put the three in jail for the night. This time they were taken to the Tombs, the "Christian Bastille," where George Francis Train was still "undergoing torture," according to his reports, "for quoting three columns of Biblical obscenity."

Bail was set the next morning in the Court of General Sessions—one thousand dollars each for the sisters and two thousand for the Colonel. William Howe pointed out to the judge that the total surety now asked of the defendants for an alleged misdemeanor was sixty thousand dollars. He asked the judge to compare that with the figure of fifty-one thousand dollars which was all that was being asked currently of "Boss" Tweed, who, as everyone now knew, had looted the city of millions. The judge was unmoved by the comparison. Bail was offered then and accepted for Victoria and Tennie, but Colonel Blood seemed unable to secure the amount required of him. He was returned to the Tombs until he could raise the bail and Victoria and Tennie were released.

Victoria may have taken some comfort during these days of repeated arrests in hearing that elsewhere in the country another woman was also suffering at the hands of the law for her principles. Susan B. Anthony, acting in accordance with the policy that had been adopted at the NWSA convention two years before, had insisted on casting a ballot in the 1872 elections. She had been arrested for illegal voting and sentenced with a fine which she was refusing to pay. Victoria remembered how she herself had advocated that militant voting policy in the days when she had been Miss Anthony's "bright, glorious spirit," and she wrote Miss Anthony a letter, offering to help in any way that she could. Miss Anthony noted receipt of the letter in her diary but made no reply.

Another letter Victoria wrote was more productive. She appealed to the Honorable Benjamin Butler, her admirer of two years before who had helped her with her Memorial to Congress, for aid in her current legal difficulties. Benjamin Butler did reply.

"I shall not be able to find time from my public duties to take part in the trial of your case," he wrote, "but I cannot believe that in ... the prosecution of yourself and your sister for sending obscene literature through the mails, in the Courts of the United States, there is the slightest need of my services or counsel. I feel as certain as I can of any question, upon construction of the statute, that the action of the United States Prosecuting Attorney was based wholly upon a misconstruction and misconception of that statute...." Butler went on to suggest how this misconception could be tested and proved and then concluded, "If I were your counsel I should advise you to make no further defense but mere matter of law.... I do not believe a legal wrong can be done you in this behalf before any learned and intelligent judge."

Benjamin Butler's letter was made public in the New York *Sun* on February 3, 1873. On the same day, Commissioner Davenport made his decision in the matter heard before him on January 10. Perhaps he was already familiar with the contents of Butler's letter, for he said that he doubted that such a case as the one in question ever had been contemplated when the statute was passed. However, the Commissioner was so impressed with "the importance of the questions involved" in the charges against Woodhull, Claflin and Blood that he was going to "hold the prisoners to await the action of the Grand Jury, to the end that a judicial determination by the Circuit Court of the United States may be had, and the rights, both of the prisoners and the public, be finally ascertained."

The *Weekly* was coming out regularly now, week after week, in spite of the repeated arrests of its editors, the time-consuming hearings and the necessary legal consultations. Stephen Pearl Andrews was still a faithful contributor, with a keen, cool eye for analyzing the technicalities of all that was happening. George Blood, an older brother of the Colonel, had joined the staff as a bookkeeper but contributed editorially now and then (and was helpful also in the care of Victoria's son, Byron). Joseph Treat, an impassioned radical, was another new recruit. And the usual helpers were delighted to carry on during these dramatic times.

The adverse decision of the Commissioner could be reported and decried at length in the *Weekly,* but Victoria was more eager now than ever to tell the "Naked Truth" to audiences wherever she could find them. And with public curiosity about the Beecher scandal growing, a great many people were anxious to hear her, however the authorities might try to intervene.

She was invited by the New England Labor Reform League, a radical organization with headquarters in Boston, to be present for its three-day meeting in late February. Tremont Temple, one of Boston's largest halls, had been engaged for the convention. However, as soon as the hall's management discovered that Mrs. Woodhull was going to be present, permission to meet there was withdrawn. Another hall was finally found.

Victoria appeared. She was modest, beautiful and magnetic as she told her story to a rapt audience. She had found another poem about truth to use as a theme and quoted some lines by James Russell Lowell which had been inspired by a mob's attack on William Lloyd Garrison during the years of the antislavery struggle.

> Truth crushed to earth shall rise again,
> The eternal years of God are hers;
> But error, wounded, writhes in pain,
> And dies among her worshippers.

So many people were eager to hear Mrs. Woodhull that Victoria had to give another speech the next evening and make two informal, unscheduled talks as well.

"Boston has had four speeches from Mrs. Woodhull," exulted the convention chairman, "and still lives!"

The League members were still rejoicing when Victoria had to leave to make a night train to New York. Almost immediately after she left, it was discovered that she had forgotten her cloak. An earnest, good-looking and very young radical named Benjamin R. Tucker was then given an opportunity to see that Mrs. Woodhull could be as magnetic and unexpected in a private encounter as on the lecture platform. Delegated to rush to the station with her cloak and restore it to her if possible, he found her in a corridor of the train and handed her the wrap. Victoria thanked him and then impulsively stood on tiptoe to kiss him full on the lips. Thrilled and bewildered, young Mr. Tucker stumbled off the train.

In Brooklyn, meantime, the Reverend Henry Ward Beecher, still as anxious as ever to "cut it and let it go," was discovering that the punishment of Victoria Woodhull was merely focusing more attention on the scandal he would so gladly have had forgotten. Seeking some means to disassociate himself and everyone around him from her, he asked Theodore Tilton to send a letter, or "card," to the newspapers, expressing regret for his association with her a year before. Beecher had already written a suggested letter. "In an unguarded enthusiasm," he wanted Tilton to say, "I hoped well and much of one who has proved utterly unprincipled. I shall never again notice her stories and now utterly repudiate her statements concerning me and mine."

Theodore Tilton, who had been obsessed by the alleged wrong Beecher had done him from the moment of his wife's confession, had become well-nigh paranoiac since Victoria's ventilation of the story. He was outraged by Beecher's suggestion that he assume responsibility, in effect, for denying the story's truth, a responsibility that Beecher still refused. He reminded the minister that it was at Beecher's own suggestion that he had become friendly with Mrs. Woodhull in the first place. Then Tilton left Beecher and began to compose his own story of what had happened between himself, his wife and the Reverend Mr. Beecher, recounting the details of Lib's confession, the way that Beecher had virtually admitted guilt in a "letter of contrition," and how Beecher, Bowen, Moulton and everyone else involved had behaved in the days, months and years that followed. He wrote and rewrote the manuscript, calling frequently on his wife to assist him in fixing dates, places and conversations.

The final version, which he called the "True Story," Tilton had bound in leather and after that he carried the volume about with him to show to friends and acquaintances. Something Victoria had sensed from the beginning of her relationship with Tilton was now becoming clearer. Tilton was more anxious than she had ever been to make Beecher's behavior public knowledge. His difficulty was that his aim was to hurt Beecher and still keep from looking like a fool himself.

Among those to whom he showed his "True Story" now was the Reverend Richard Storrs, a Brooklyn minister of eminence. Storrs had long been a friend of Beecher and had taken it for granted that the scandal story was a Woodhull fabrication. Dazed, he read Lib Tilton's statement that "in July of 1870, prompted by my duty, I informed my husband that H. W. Beecher, my friend and pastor, had solicited me to be a wife to him, together with all that this implies." For the first time Storrs began to wonder if the story might not be based on fact.

"Oh, Theodore," groaned Beecher when he learned that

Tilton had showed Storrs the "True Story," "of all the men in the world I wish you had kept clear of Dr. Storrs."

Still, when a friend wrote to Tilton soon after that to ask why he had made no public reply to Mrs. Woodhull's charges, Tilton did not send the "True Story" to the newspapers as an answer. Instead, he composed a lengthy communiqué which he titled "Letter to a Complaining Friend," and sent this off to the press. In this, he told his friend that it was not so easy to give the lie to a wicked story and end it forever, for after all, the story as told by Victoria contained so many statements that it would be strange if some were not true. Further, he said, "when the truth is a sword, God's mercy sometimes commands it sheathed. If you think I do not burn to defend my wife and little ones, you know not the fiery spirit within me. . . . But my wife's heart is more a fountain of charity, and quenches all resentments. . . . From the beginning, she has stood with her hand on my lips, saying 'Hush!' So . . . I shall try with patience to keep my anger within my breast, lest it shoot forth like a thunderbolt through other hearts."

The letter clarified nothing and refuted nothing and merely served to keep general speculation busy. In Troy, Edward H. G. Clark read it and decided to use Tilton's metaphorical thunderbolt as the title of a pamphlet he was preparing on the Beecher-Tilton-Bowen-Woodhull-Claflin drama.

And the drama went on. New crises were continually precipitated, often by those most eager to shut off all the ventilation. A friend of Beecher and a prominent Plymouth Church member, Sam Wilkeson, bethought himself of a document that had come into being two years before during a period of uneasy truce between Beecher, Tilton and Henry Bowen. The three men had called it a "Tri-Partite Covenant," and in it Bowen, promising to stop his whispering about Beecher's past adulteries, had declared he knew "nothing derogatory to Beecher's reputation as a clergyman or a man." Tilton had sworn to his faith in Beecher as a "grandly good and generous man," and Beecher had said that he rejoiced in resuming his old relations of "love, respect and alliance" with both men and promised to repair any damage he had done to their "standing and fame as Christian gentlemen." It seemed to Mr. Wilkeson that this document could be used to deny gossip about how Tilton and Bowen mistrusted Beecher and so might help damp the scandal. He obtained a copy and had it published.

This action incensed both Henry Bowen and Theodore Tilton since both felt that it gave the impression that they had gratuitously slandered Beecher and been graciously forgiven. Tilton, especially, objected so violently to being cast as a sinner rather than the sinned-against that he threatened to make public Beecher's "letter of contrition." Somehow, with Frank Moulton's help, Beecher managed to dissuade Tilton from this step. But he could not stop Tilton from carrying about the leatherbound "True Story" and displaying it privately.

All of this, and a great deal more in the way of interpretation and speculation, was reported energetically in the *Weekly*, which featured long columns headed "Beecher-Tilton-Bowen," or the "Brooklyn Business" in every issue. There were periodic rehashes of past revelations and detailed accounts of the persecution suffered by the editors of the *Weekly*. There was no lack of material. What the *Weekly* was lacking more and more these days was money. The long-drawn-out legal proceedings and fees to lawyers were straining all of Victoria's financial resources.

Appeals for money to keep the paper going and to help the editors with their legal expenses began to appear regularly in the paper. Photographs of Victoria, Tennie and Colonel Blood were offered for sale at one dollar each and so were the books that Victoria and Tennie had published in 1872. The advertising copy cited the "bravery, originality, profundity and philosophy" of the books and called them "immortal." There was also a special offer which promised the photographs free with any purchase of both books.

George Francis Train, a onetime benefactor, was finally brought to trial on the obscenity charge against him in April. He had been in prison fourteen weeks, during which time he "obstructed business, distracted judges and made a travesty of justice, uttering his vaporings and trumpetings," according to the New York *Times*. At his trial, his attorney argued that he was mentally unbalanced and this brought a recommendation from the judge that Train be institutionalized. Train sprang to his feet and moved that the judge be impeached "in the name of the people." This motion was disregarded. After that, Train had to busy himself to escape commitment to an asylum. He no longer had time or money with which to help Victoria and Tennie.

In May, Edward H. G. Clark released his *Thunderbolt,* which provided an exhaustive and generally objective survey of the Beecher-Tilton-Woodhull scandal for all those people who would have blushed to seek their information in the *Weekly*. Clark had read and studied Tilton's "True Story," as well as all Victoria's writings on the subject and he spared no one in his analysis. He called his longtime friend, Tilton, a "wretch," and accused him of cowardice and wishy-washy romanticism. Mrs. Woodhull, Clark declared, "ought to be hanged," and then she "also ought to have a monument to her memory erected at the foot of the gallows." Still, little as he sympathized with Mrs. Woodhull, the chief burden of Clark's message was that "Through Victoria Woodhull and Tennie Claflin American law has been outraged, the rights of the press assailed, freedom of speech endangered and the functions of republican government usurped, to cloak the reputation of one or two prominent individuals."

The *Thunderbolt* also provided a great deal of material for the *Weekly*. But money grew scarcer and scarcer.

Suddenly and unexpectedly, the Challis libel case was called for trial on June 2. The defendants and their counsel, William Howe, arrived at the courtroom that day only to discover that the judge scheduled to hear the case was none other than the same General Davies, who, as District Attorney, had instituted the proceedings against the sisters and Colonel Blood six months previously. Mr. Howe pointed out this impropriety to Judge Davies and the case was transferred to Judge Barret's court. Mr. Howe told Judge Barret that the case had been called with so little warning that he had been unable to get all the affidavits he needed since some witnesses lived out of the city. Judge Barret postponed the case until the next day.

The next day a new difficulty was pointed out by Mr. Howe. The Mr. Maxwell who had testified at the Challis libel hearing was currently under indictment for perjury in another matter. Efforts by the defense counsel to have that case tried had been unavailing. The District Attorney admitted that he had reasons satisfactory to himself for not trying Mr. Maxwell. The judge agreed that it would be proper to have the veracity of Mr. Maxwell established before proceeding with the Woodhull-Claflin case since his testimony had a direct bearing on the latter. The case of Challis vs. Woodhull, Claflin, Blood, et al., was postponed for two weeks.

Two years before, a reporter had called Victoria "a splinter of the indestructible." More and more, after her weeks in jail, repeated arrests, further nights in jail, lecture tours, money worries, aborted hearings and postponed trials, it seemed an apt description.

Then, on the hot and muggy Friday after the Challis case had been postponed, Victoria and Tennie made a visit to the offices of the New York *Sun,* a paper for which Tennie's current gentleman friend worked as a reporter. The sisters had a "card" to present for publication in the paper, a public letter asking why justice was so obstructed in their case and why a witness on whom their case depended was deliberately kept from trial by the District Attorney. They talked excitedly for a while to various *Sun* employees, including Tennie's sweetheart. Then, their card having been accepted, they left to travel home on the stage.

A heavy rain was falling but the air was as sultry as ever. On the stage, Victoria complained to Tennie of pains around her heart. Tennie was sympathetic but unworried. The weather was so oppressive and they had been under a strain so long it was surely no wonder if she did not feel well. Arrived at home, Victoria refused supper, took a cup of tea and then started upstairs to bed.

She had reached the upper landing when she suddenly fell unconscious to the floor. Tennie, Colonel Blood and Roxanna rushed up the stairs to her. They took her wrists and felt no pulse. They leaned over her face and it seemed that she had ceased to breathe. Colonel Blood, in wild alarm, hurried to find someone to send for Victoria's doctor or any doctor who could be found. Tennie, almost hysterical, ran out to wire her sweetheart on the *Sun* that Victoria was dying, possibly already dead.

So the news was flashed out by telegraph to appear in newspapers across the country the next day—"Mrs. Woodhull Dying!"

Editors relieved themselves of their feelings about The Woodhull according to their temperaments. Some, like the editor of the Pittsburgh *Leader,* suggested that the illness was "merely a characteristic attempt of the 'obscene sisters' to create a public sympathy of which they can avail themselves at their forthcoming trial."

Others were more inclined to some charity now that Victoria was presumably passing from the scene. The New York *Graphic* called her "exceptionally endowed and truly remarkable.... Her career has been as wonderful as it is open to censure." In the New York *Sun* it was suggested that "If Mrs. Woodhull had been born and educated in a different sphere—if her surroundings had been refined and inspiring—she would have developed into a great and glorious character. As it was, she simply leaped from one excitement to another, wasting her life."

The most dramatic eulogy of all was in the lively *Democrat.* "At the door of death! ... Mental anxiety, overwork and the unnatural excitement of weeks in prison or at the bar of incompetent courts, have combined against her vitality, and one

of the bravest, if not the most discreet, women of the world
is prostrate. . . .

"No more libels on the Biblical bulls and boars of Brooklyn!
No more dragging the tomcats of Puritanism by their tails from
rooms made sacred to lust by standing a Bible before the door
to retard the step of the man whose wife was being debauched
within. No more pointing to pillows of satin on beds of slush,
wherein reposed the self-annointed Lord, for the wicked Woodhull is dying! . . ."

20 § On the Incoming Tide . . .

AN atmosphere of doom pervaded the house. Doctor
Cummins, Victoria's regular physician, arrived, and so did two
other doctors. Examining Victoria, they found a feeble action
of the heart and tried restorative measures. As they moved her
body, a slight trickle of blood oozed from her lips and the doctors conjectured that she had ruptured a blood vessel in her
lungs. Soon after that, they found that her circulation and
heartbeat had been restored. She was removed to her bed, still
unconscious. Medicines were prescribed and various thera-
peutic measures suggested, such as hot-water baths for her feet
and hands and mustard plasters for her chest.

All night long and all the next day Colonel Blood and
Tennie sat beside Victoria's bed ministering to her while
Roxanna and other members of the family wailed or shrieked
elsewhere in the house. Late Saturday night, more than twenty-
four hours after her collapse, Victoria roused to conciousness
briefly, then lapsed again into a coma.

Through the next day and the next her condition remained
almost unchanged. She woke briefly now and then, murmured

about the law suits pending against her and Tennie and about the fate of the *Weekly* after her death, and then drifted back into unconsciousness. The attending doctors held little hope for her life.

On Monday, an unsympathetic newspaper in Albany, New York, commented that "although the news came two days ago that Victoria C. Woodhull was dying, we have yet to announce her death, and it seems probable that she may again return to the fray and fight anew her immoral battles before the hand of death lays her low." Since Victoria remained unconscious for the fourth day, Tuesday, such a surmise seemed unjustified and cruel.

And then, on Wednesday, after rousing briefly from her coma and speaking a few words, Victoria slipped into a real and refreshing sleep. When she woke, she was herself again. She could smile faintly at the baskets of flowers that had been delivered by her admirers, and frown at the information that reporters and curiosity seekers had joined with friends in invading the house to find out if she were really ill or only shamming.

Soon she was sitting up in bed, pale and weak, but with her usual spirit evident. She was concerned again about the upcoming trials both on the Challis libel charge and the Federal obscenity charge, concerned about all the matters which had been agitating her before her collapse.

"Will the Great Scandal she has raised die with the Woodhull?" the Pittsburgh *Leader* had asked when her death seemed imminent. "We neither believe nor hope that it will. The truth is that this scandal has got out of the Woodhull's hands and is now the concern of the church and the nation."

Victoria read the comment as she convalesced and gave no sign of being disturbed by the suggestion. She had "ventilated" the Beecher-Tilton story in the beginning to rouse society to the mustiness of some of the rooms in which it lived. If the church and the nation were now going to continue the "ventilation," surely she had succeeded in her original intent.

Besides, it hardly seemed to her that she was altogether out of the matter, as yet. Henry Bowen, reacting against the publication of the Tri-Partite Covenant, was concerned about finding tangible evidence that Beecher's private behavior had justified any "whispering" he might have done about him. Bowen wrote to Victoria asking if he and another Plymouth Church member, Horace B. Claflin (related to Victoria's family only through the founding Mackclothlan, seven generations back), could have a meeting with her.

Victoria had a new friend and advisor these days, a wealthy merchant named George Ellery. Ellery's daughter, one of Victoria's devotees, had urged her father to help Victoria in any way he could. Informed of Bowen's request, Ellery's first advice was that Victoria postpone any meetings with Plymouth Church members until she was stronger. But since a date for a meeting had already been set, Ellery offered to be present to protect Victoria's interests.

Mr. Bowen and Mr. Claflin were accompanied by several friends and relatives of Bowen when they arrived at 6 East 34th Street, where Victoria and her family were currently living. They were greeted at the door by Tennie and ushered into the parlor. Immense oil paintings dominated the room, and the callers might have gazed at a huge picture of the Virgin and Child as they waited for Victoria. But Utica Claflin Brooker was staying with the family just then, and for the last several years Utica had been drinking more and more heavily. Thoroughly intoxicated on this particular day, she burst into the parlor with a whoop, disconcerting the already uneasy group.

At last Victoria, pale and drawn from her illness, appeared with Mr. Ellery. She learned that what Mr. Bowen wanted was letters, any letters that she might have from the Reverend Mr. Beecher which indicated that his private attitudes toward love were freer than his public utterances.

Victoria suggested that Mr. Bowen was interested in obtaining any such letters in order to suppress them in Mr. Beecher's interest. Bowen denied ever having acted in any way to try to protect Beecher or having taken any part in Victoria's persecution. He wanted such letters, he said, for his own vindication.

"I have asked no one to help vindicate me," cried Victoria, her cheeks flushing. "Eight months ago I began this fight and stood my ground without assistance. . . . You are all millionaires. You, and the press, with a few exceptions, have hounded me and blackguarded me as no woman was ever hounded before." She lifted her head and her eyes flashed. "But I have touched bottom at last. I am on the incoming tide. Why come to me to vindicate you?"

Mr. Bowen persisted, invoking, in the customary ritual, his innocent family that would be injured if Victoria did not help him. Finally, Victoria admitted that she had several letters from Beecher. Bowen asked if any of them offered the kind of evidence for which he was looking.

"Anyone of sense would know that after several months' intimacy with Mr. Beecher, being with him frequently and alone, that our correspondence was not one of mere platonic affection," answered Victoria.

She then produced two letters and showed Bowen the signature on each so that he could identify it as Beecher's. After which, she handed the letters to Ellery and spoke to Bowen with a certain meaningfulness.

"My case is set for trial next week," she said. She was not referring to the Challis libel case, which had been postponed again, but to the trial in the matter of the Federal obscenity charge, for which a date had at last been named. "I will reserve what evidence I have till after that, but if you will get the trial out of the way, I will produce it."

Mr. Bowen and his associates were presumably digesting this information as they took their departure.

June 26, 1873, the day of the obscenity trial, was again hot and muggy. The courtroom was crowded when Victoria, Tennie and Colonel Blood appeared. It was noted that Victoria still looked wan and that she took off her bonnet to fan herself with it, but Tennie was lively and interested.

A dashing young Irishman named Charles Brooke had taken

over as trial attorney for the defendants. A jury was quickly chosen and Mr. Brooke began at once to follow the line of defense that had been suggested by the Honorable Benjamin Butler. The statutes of 1865 and 1872, he said, under which the defendants had been charged, bore on the sending of obscene material through the mails in the form of "book, pamphlet, print or other publication." Brooke submitted that *Woodhull & Claflin's Weekly* was neither a book nor a pamphlet and that "other publication" was too vague a term on which to base an indictment.

The judge, criticizing the acts of 1865 and 1872, admitted that since the act of 1873 added "paper," it had to be inferred that the previous acts had not included it. Since the act of 1873 had been passed after the beginning of the prosecution, the judge said that the prosecution had no case. He instructed the jury that no testimony had been presented. A verdict of "not guilty" was rendered.

And as quickly and simply as that, with no argument as to the definition of obscenity, no discussion about Deuteronomy XXII, and no decision as to whether Victoria and Tennie had been guilty of mailing obscene material, the charge which had caused Victoria, Tennie and Colonel Blood so many days and nights in jail, was dismissed.

Four days later, on June 30, the Brooklyn *Eagle* printed Henry Ward Beecher's first public disclaimer of the story published in *Woodhull & Claflin's Weekly* of November 2, 1872, and thereafter circulated in so many different ways.

To the Editor of the Brooklyn Eagle.... I have just returned to the city to learn that application has been made to Mrs. Victoria Woodhull for letters of mine supposed to contain information respecting certain infamous stories against me. I have no objection to have the Eagle state in any way it deems fit, that Mrs. Woodhull, or any person or persons who may have letters of mine in their possession, have my cordial consent to publish them. In this connection, and at this time, I will only add that

the stories and rumors which have for some time past been circulated about me, are grossly untrue, and I stamp them in general and particular as utterly false.

Respectfully,

Henry Ward Beecher.

The appearance of that simple statement brought rejoicing
to Beecher's defenders everywhere. They had been waiting
eight months for just such a forthright denial. Now it seemed
that there was no doubt that all doors and windows were
slammed shut against the "wicked Woodhull."

But there were others, not so convinced of Beecher's innocence, who saw an interesting connection between the quick
dismissal of the charges against the *Weekly*'s editors and the
issuance of Beecher's denial, and who wondered if someone had
seen to it that any damaging letters had been safely returned
to Beecher before he spoke out so freely and frankly.

There were no references to such speculations in the *Weekly*,
however, which pounced at once on Beecher's letter to the
Eagle and proceeded to chew it to pieces. Mr. Beecher was
asked editorially if the stories and rumors he stamped as utterly
untrue included Theodore Tilton's "True Story," currently
available for perusal in the *Thunderbolt*. He was asked how
he explained Mrs. Stanton's refusal to publicly deny the story,
and what sort of genesis he offered for the Tri-Partite Covenant.

"I have touched bottom at last. I am on the incoming tide,"
Victoria had told Henry Bowen. After the dismissal of the
obscenity charge, it did seem that she was.

But Claflin family quarrels and difficulties were always sim-
mering in the background whatever Victoria was doing, and
there was never any telling when they would erupt volcanically.
One night in early July, Utica had again been drinking to
excess and suddenly progressed from haranguing her sister,
Margaret Ann, to attacking her physically. Margaret Ann at last
managed to disengage herself, rushed out of the house and soon
returned with the police, asking them to arrest Utica for dis-

orderly conduct. Utica, still fiercely jealous of Victoria, shouted that Victoria and Colonel Blood were to blame for the disturbance. Roxanna Claflin added her voice to the chorus. Ultimately, the uproar was such that the incident made the papers the next day.

Once again, as so often before, Victoria was faced with the problem of trying to explain her family to the world. She wrote in a letter to the *Sun:*

"Mrs. Brooker in a drunken or insane rage, attacked Mrs. Miles, her sister, with a heavy chair; for which, and her subsequent acts, Mrs. Miles had her arrested for disorderly conduct. It was, however, at my special solicitation that Mrs. Miles did not appear against Mrs. Brooker. It was expressly understood that she should not return to the house to further molest us, but no sooner was she released than she did return, and at once began her insane and disorderly conduct. Her complaint is purely malicious, and by her own avowal made to affect the public against me."

Victoria had firsthand experience of the ravages of alcohol from her years with Canning Woodhull. She was alarmed by Utica's intemperance and knew that she was making herself ill. But neither Victoria nor anyone else in the family was prepared for the event when Utica suddenly collapsed completely a day or so later.

Only a month before, the family had been sobbing and wailing at the prospect of Victoria's death. Now Roxanna and Buck Claflin, Margaret Ann, Polly, Tennie, Colonel Blood and Victoria were gathering around Utica's bed, venting their emotion in various ways.

"Oh, my sister, do you know how I have always loved you?" cried Victoria, forgetting the unhappy relationship of recent years and remembering their childhood days together. She put her arms around the prostrate figure. "Do you know I would die for you?" Utica was too ill to speak. Tears oozed from under her closed eyelids.

Victoria finally grew so distracted that at the unlikely hour of eleven o'clock at night she started off for the office on Broad Street. She was on the Broadway omnibus, opposite Trinity Church, when she distinctly heard Utica's voice.

"Vicky, it's all right now."

Victoria had no doubt as to what the message meant. "My God," she exclaimed, "Utica is dead."

Returning home, she found it so. Utica had died at eleven-thirty, precisely the time Victoria had seen marked on the Trinity Church clock when she heard Utica's voice. Roxanna, Margaret Ann and Polly were walking the house, crying out to God, Jesus and all the powers of heaven and earth to restore their darling. In their grief, they asked how it was that Utica, only thirty-one years old, should have succumbed so swiftly. They wondered wildly, glancing toward Victoria, if she could have been poisoned.

Sick and shocked herself, Victoria knew her family. If the idea of poisoning had entered her mother's and sisters' minds, they would not let the matter rest but would cry their suspicions up and down the city. She and Tennie arranged at once for an autopsy the next day.

The *Weekly*, which chronicled the circumstances of Utica's death in lengthy and dramatic detail, reported the findings of the autopsy. It had revealed that Utica died of Bright's disease, brought on, without any doubt, by her intemperate use of alcohol and other narcotics. There was no sign whatever to substantiate another rumor that Utica had died "rotten with sexual disease." The *Weekly* did not mince words in refuting that charge. "The uterus and the vagina were pronounced by Dr. Cushman . . . as natural as those of a virgin."

Victoria also had views on the cause of Utica's death, which the *Weekly* reported. Victoria thought that Utica had been a victim both of her own nature and of society. Proud and ambitious, she lacked concentration. Yearning for love, she had married twice, and "while either of those to whom she was married would have made any ordinary woman happy, in marriage as the world goes, to her they were restraints that at the same time both curbed and nettled her proud spirit and kept her constantly on fire." Her tomb bore the words, "Utica V. Claflin Brooker. Died, July 9, 1873, aged 31 years." It seemed to Victoria that the epitaph might well have continued: "Cut off at this early age by marriage."

The reporter of all this, obviously not Colonel Blood, who never had such a rhapsodic style, concluded: "And what more can I say to the readers of the *Weekly* in behalf of our dear, suffering Victoria?" He spoke of the agony in "her sweet, sad face," the sorrow that came not just as an "outburst of blind affection for kindred," but also the "consequence of the accumulated wrongs and injustice that surround her on every hand." Then he quoted Victoria's words as she was "weeping over the remains of her sister."

"Do you wonder, my brother," she said, "that I should feel desperately in earnest to reform the evils of our social life when I remember what I have suffered in my own family? Opposed and misunderstood by my parents and sisters, compelled to bear an idiotic child by a drunken husband. Oh, my God! and the world thinks me only ambitious of notoriety."

21 Tell Me Where I Am ...

"VIRTUE, what it is and what it isn't," was the title of a short article by Tennie in an August issue of the *Weekly*. "It [virtue] means that a woman has never been approached in a special way by a man and nothing but just that," wrote Tennie. "Apart from that question, the woman may have all the nobler qualities of her sex, be a pattern of generosity, inspiration, religious emotionality even, and she is not virtuous and can never become so; but if she is 'sound on the goose,' she may be a virago, a thief even, a fiend or a hag, but she is *perfectly* virtuous."

Tennie's tone did not change, no matter what shocks, difficulties or tragedies befell. She remained down-to-earth and practical. Victoria reproved the readers of the *Weekly* for neglecting Tennie in their letters of sympathy and wrote of "the large, blue sorrowful eyes of her who has so faithfully stood by my side during these three eventful years," adding that their gaze saddened her, because "she, equally with me, is not enshrined in the freedom-loving hearts of the country." Victoria wanted sympathy and recognition for Colonel Blood too, "without whom we had both of us fainted by the wayside."

But there were never the long columns in the *Weekly* describing Tennie and Colonel Blood's sufferings that there were to detail Victoria's. So the sympathy continued to go to Victoria. And the sorrow in Tennie's large blue eyes notwithstanding, the younger sister seemed able to remain "sound on the goose" in a way that Victoria did not.

For a change was manifesting itself in Victoria these days. Ultimately it would transform her so that many of those who had admired her and followed her lead would look at her in amazement and follow her no longer. Those who loved her could look back later and recall how the signs of the change had appeared one by one. Defending her, they would say that the consequences of her Beecher-Tilton revelations had been too much for her. No one seemed to consider the possibility that, having gone as far as she could in launching one phase of the "social revolution," and the matter then being taken out of her hands, she had lost interest in the subject. To no one did it seem to occur that she might have become simply bored with her concerns of the last few years and was turning to something new.

What seemed to be working on Victoria now was the shock of her own nearly fatal collapse followed so suddenly by Utica's death. Victoria never admitted that the fear of death, her own individual, personal blotting-out, entered her heart at this time. What she did say publicly made it clear that a new concern with mortality was agitating her. And, true to what she had learned from Colonel Blood when he gave her principles to banish the confusions of her life, she was seeking a principle that would take care of this new fear.

A large spiritualist camp meeting was being held in Vineland, New Jersey, in August, and Victoria, president of the spiritualists, was scheduled to make the chief address. That she was still highly newsworthy was attested by the fact that three New York newspapers sent reporters to cover the meeting. It was a six-hour trip—"from New York, by New Jersey Southern Railroad, take boat, pier 28, 9:30 A.M. to Sandy Hook, thence by car to Vineland, 3:20 P.M. Fare, $3.25."

A rude wooden platform was set up in the piney barrens amidst hundreds of encircling tents. Victoria was the focal figure on the platform while others went through the preliminary business of the gathering. Then she rose to make her speech, its title, "The Scarecrows of Sexual Freedom."

Nothing that she said in the main body of her talk was too unusual, for her. She spoke of the bogeymen that had been set up by society to protect the institution of marriage, thus making the family a "community of hot little hells." What were these scarecrows? The fear that a child might not know who his father was? But what difference would that make? True solicitude for children would not concern itself with that question but take heed of the homeless, half-starved, untaught little ones to be seen on any city street. Victoria laughed at the scarecrow labeled "License." Anyone had the right to be promiscuous who wanted to be. The only sexual crime was sexual intercourse obtained by force.

"This is my lover," she said, pointing to Colonel Blood on the platform behind her, "but when I cease to love him, I will leave him, though I trust that will never be."

All of this caused the *Herald* reporter to call her speech "the most outrageous address ever yet delivered by her." But shocked by her free-love pronouncements, he hardly seemed to notice her new vision of what true devotion to free-love principles might mean.

Immortality, nothing less, was what Victoria was seeking in free love now. "In a perfected sexuality shall continuous life be found," she said. "So also shall life not come to an end when its springs shall not cease to send forth the vitalized waters of life, that earth's otherwise weary children may drink and live.... Then shall they, who have in ages past, cast off their mortal coils be able to come again and resume them at will; and thus also shall a spiritualized humanity be able at will to throw off and take on its material clothing, and the two worlds shall be once and forever united."

Victoria did not dwell overlong on this new vision of immortality; nor did the spiritualists, accustomed to thinking in the extra dimension of the supernatural, seem surprised by it. Eagerly, they listened to Victoria speak again the next day and the next. At the close of the three-day meeting, they ended their convention with a benediction in her name.

"And now may the life, and power, and wisdom, love and mercy of Victoria C. Woodhull, save us all from our married curses and bring us into individual and universal freedom, with love and good will for all. Amen."

A wholly different mood prevailed among the spiritualists who gathered in Chicago a few weeks later for the annual convention of the National Association of Spiritualists. Victoria, Tennie and Colonel Blood sensed the hostility as soon as they arrived in the city. A mistrust of Victoria was prevalent that far exceeded the uneasiness she had felt a year before in Boston.

Some of the unfriendliness in the atmosphere could be traced to a Mr. S. S. Jones, publisher of a magazine called *The Religio-Philosophical Journal,* in which he had denounced Victoria's free-love ideas. Colonel Blood undertook to deal with Mr. Jones. Accompanied by a friend to act as a witness, he went to Jones, to whom he was unknown, and asked to rent several rooms in a building owned by him. Blood said that he wished to use the rooms to house women for the purposes of prostitution. Jones made no objection and proffered a lease. Colonel Blood then went to the authorities and was able to lodge a complaint against Jones which resulted in that man's imprisonment over the weekend.

But there were other critics, as well. At the opening meeting of the convention, various delegates arose to protest what they felt was Victoria's use of the society to gain her own political ends. A Mrs. Mills spoke against the Woodhull program for the society. Tennie, Colonel Blood and Victoria stared at her as she began to speak. Mrs. Mills' voice faltered. She put a hand to her mouth and said uncomfortably, "I can't talk with these in the way." Then she took a dental plate from her mouth and laid it on the table before her. Many delegates laughed. After this inauspicious beginning, Mrs. Mills stumbled through her remarks and hurried to her seat at the back of the platform, Tennie, Colonel Blood and Victoria still watching her. She then discovered that she had forgotten her dental plate on the table. There was more laughter, and an uneasy feeling among some delegates that Tennie, Colonel Blood and Victoria had somehow invoked spirit aid to discomfit Mrs. Mills.

The undercurrent of hostility against Victoria persisted, even so. Before the evening meeting convened, a male delegate went about among the assembled spiritualists suggesting that Mrs. Woodhull be asked to explain exactly what she meant by free love. He said he would like to hear her talking frankly and uncovering "individuals from Butler down." He also was giving it out as his opinion that to further her own ends, whatever they were, Victoria "prostituted herself sexually to do it."

"Can anyone tell me where I am?" Victoria asked as she faced the convention at last. Very pale, staring as though unseeing at the crowd before her, Victoria's feeling now was that she belonged nowhere. Those who called themselves respectable Christians persecuted and ostracized her. She was no more welcomed by those who lived outside the respectable ranks. She told of getting onto a Broadway omnibus one day and sitting beside an elegantly dressed lady without noticing who the lady might be. Suddenly the woman put her fan to her face and whispered behind it to Victoria. "For heaven's sake, Mrs. Woodhull, do not recognize me. It would ruin my business." Then Victoria had recognized her as the keeper of a fashionable house of assignation. The madam was concerned lest some of her customers might be on the bus also. If they saw her talking to The Woodhull they might cease their patronage, fearing exposure.

"I am ostracized by those whom the world calls prostitutes almost as fearfully as I am by those whom I call the real prostitutes. Sometimes I doubt if I belong anywhere," said Victoria.

Then she addressed herself to the man who had accused her of prostituting herself.

"A man questioning my virtue! Have I any right as a woman to answer him?" she asked.

"I hurl the intention back in your face, sir, and stand boldly before you and this convention, and declare that I never had sexual intercourse with any man of whom I am ashamed to stand side by side before the world with the act. I am not ashamed of any act of my life. At the time it was the best I knew. Nor am I ashamed of any desire that has been gratified, nor of any passion alluded to. Every one of them are a part of my own soul's life, for which, thank God, I am not accountable to you. . . ."

She spoke of the difficulties of the last year. "When I came out of prison I came out a beggar. I appealed to the Spiritualists, to the reformers of the country, to send their money that I might send you my paper. But did you do it? No: you left me to starve in the streets. . . . I went to your bankers, presidents of railroads, gamblers, prostitutes, and got the money that has sent you the paper that you have been reading. . . . I used whatever influence I had to get the money and that's my business and none of yours; and if I devoted my body to my work and my soul to God, that is my business and not yours. . . ."

She asked if any of those listening to her were ready to put their bodies in the gap as she had. And she said, "This sexual intercourse business may as well be discussed now, and discussed until you are so familiar with your sexual organs that a reference to them will no longer make the blush mount to your face any more than a reference to any other part of your body." What was she after? "I'll tell you what I'm after," she said. "I am seeking the truth about sexual intercourse, and I will follow it if it lead me either to heaven or hell." Nothing, she told her listeners, was so destructive as intercourse carried on habitually without perfect and reciprocal consummation. Every man should have thundered in his ears the need for the female orgasm.

And then, suddenly, she was striking again the note that she had struck in Vineland, New Jersey. Perfected sex brought more than simple, earthly happiness. Perfected sex was nothing less than "The Elixir of Life."

"Take this as coming from the wisest and best of spirits," Victoria counseled her audience, "to whom for six years I have yielded a willing and appreciative obedience, that I am commanded to declare unto you that in the despised problem of sexuality lies the key that shall serve to open the doors of materiality."

Where was she? When she had finally finished astonishing her audience, the delegates gave their answer. She was still among those who loved her best. With one ringing affirmative after another, the delegates voted to support the entire Woodhull program of social reform. Then, in spite of instructions to the contrary, they triumphantly reelected her president of the American Association of Spiritualists.

Somewhat cheered, Victoria, Tennie and Colonel Blood returned to New York. They learned that the Challis libel case was still postponed indefinitely, but the need for money to meet living expenses and to keep publishing the *Weekly* was as acute as ever. The only answer seemed to be that Victoria undertake another lecture tour. Colonel Blood was delegated to book a series of engagements for her in New England, and,

perhaps to minimize any difficulty in securing halls, it was decided that her topic would be finance, another of the *Weekly's*
continuing concerns, after all, and one well-suited to the nation's first lady broker.

Colonel Blood went first to Boston and there he ran across
young Benjamin Tucker, the earnest youth who had been so
impressed by Victoria's speech on "Truth Crushed to Earth"
almost a year before, and also by her kiss when he returned her
cloak to her. Colonel Blood was pleased by Tucker's manner
and asked if he would like to help in the management of the
tour. Tucker was not especially interested in Blood's financial
theories but was willing to serve radical causes however he
could. He agreed to help and was soon traveling off to Salem,
Massachusetts, to engage a hall for Victoria's first lecture and to
arrange for advertising and posters.

Tucker had the kind of difficulty long familiar to Colonel
Blood—a hall engaged and then the engagement canceled when
it was learned that Mrs. Woodhull was to be the speaker. But
Tucker persisted, showed a copy of the intended speech to the
mayor, and finally managed to have the objections withdrawn.
Then he traveled back to Boston, where Victoria had just
arrived.

Years later, Mr. Tucker would write his recollections of his
second meeting with Victoria Woodhull and of the events that
followed. He was a man in his seventies by that time, in retire-
ment abroad after a newspaper and publishing career in New
York but he remembered quite well the young man he had
been in 1873.

Nineteen years old, he was a youth who had read widely in
all the more advanced literature and become thoroughly committed to the doctrine of free love intellectually. But in spite
of all the glib arguments he could recite in its favor he had had
no personal experience with love and was not only a virgin but
thought himself quite indifferent to girls. Mental activity absorbed all his energies, that and a game of billiards or some
cards now and then.

He felt a strange agitation, however, when he learned from the landlady of his boardinghouse that Mrs. Woodhull had called to see him in his absence and left word that she was staying at the Parker House. Tucker rushed through his dinner and hurried to the hotel.

He found Victoria and Colonel Blood in their rooms, along with two lady callers. But Victoria quickly dispatched the ladies, with Colonel Blood accompanying them as an escort. As soon as they left, Victoria turned the key in the door and hung a wrap over the knob to cover the keyhole. Then, "quiet, earnest and charming," she walked to the chair where young Tucker was sitting, leaned over and kissed him and said, "There, I've been wanting to do that so long!" After that, "with a grace all her own," she gently swung herself around and placed herself upon the young man's knee.

Dazed, the young man sat unmoving while she talked easily of various matters. At last she left his knee, moved around the room a bit and then took a chair near him. The conversation came to her Beecher-Tilton exposure. In that connection Victoria remarked quietly that "she herself had had sexual relations with both Tilton and Beecher." Tucker, who had assumed such a relationship with Tilton, was surprised to hear that there had been a similar one with Beecher, but he was far too shy and tongue-tied to make any comment. At some point Victoria must have removed the coat from the doorknob and unlocked the door, for Colonel Blood found nothing to excite comment when he returned. He asked Victoria if she would like something to eat after her day's journey.

"Oh no," she answered, "we have just had refreshment that you know not of."

The poor, bewildered youth could only rise in embarrassment and take his leave, pondering the fact that they had had nothing to eat at all.

The next morning, however, he called on Mrs. Woodhull again, as had been arranged the night before. Colonel Blood was not present and Victoria quickly made her meaning clearer.

"Do you know I should dearly love to sleep with you?" she asked.

Stammering, the young man confessed that if her wish were to be gratified it would be his first experience in that line. He was trying to explain why when Colonel Blood appeared and the matter was postponed until the afternoon. At that time Victoria, lying on a sofa, complained of a headache and asked Tucker to stroke her forehead for her. This Tucker did. Colonel Blood was writing at a desk across the room, but soon he gathered up his papers.

"There's altogether too much magnetism around here for me," he said. "I must go down to the reading room to finish my work." He took his leave.

After that "affairs moved rather more rapidly," according to Tucker's later recollections. It was necessary for Mrs. Woodhull to make most of the advances, but soon what Tucker later called, in quotes, "his ruin" was accomplished.

He was "a proud and happy youth," but still he managed to ask, "What will Colonel Blood think of this?"

"Oh, that will be all right," Victoria replied gently. "Besides, he cannot deny that it's largely his own fault. Why, only the other day he wrote to me of you in glowing terms, declaring, 'I know very well what *I* would do, were he a girl. . . .' "

"In a perfected sexuality," Victoria had told the spiritualists, "shall continuous life be found." She had not changed in her willingness to live by her beliefs, or to believe as she wished to live, whichever happened to come first.

22 The Elixir of Life

THE Victoria whom Benjamin Tucker remembered and described was a curiously quiet figure. Theodore Tilton had known and written about a woman of "mad and magnificent energies," a woman who could hold a roomful of listeners entranced as she stood before them, gesturing an imaginary Jacob's Ladder into being in the air, with spirits descending and ascending from one world to another. Susan Anthony had saluted her as a "bright, glorious spirit." Benjamin Butler had been delighted by her fervor. Stephen Pearl Andrews would testify to the skill with which she had established a salon where some of the most original and radical thinkers of New York were happy to forgather. A member of the audience in Boston, to which she had first revealed the Beecher-Tilton story, saw her as a flame.

But Benjamin Tucker saw her almost as a shadow, gently and undemandingly affectionate to him and muted in all her responses to the world. And he was close to her, her "boy lover," for almost a year.

A few days after Victoria had accomplished his seduction, he accompanied her and Colonel Blood to a spiritualist camp meeting at Silver Lake, Massachusetts. She gave again the "Scarecrows of Sexual Freedom" speech that had excited the spiritualists at Vineland, but Tucker had nothing to say later of any enthusiasm kindled by the same speech at Silver Lake. After the camp meeting, Victoria and her husband returned to New York and Tucker went home to Boston, but before parting Tucker told Victoria that he would be in New York soon after the beginning of 1874.

A blizzard had muffled New York in snow when Tucker arrived in February. He waded through drifts to the offices of the *Weekly,* now located on Nassau Street, and found Tennie and Zulu Maud there but no Victoria. He learned that she had been away since the end of November on a lecture tour in the Middle West but she and Colonel Blood were expected back that very evening.

Tennie was enthusiastic when she discovered who the caller was. "What! Is this Bennie Tucker? Why, Vicky just thinks the world of you. She'll be awful glad to see you. But isn't this weather terrible? Just look at this!" Tennie pulled up her skirts above her knees to show the young man from Boston her snow-drenched stockings and underwear. Then she swept him out to lunch with her and Zulu Maud. Back in the office after lunch, Tucker met Johnnie Green, Tennie's sweetheart on the *Sun,* and George Blood, the Colonel's brother, who was taking care of Victoria's son, Byron, while she was away.

The next day Tucker was reunited with Victoria. For the next five or six months he spent most of his waking hours either in her company or with some member of her family.

During that time he heard a good deal about the Beecher-Tilton scandal, which was continuing to generate its own momentum, week after week, month after month. A new crisis had been precipitated in October, 1873, by the Plymouth Church membership committee. Eager to underline Beecher's repudiation in the *Eagle* of all the rumors about him, the committee had expelled Theodore Tilton from church membership for having slandered his pastor. Tilton, furious at being made a public scapegoat still another time, went again to the Reverend Mr. Storrs to air his complaints. Storrs agreed with Tilton that the Plymouth Church committee had acted in an arbitrary manner and Storrs set wheels in motion to call an

Advisory Council meeting of Congregational ministers to review the actions of Plymouth Church.

It was then Beecher's turn to react in outrage. He refused
to be called to account by fellow ministers. He insisted publicly
that he would have nothing to do with the council and would
not appear before it. "I won't," he said, "I won't. I say to them
that gave me these words of cruelty and wrong, 'God will smite
thee, thou whited wall.' " But Congregational ministers all
over the country, tantalized by what they had heard and read
of the Beecher scandal, journeyed to Brooklyn and the council
convened. At the same time, Beecher bravely embarked on the
annual Plymouth Church pew sale and his loyal church members did not fail him. A total of $59,430 was raised, several
hundred dollars more than the previous year's total. "Well,"
cried Beecher to a reporter, "it's going better than I expected.
What do you think of these for panic prices?"

The *Weekly* continued to chronicle all such news relating to
the "Brooklyn Business," and still advertised a pamphlet that
had been prepared to tell the "full story" of the Beecher-
Tilton-Bowen scandal. But the commotion was more and more
at a distance. The prophecy of the Pittsburgh *Leader*, "that this
scandal has got out of Woodhull's hands and is now the concern of the church and the nation," had come to pass.

Young Tucker heard far more about the Challis libel case
against Woodhull, Claflin, Blood, et al., which was at last
scheduled for trial. Charles Brooke was again acting as the
sisters' counsel and Tucker was often Victoria's escort as she
visited Brooke's office for consultations. After the trial started,
on March 4, 1874, he was a daily attendant in the courtroom.

The outlook for the defendants seemed bleak. An unfriendly
judge was allowing any kind of extraneous evidence to be
introduced so long as it told against them. Victoria was questioned at length about her social theories and her marriages.
Tennie's past was examined and someone at last discovered
the long-ago manslaughter charge against her in Ottawa,

Illinois. The judge himself interrupted proceedings from time to time to deliver moral lectures.

But so much bias ultimately began to arouse sympathy for the defendants among the jurors. Charles Brooke made a concise summation, pointing out that no testimony had been offered to prove that the story printed in the *Weekly* about Challis was untrue. The jury withdrew, debated all night, and the next day brought in a verdict of "Not Guilty."

The judge did not try to hide his surprise and displeasure. Victoria and Tennie burst into tears of relief. Roxanna thanked the jury effusively. Young Tucker and others of Victoria's group who were present shouted "Hurrah!"

After the trial, Victoria moved the family to a house on East 18th Street. There was no longer any of the elegance that had once surrounded them in the mansion on 38th Street. Benjamin Tucker noted "bohemian disorder" everywhere. As warmer weather came, he was the one frequently detailed to take a washstand pitcher to be filled with beer at one of the saloons on nearby Third Avenue. He made no objections to this or to other aspects of life that were unfamiliar to him. But he did object when Victoria suggested one day that he might like to sleep with Tennie.

"I don't care to," he said.

"Oh, don't say that," replied Victoria. "Nobody can love me who doesn't love Tennie."

But Benjamin Tucker, committed to free-love doctrine, had gone as far as he could in submitting to Victoria.

In the early summer of 1874, Victoria traveled to the Far West to make a series of lectures in Salt Lake City, Utah, and in San Francisco and San Jose, California. Her absence did not seem to trouble Tucker, who remained in New York, nor was he impressed by the clippings she brought back which related how hostile and curious crowds in every city had been won over by her earnestness, passion and oratory.

Years later, in recalling her, Tucker would grant that she did have a gift of spontaneous eloquence. He would also allow that she was sincere in her advocacy of free-love doctrines. He felt that she, and Tennie too, had a general understanding of the material contained in their speeches, and in the articles and books that appeared under their names. But he found it impossible to believe that they had written any of the material themselves. Just who did write it he did not conjecture, although he had been close to the family for months. What he did say was that he finally began to doubt whether Victoria could read or write at all.

Still, in the summer of 1874, he lingered near her. His family had planned a trip to Europe for him that summer as a proper part of a young man's education, and he was scheduled to sail in July. One day, Victoria suddenly said, "Why shouldn't we all go to Europe on a short vacation?"

Tucker had no objections. Tennie, the most persuasive in such matters, went off to see what steamship line would give the Claflin group reduced rates as journalists. Before long, passage was booked on the *Lafayette* for Victoria, Colonel Blood, Tennie, Roxanna Claflin, Zulu Maud and young Tucker.

The impending trip was announced in the *Weekly* with warnings that no one should leap to the conclusion that Victoria and Tennie were quitting New York permanently. Such rumors had circulated after Victoria's trip to the West in the spring, and the *Weekly* made it clear that however some people might wish that the sisters and their paper were going to leave the scene there was no possibility of that happening.

After that, the *Weekly* seemed to forget the travelers for a month. The usual contributors maintained their efforts and faithfully reported on continuing developments in the Beecher-Tilton difficulties. The Advisory Council of Congregational ministers had considered the expulsion of Theodore Tilton and offered a mild censure to Plymouth Church's membership committee for its handling of the matter—nothing more. A Beecher defender, eager to make the most of this small victory, rushed into print with some intemperate remarks blaming the whole scandal on Tilton and calling him a "knave" and a "dog."

The ball was in Tilton's court and he responded by making good at last on his threat to publish Beecher's damning "letter of contrition." And this finally put such a burden of repudiation on Beecher that he took the dramatic step of setting up an Investigating Committee of his own church members to examine the rumors and charges about his behavior and make a decision. No one seemed to take any notice, at the time at least, of the fact that Beecher personally appointed the committee members. His action acknowledged the extent of the gossip and the decision of the committee was eagerly awaited by the public at large.

But from the travelers in Europe there was no word.

Benjamin Tucker wrote about the trip in his later recollections. The little party had engaged in the usual sort of sightseeing in Paris. This offered Tucker further opportunities to observe Victoria's lack of cultural or historical background. Only three years before, in New York, she and Tennie had marched in a parade commemorating the martyrs of the Paris Commune. But driving about Paris, noting evidences of destruction caused by the last-ditch fight of the Commune supporters, Victoria denounced the damage. Young Tucker concluded that she knew nothing about the Commune and its efforts to bring a reform government to France.

After a fortnight, Victoria, Tennie, Colonel Blood, Roxanna and Zulu Maud left for Le Havre to sail back to America. Benjamin Tucker remained in Paris to continue his tour of Europe and to reflect as he did so on the nature of the woman with whom he had been so intimately associated for months.

"Slowly," he confessed later, "I came to the realization that however worthy the ends that the Claflin sisters claimed to be pursuing, the means to which they resorted were unjustifiable and even disgraceful; and in consequence, I resolved to break away."

So young Benjamin Tucker, fastidious and bookish, disappeared from Victoria's life. Was the vague, dreamily affectionate, ignorant woman whom he remembered truly the Victoria

of this particular year? Or was Tucker, insulated by his youth
and academic radicalism, simply unable to see and feel more?

A stormy, foggy westward crossing brought Victoria, Tennie,
Colonel Blood, Roxanna and Zulu Maud back to New York.
Arrived there, Victoria found that the "ventilation" which she
had begun two years before had at last, thanks to so many
efforts to close it off, built itself into a tempest that was sweeping all before it.

Beecher's handpicked committee of Plymouth Church members had been supposed to investigate the rumors against their
pastor in private and secret sessions. But there was some leak
in the security. From the moment the Investigating Committee
began its meetings, all newspapers everywhere were full of its
proceedings, reporting the witnesses who appeared, their testimony, their behavior both before the committee and away
from it.

Elizabeth Tilton, who had started it all with the confession
she made in 1870, and who had recanted that confession, then
confessed again, then re-recanted, had finally been persuaded
to leave her husband and stand by Beecher, maintaining that
Theodore had slandered Beecher. She testified to the committee that there had never been anything improper in her
relations with the minister.

Theodore Tilton, on the other hand, now openly accused
Beecher of "criminal seduction." Frank Moulton, the helpful
friend, testified about the role he had played as mediator in
the constantly changing relationship between the two men.
Servants from the Tilton house testified. Everybody testified
who had anything to say, however remote, about the scandal.
Details were piled on details in the public print, putting to
shame the revelations in the *Weekly* of November 2, 1872.

Henry Ward Beecher himself testified, saying, among a great
many other things, "I can see now ... that Tilton is and has
been from the beginning of this difficulty a reckless schemer,
pursuing a plan of mingled greed and hatred, and weaving about

me a network of suspicions, misunderstandings, plots and lies, to which my own innocent words and acts—nay even my thoughts of kindness toward him—have been made to contribute."

Victoria could read all about it in any daily paper that she chose to pick up, assuming, of course, that in spite of Benjamin Tucker's observations, she could read. One way or another, she was sure to know what was being written and to hear that Mr. Beecher had declared that "the circle of which Mrs. Woodhull formed a part was the center of loathsome scandals, organized, classified and perpetuated with a greedy and unclean appetite for everything that was foul and vile...." She could also learn that Beecher demanded of his committee that the "open pool of corruption," the vapors of which the nation had been breathing for weeks, be closed up at last. "Whoever is buried with it, it is time that this abomination be buried below all touch or power of resurrection."

The church committee was ready to agree with its pastor, ready to report that it had found no evidence of misconduct on Beecher's part and that he had been woefully slandered.

Before it could make its report public, Theodore Tilton anticipated the verdict and made his last and most desperate bid to be recognized as the victim and not the villain.

On August 24, 1874, Tilton swore out a complaint in City Court against Beecher, charging him with having wilfully alienated and destroyed Mrs. Tilton's affections for him, her husband, and demanding $100,000 for having "wholly lost the comfort, society and assistance of his said wife."

"To Mr. Beecher, as an individual, my most humble apology," Victoria had written almost two years previously when she made the first public revelation in print. Now, in the *Weekly*, she told the Reverend Beecher how he had erred when she had opened the doors and windows to his private rooms, and how he might have avoided the consequences which had mounted to such climactic proportions.

"Had Mr. Beecher, instead of moving heaven and earth to crush us ... come boldly to the front and declared that he would not be arraigned, and that he would not admit the right of anybody to question or compel him to plead by stooping to answer what anybody might charge against him, he would have risen as high as he must now fall low for choosing the opposite course. ... The public had no business with his matters ... and it was to induce him to tell the public just this truth, which it would not accept from us, and which they so much needed to have told them by just such a man ... that we pressed this matter home upon him. ...."

However shadowy a figure Benjamin Tucker had found Victoria as they tasted the "Elixir of Life" together—and whoever was writing her material for her these days—she still sounded very well in print, retreating not an inch from her doctrine of personal freedom in sexual matters.

23 } No Moral Fall, but Physical ...

VICTORIA's health, which had sustained her so buoyantly until her sudden collapse in 1873, grew more and more unreliable during the fall of 1874. Another lecture tour was imperative to sustain the *Weekly* and meet the family's living expenses, but she embarked on it wearily, almost ill before she started. Tennie, as fresh, plump and charming as ever, went ahead as advance agent, booking halls and placing advertising. Colonel Blood lent Victoria what support he could as they traveled from town to town. Sometimes he opened the evening's proceedings, offering Woodhull-Claflin books and pamphlets for sale to help increase the evening's financial take. Zulu Maud, thirteen now, also accompanied her mother, and often she was part of the program, reciting poetry before Victoria appeared on the stage.

Then, in Philadelphia, where a group of Victoria's admirers had scheduled a testimonial dinner for her, Victoria was ill enough to summon a doctor, who promptly refused her permission to attend the banquet. Tennie took Victoria's place and did very well, according to report, exhibiting her own "inimitable freshness and audacity." Fortunately she did not "frighten outsiders by the tremendous volume of her voice as she has done sometimes heretofore." Tennie's voice was "something astounding to hear when at full capacity," one reporter commented.

But Victoria's voice was going to have to be hushed for a while her doctor said. She was to do no more traveling and undertake no more speaking engagements until she was stronger.

"What will become of the Weekly?" was the desperate editorial question when these orders were reported in its pages. With the issue of December 5, 1874, the paper was reduced from its original sixteen-page size to eight pages. Included in this half-size issue were the most anxious appeals yet for money. If readers and sympathizers would only send in gifts to a total of $1,000, the *Weekly* could be maintained, the editors pleaded, and advertisements for Victoria and Tennie's books were even more prominently featured.

Victoria knew a good deal about the power of money. She and Tennie had first captured the attention of the nation by their invasion of the "walks of 'change," and their ability to win the power of money for themselves. Principle, "women have every right," attracted much more attention against a golden background. But gradually principle had taken over and the gold had faded. All that remained was Victoria's power of persuasion on the platform. "A melodious voice, expressive face, and graceful form...." "Accursed of the ministry, the slandered object of a subsidized press... at the close of her speech... a heroine, the idol of her worshippers." And now she could not even speak to earn money.

Elizabeth Cady Stanton had become more and more forthright in her public utterances about the Reverend Mr. Beecher's behavior since the airing of the scandal in his private life. She answered a letter from Victoria about this time.

"Dear Friend," she wrote (for she had not forsworn her as most of the suffragists had), "you ask my views of the great social earthquake that has recently jarred so many theories and reputations that once stood firm. . . . The true relations of man and woman, the foundations of the family and home, are of more momentous importance than any question of state or church can possibly be. . . . The true social code, whatever it is, must be the same for both sexes. . . ."

Mrs. Stanton predicted, however, that in the present situation Mr. Beecher would maintain his position of unsullied innocence in the face of any facts, or rather, "it will be maintained for him," by Plymouth Church, the *Christian Union*, the publisher of the projected *Life of Christ*. "The bondholders," Mrs. Stanton wrote, "stand around Mr. Beecher, not loving truth and justice less but their own pockets more."

Victoria hardly needed this letter to realize that in his hour of trial the Reverend Beecher had all the money that he needed on which to draw. He had money ranged in a solid wall around him.

He had something more, as well, on which to lean as the alienation of affections trial approached. The night before the trial was scheduled to start was a Sunday. Beecher led a prayer meeting at Plymouth Church and took as his text, "A Taste of Honey," from the verse: "Then Saul said to Jonathan, Tell me what thou hast done. And Jonathan told him, and said, I did but taste a little honey with the end of the rod that was in mine hand, and lo, I must die."

No one in his audience seemed to find this a curiously confessional sort of text to choose on such a momentous eve. Instead, everyone was passionately sympathetic as Beecher drew from the text a moral about the "little sins" which destroyed the harmony of friendship and marriage. "Oh, the friendships that have been severed by the constant gnawing, gnawing, gnawing of little faults," cried Beecher. "Beware, beware, my hearers, of little sins!" Then, with his usual swift change of pace, he whispered, "Let us pray."

Money—*and* the Bible. Victoria, who had been raised in an atmosphere saturated with revivalist prayer and Biblical injunction, had abandoned any religion but that of spiritualism when she linked her destiny with Colonel Blood's. Now she saw herself suffering ostracism, abuse and poverty as the result of her revelations about Beecher, while Beecher, who should have been scorned for his hypocrisy, seemed as untouchable as ever—behind the shield of the Bible.

The trial, which began January 11, 1875, at the Brooklyn City Courthouse, had been looming for weeks as the greatest attraction to take place in either New York or Brooklyn for years. The newspapers had already aired almost every aspect of the relations between Beecher, Tilton, Mrs. Tilton, Henry Bowen and Frank Moulton, during the days when Beecher's committee had been investigating the scandal in Plymouth Church. This simply meant that everyone was familiar now with the characters and with the plot to date and eager to see the principals in person and get on with the story. Beecher had engaged five of the highest-priced lawyers in the city to defend him, including William M. Evarts, who had been chosen by the government some years before to prosecute Jefferson Davis. Tilton had three lawyers, including William A. Beach, who was almost as renowned as Evarts. Drama was guaranteed and tickets for seats in the courtroom were selling at black-market prices as high as five dollars each. Crowds crossed from New York to Brooklyn on the ferries as soon as the trial started and each day hundreds of would-be spectators were turned away from the courtroom, to mill around the courthouse and patronize the refreshment booths and souvenir stands which had turned the area around the courthouse into a fair grounds.

Victoria, her health somewhat improved, was already out of the city by that time, off on another lecture tour which was to take her from New York to Illinois, Kansas, Missouri, Nebraska, Iowa and Michigan. But so far as news of the trial was concerned, it did not matter where she was. She could read about it in the newspapers of any city or town through which she passed. Not since the war had any event been reported so fully across the nation. The long opening statements by the opposing counsels were recorded. Then the procession of witnesses began—a dozen for Tilton, thirty, forty, fifty and then still more for Beecher. Their testimony was all reported.

Victoria's name was part of the proceedings from the beginning, not only because she had been the first to publish the scandal but because Beecher's attorneys seemed to be working on the theory that if Tilton's name could be linked with that of the notorious Woodhull his whole case would be discredited by that fact alone. As a result, Victoria could now read Tilton's sworn testimony that all of his relations with her had been entirely proper and that the only motive for his association with her had been to suppress the scandal. She could read of how Beecher's counsel was trying to prove that Tilton was lying about this, pouncing on anything he said that might imply he had been friendlier with her than he admitted. It seemed a roundabout and irrelevant way to prove Beecher's innocence in relation to Mrs. Tilton, and in New York, the *Weekly* pondered the point, as it pondered on many another of the strange meanderings of testimony and counsel in Brooklyn.

Why Victoria herself, such a prominent figure in the case, was not being detained in New York as a possible witness, was a question with which other newspapers dealt more fully than the *Weekly*. They found the conclusion obvious. Mrs. Woodhull was so unpredictably candid that both sides were equally fearful of summoning her to the witness stand. As the original publisher of the scandal, she was hardly likely to help Beecher's case. And Tilton's counsel, pursuing the line of disavowing any warmth between her and their client, wanted no part of her either.

And so Victoria traveled on through the Middle West until a severe cold spell brought on a new physical collapse. She was hardly able to breathe as she struggled against the icy wind from the station in one small town to the hotel. Arrived at her room, she began suffering from pains in her chest. Soon, wholly unable to speak, she was forced to cancel her engagements in the next few towns and return to New York.

As she convalesced at home, a name from the past began to haunt her and Tennie—Commodore Vanderbilt. The sisters spoke together of how the merest fraction of his vast wealth, a token which he would not even miss, would lift the anxiety about money from their shoulders. Soon, with Colonel Blood's help, they were composing a letter to the Commodore.

"Dear Commodore—It was you, Commodore, who first extended your hand to aid two struggling women to battle with the world; it was you who encouraged them to break away from the fetters that held them captive to public opinion, and to go out into the world to claim a recognition as individuals upon the talent that they possessed ... you who stood by them when they ventured into the financial heart of the nation ... your check ... your name ... that gave prominence to their venture ... and again, it was your assistance that enabled them to begin the publication of their paper.... To you they owe their all...."

They assured Vanderbilt that it was a foregone conclusion that his name would go down in history as the founder of a great railroad empire, but they asked if he did not want more. Did he not wish to be remembered as Napoleon, Luther, Garrison were, for the espousal of revolutionary principles? They came to the state of women in society and the need for a great change in the relation of the sexes.

"In our feeble and almost unaided way we have for several

years been endeavoring to impress these truths upon the world.
... But there needs to be some great Patron Saint to endow the
work to give it vitality and material strength. ... Commodore,
we appeal to you to become this great Patron Saint. ... To do
all this would require a paltry sum only when compared to
your many millions. ... Let us again beseech you to become the
Patron Saint of this great cause ... and by so doing, build for
yourself a monument of fame before which all future ages will
bow with blessings on their lips and with gratitude and rev-
erence in their hearts.

"Affectionately yours," they signed the appeal, "Victoria C.
Woodhull and Tennie C. Claflin."

There was no response from the Commodore. His young wife,
who had borne patiently with his attendance on Tennie during
the opening days of the brokerage office, was winning the rewards of her restraint. When the Commodore was ill these days,
he followed her wishes and consulted orthodox medical men.
Troubled, he was at last willing to talk with his wife's minister,
and thoughtful, just as Victoria and Tennie had suggested
that he might be, of building for himself a "monument of
fame," he was planning to endow a university.

Victoria rose from her bed and traveled back to the Middle
West to resume her lecture tour.

The great trial in Brooklyn went on. In the *Weekly*, it was
pointed out how exhaustively the newspapers of the nation
were reporting the provocative, insinuating details of each day's
testimony, when, only two years before, "We were deserted,
left alone to stand the odium" of having dared to speak of the
scandal at all.

Still, there was comfort to be found in noting results already
gained—comfort, at any rate, for someone as cool and detached
and financially untroubled as Stephen Pearl Andrews, or other
secure contributors. "The agitation and discussion that have
grown and will grow out of that publication, will develop a

good in the world that nothing else could have done so well. Already Anna Dickinson has been given courage to go on the rostrum and speak to the public about prostitution. . . . Susan B. Anthony has also begun to discuss 'social purity' in the same way, both of which were impossible discussions for public treatment, especially by women, three years ago. . . ."

Two servants who had worked for Victoria in wealthier days were called to the witness stand by Beecher's counsel in April. Victoria, home again in New York, was suddenly roused to her first public utterances (aside from those in the *Weekly*) about the proceedings in Brooklyn. Both the manservant, James Woodley, and the maid, Lucy Ann Giles, testified to having overheard various conversations between Theodore Tilton and Victoria Woodhull in connection with the scandal in Brooklyn before the *Weekly* published its account. They also testified to having witnessed "amorous glances," "embraces," and certain bedtime arrangements between the two that were out of the ordinary.

The purient style of the testimony and the way in which it suggested illicit love while stopping short of any direct statement may have been what aggravated Victoria. She wrote a long, sharp letter to the New York *Herald* denying everything that the servants had said. Mr. Woodley had not even been in her employ at the time stated, she wrote. Miss Giles had never made up a sofa-bed for Mr. Tilton in the living room of her house on 38th Street, nor had Mr. Tilton spent a subsequent night in Mrs. Woodhull's bedroom.

"I am sure," Victoria wrote, "there is one thing for which the public will give me credit. It is well enough known that I am my own mistress, and that I always remain in control of my own person, and that *I* would not lie either for myself or for anybody else in a matter such as is presented in this testimony—that is, if Mr. Tilton and I had occupied the same bed those two nights I would not deny it."

It was a telling point, even though not many weeks later she would be freely admitting that for three months she and Tilton had hardly been out of each other's arms. But even more pertinent was her conclusion about the dire straits of Beecher's defense. "It seems to me that a case compelled to resort to these alternatives—to supposed 'amorous glances,' and 'tender embraces' and 'preparations for retiring at night' in places and in ways to which none but a fool would indulge—is in an emergency."

The *Herald*, publishing this letter, said it was a pity that Mrs. Woodhull was not being called on to testify for herself. "There is a charming frankness about this lady, who at least has the courage of her convictions."

Another long letter from Victoria was published by the *Herald* just two days later. It was a letter which she subsequently said had been written weeks earlier, directly after Tilton's testimony about her. She had planned to publish it in the *Weekly* but circumstances had moderated the harshness of her feelings and she had put it aside. Then "through the treachery or carelessness of a third party," it was sent to the *Herald*, which found it even more newsworthy than the previous communication.

Addressing herself "To Theodore Tilton:" Victoria warned Tilton that those "whom the Gods would destroy they first make mad," and told him that his "shameless departure from the truth . . . to shield himself from the odium which he has conjured up in his own mind as existing on account of his relationship with me, is patently a symptom of madness. . . . I wonder if he imagines that I shall remain silent under these new imputations as I have done thus far under others he has cast upon me."

Item by item, she denied the statements he had made about her on the stand. They had not met as he said; he had falsified the events leading up to her Steinway Hall lecture; neither had they parted as he testified, because of her "Tit for Tat" article and his disapproval of it. "Oh no. At this really last interview Mr. Tilton knows well enough that there was no display of attitudes on his part. He had learned their inutility with me long before. He knew well enough that this interview was intended by him to be one of the most affectionate we ever had."

She scoffed at his implications that his business and professional career had been hurt by his association with her. She remembered the way she had warned him against political aspirations tied to Greeley's bid for the Presidency. No, she had not hurt him. "Mr. Tilton's real downfall dates from the time the Greeley movement collapsed, and not when his intimacy with me began."

"At another time, I shall consider further of his condition during the period of his relationship with me," she wrote, "shall show how he was complimented upon all sides for the piquancy and brilliancy of his editorials, and how a very dear friend and competent critic withal, then absent in Europe, wrote that his articles sparkled in every line like rare old wine, which was to be accounted for only upon the theory that he was newly and madly in love, for nothing else could have inspired him to write so grandly."

Victoria granted that her threatened publication of the scandal first brought Tilton to her, but she denied in toto his inference that he had then stood "with his hand on my mouth," to prevent her from carrying out her threat. "He would have consented to aid in its publication in any way.... The only wish of his that I ever learned was that he should not be involved as an authority."

Tilton now called his association with her "foolish and wrong." Victoria granted his right to call it anything he wished, "but the attempt to make Mr. Beecher equally responsible with himself for that which made it foolish and wrong is preposterous and absurd. It is a little schoolboy's sniveling—'He made me do it; if it hadn't been for him I shouldn't have done it.' ...I have said before that I believed Mr. Tilton would make quite a man if he should live to grow up. I confess to considerable skepticism upon that point since reading his evidence upon his trial."

A third letter from Victoria followed this dressing-down of Tilton. She had been "astonished, confounded and abashed" to see her letter to Tilton published in the *Herald* she wrote to the editor. At the very beginning of the trial she had gone to the West, "to be away from the terrible scenes of which I knew these two cities would be the centre." But no matter how far she went, she had read of the case and the words of Tilton had seared her soul. Returning to New York, her heart "bleeding at every pore," she had poured out the indignant truth in the letter which she had planned to publish in the *Weekly:*

"But on the verge of its publication . . . I remembered . . . how when they had cast me into prison and turned the whole world against me . . . in the grated cell, before our iron bed, upon that stone floor, my darling sister and my angel mother kneeled with me . . . and how, as we prayed, our cell was lighted with a spirit light . . . while a still, small voice whispered . . . assuring us that help would come . . . to deliver us safely from all the trials that were prepared to crush us. . . . I remembered all this . . . and then, with the proofs of the article in my hand, I went before the throne of grace and asked that Jesus . . . should come and show me the right. . . . And He did come and He said, 'Stay thy hand my child. All these things are committed to My charge. In the fulness of time all hidden things shall be revealed and you shall be justified as you now stand condemned. Wait!' "

All the way through to its conclusion, this third letter breathed the same strange, new tone. Victoria's visions had almost always been secular before. Demosthenes was her counsel. Sometimes she communed with such militant spirits as Alexander the Great or Napoleon. Now, suddenly, as organized religion rallied in Brooklyn to support one of its chief representatives, Victoria's visions were those of Jesus.

This new emphasis on religion was the second sign of the change that was coming over Victoria and it was a far more shocking manifestation of it to the free-thinkers who admired her than any of her theories of immortality could be. The shock was brought sharply home to them by a surprising announcement in the *Weekly.*

A series on some of the symbolism in the Bible was to be a forthcoming feature. "No enlightened person now assumes that the world was created as it was once held to have been and as recorded in Genesis." Understanding the symbolism was everything, but, until now, the Bible had been a "Sealed book." "From the fall of man by the original sin, on through and closing with the Revelations of St. John the Divine, there are great and grand lessons but little understood ... it was the fall of universal man represented by Adam, and of universal woman represented by Eve ... nor was this fall of moral nature, but was brought about by improper physical habits."

The *Weekly* did not propose to interpret the Bible from beginning to end but rather to study the last and most important part of it, the visions of John upon the Isle of Patmos. "We do not hesitate to declare our belief that this remarkable series of visions symbolizes the great events that have occurred in the world's history, and those that are to occur hereafter; nor that the outpouring of the seventh vial of wrath has already begun upon the earth."

"The seventh seal" was soon to be broken, according to the *Weekly,* and with that a new heaven and a new earth would be ushered in, wherein "the tree of life ... by the river of life ... shall yield her fruit every month."

Victoria had rejoiced in the physical from the time she met Colonel Blood. Seeking a promise of immortality she had found it in a "perfected sexuality." Now, ill, poor and discouraged, she was turning to the Bible for strength. But even there she looked for the physical interpretation. She was changing, but she had not accepted the moral shibboleths of respectability yet. Man had fallen and woman with him—"nor was this fall of a moral nature, but was brought about by improper physical habits."

24 ❧ *The Dismal Swamp...*

VICTORIA had on a "dark purple dress," according to the *Tribune,* "and wore a thick blue veil thrown back over her bonnet." The *Herald* reported "a smartly dressed lady, wearing a red and yellow flower on her bosom, a black hat enveloped in a blue gauze veil and a suit of gray surmounted by a blue velvet jacket." The *Sun* reporter, to whom she had never looked better, described her "black straw hat with a dark veil, a black silk dress with a sleeveless jacket and a little bunch of flowers. The *Evening News* had a reporter on the scene with a more discriminating fashion vocabulary and was able to note "a dark blue promenade suit, basque cut . . . with narrow bands of velvet running down to the waist . . . a small tea rose with a geranium leaf at her throat, and a black chip hat."

Confused as these fashion notes were, they spoke of the consuming interest with which everyone in the Brooklyn City Courtroom stared at Victoria Woodhull when she was called finally to make an appearance there on May 12, 1875. Her name had been "woven into the warp and woof of the Brooklyn scandal," and her entrance caused one of the biggest stirs in the courtroom since the start of the trial. The counsel for both sides turned in their chairs to stare. Jurymen whispered, smiled and bent their gaze on her. Spectators rose to their feet throughout the room so as to have a better view. The defendant, Mr. Beecher, was not in court that day, but his wife, the stern-faced Eunice Beecher, who sat through each day's proceedings whether her husband was present or not, glared at Mrs. Woodhull and it was noted that "her lips curled and a bright glitter grew in her eye." Theodore Tilton, sitting among his counsel, at first feigned an unawareness of Mrs. Woodhull's presence, then, when this became impossible, "he pursed his lips and peered at her in an inquiring way," a look which was later to become "anxious, half-despairing."

It was necessary for reporters and spectators alike to make as much as they could of such details, for Victoria had not been summoned to go on the witness stand, but only subpoenaed by the defense to deliver up any letters that she had in connection with the case.

She was escorted to a seat among Beecher's counsel. One of Beecher's lawyers addressed the judge, informing him that Mrs. Woodhull preferred not to surrender the letters that she had with her unless so directed by the court. The judge declined to make such a direction. One of Tilton's lawyers arose and insisted that if the defense wanted Mrs. Woodhull to produce any letters they should put her on the stand as a witness. Since this would make her available to the plaintiff's attorneys for cross-examination, defense counsel smiled and rejected the gambit. Victoria arose, and in a low voice asked if she might speak. When the judge nodded, she began to talk rapidly, but still in such a low tone that few could hear her. Her first remarks were about the imprisonment and persecution she had suffered. Then she spoke of the letters from Theodore Tilton which she had with her. There was nothing discreditable to either the writer or to her in the letters, she said, and she had no objection to producing them, but she thought their privacy should be respected unless the court ordered otherwise.

The judge indicated that she could do as she wished. She spoke briefly to the attorneys, then reached into her morocco wallet and brought out a packet of letters. One by one, she handed them to the attorney, who scanned them and then tossed them impatiently to a colleague. She handed him the last letter and he looked up with displeasure.

"These won't do, Mrs. Woodhull."

"Very well, sir," said Victoria. "I am not to be the judge of that. They may not do for Mr. Beecher, but you were anxious to have them."

With that she turned and made her way out of the court-room, seemingly annoyed by the continuing attention she attracted.

The six letters which she had produced were published the next day in most newspapers, both in the city and across the country. They seemed vaguely innocuous after the stir they had created. One could read into them evidence of a once warm relationship between Tilton and Victoria but there was nothing that proved it directly.

"My dear Victoria—Put this under your pillow, dream of the writer, and peace be with you. Affectionately, Theodore Tilton."

"My dear Victoria—I have arranged with Frank that you shall see Mr. Beecher at my house on Friday night. He will attend a meeting at the church till 10 o'clock, and will give you the rest of the evening as late as you desire. . . ."

"My dear Victoria—Emma [Moulton] is expecting you at dinner this evening. It will be a picnic frolic for the three of us, held in the library, around the center table and graced with Frank's burgundy. I will call for you in a carriage at your office at a quarter past six o'clock. . . ."

"Victoria—I have a room temporarily at the Fifth Avenue Hotel, where I shall abide for a few days and until Frank's return. I will ride up with you in your carriage this afternoon at five o'clock. If I don't call for you, please call for me. Hastily, T.T."

Still another letter made arrangements for another meeting, and the final letter, longer than the others, referred to some advice given Victoria by Mrs. Hooker, who "is no fuller of good will toward you than your uprightness and singleness of mind merit." That letter also mentioned the biography which Tilton was writing of Victoria and asked if she would see Mr. Beecher that evening, as arranged.

The *Weekly,* reporting on the delivery of the letters, found significance in the fact that neither Tilton's counsel nor Beecher's wished to examine Mrs. Woodhull about them. Plainly they contradicted Tilton's testimony about his relationship with Victoria and also contradicted Beecher, who had testified that all of his meetings with her but one had been accidental. "So the case is closed," declared the *Weekly*, "leaving mystery upon mystery unsolved, fact after fact concealed, and perjury piled on perjury, challenging the future for determination."

The case of the letters may have been closed, ending Victoria's only personal participation in the great Brooklyn extravaganza, but the trial still went on. Not until June, five months after the trial's start, did the counsels begin their summing up. Day after day, Beecher's attorneys expended their eloquence and learning in their client's behalf and in behalf of all that they called decent and pure in American life. William Evarts, Beecher's chief counsel, declared that it was impossible that Beecher could have committed adultery. To believe that he had done so was "wicked, wicked as it can be, wicked in heart, wicked in soul, wicked in hate to God, to society, to human nature, wicked in everything."

Tilton's chief counsel, William Beach, was less sweeping but had his own telling points. "Great and good as Mr. Beecher may have been," said Mr. Beach, "he is yet, in the eye of God and in the eye of man, a fallible sinner.... Are we to have a new version of the Scriptures?... new teachings in regard to the fall of man? Are we to be told that there is no sin among the apparently pure and great?" The church had stood through many catastrophes, William Beach said. It could even stand the loss of a man like Henry Ward Beecher. The real question "is whether the wealth and influence of Plymouth Church, and the power of a great name, shall overcome the force of proof, the lessons of the law, and the instincts of justice." Again he pointed out, as he had so many times before, that Tilton was not on trial for his faults. Even if he *had* loved Victoria and broken his marriage vows and "was odious and debased in his habits," that did not change the fact that Beecher had invaded his home and that was what the complaint was about.

June was almost over when the judge gave his charge to the jury, warning the jurymen not to be influenced by extraneous testimony about Tilton's character or any previous clearing of Beecher's name by Plymouth Church. "In any view of the case," Judge Neilson said, "you may be disposed to ask why Mr. Beecher, if innocent, should have garnered up in his heart all that pain and fear so long, when he might have made proclamation to the world and trampled out the scandal as with iron boots."

The jury retired. And then for eight days—days of a heat wave so extreme that several jurors fell ill of the colic and one juror fainted—they deliberated their decision. The whole nation waited and reporters crawled out onto window ledges and hung from the courthouse roof with spyglasses, trying to peer into the jury room and deduce from the postures of the jurors some clue as to their voting.

At last, on July 2, the jurors dragged back into the courtroom to report no decision. They had been eight to four against a verdict for Tilton at the beginning of their deliberations. Fifty-two ballots later the balance had shifted to nine to three against him but no further shift was deemed possible.

Tumult exploded in the courtroom, the "Plymouth section" rejoicing as though at a complete vindication of its pastor. Women sobbed and kissed each other and "gray beards of ordinarily dignified demeanor were frisking from table to table." Amidst the uproar, Theodore Tilton walked quietly out of the courtroom, alone except for a group of reporters who trailed him, trying unsuccessfully to get a statement from him.

The corruption and rottenness of society that Victoria had tried to "lance like a boil" almost three years before had indeed been exposed. But that the corruption and rottenness had anything to do with the Reverend Beecher had been denied. Or so it seemed to Beecher and his supporters. They gathered that evening for a triumphant prayer meeting at Plymouth Church and Beecher led them in the hymn, "Christ leads me through no darker rooms than He went through before."

The vindication, by a nine to three vote, was not nearly so complete as Beecher and his admirers tried to believe. The press, which had covered the trial with so many millions of words, was divided in its editorial views as never before when the trial ended. The Eastern newspapers had been generally pro-Beecher at the beginning of the scandal but the testimony they had presented day after day had pushed many to a more doubtful attitude. The conservative New York *Times* ran a detailed analysis of the case after its completion and concluded that the facts "tell heavily against Mr. Beecher," and that "every theory which he put forward to account for his conduct *before* the trial was expressly contradicted by himself or his counsel *during* the trial." Other newspapers were even more blunt, calling Beecher "a dunghill covered with flowers," and declaring that "Plymouth Church is about as deep in the mud as the pastor is in the mire." Newspapers in the Middle West and the West were even harsher in their comments.

Before the year was out, Beecher would find it necessary to stage still another trial of his own in Plymouth Church. To this he invited more than two hundred Congregational ministers. They spent days reviewing the masses of testimony recorded at the civil trial, and finally gave Beecher the unanimous verdict that he craved, each and every minister declaring himself satisfied that Beecher was wholly innocent of the charges against him. But still Beecher's reputation would not be what it was before the scandal. He would undertake a grueling lecture tour, using all his charm and eloquence to win hostile audiences to his support again. And still his reputation would not be the same.

The scandal and trial changed life for Theodore Tilton and his wife also. However extraneous some of the testimony about Tilton's behavior had been to the issues of the court case, Tilton was tarred with it, himself discredited as he had sought to discredit Beecher. The notoriety he had gained insured him a great many lecture engagements during the next few years, enough so that he could support his children and send them to private schools. But for Tilton there was an ugliness to life that there had not been before and that was hard for a man of his nature to disregard. At last he fled to Paris, to live out his life as a brooding, poetry-writing, chess-playing expatriate.

Things would be even more difficult for Lib. She had left her husband to sustain Beecher in his contention that he had been slandered by Tilton, but she was abandoned by Beecher as soon as the trial was over. Living with her mother in Brooklyn, she supported herself by teaching in a private school. Three years after the end of the trial she made another—and final—public confession, admitting that "the charge brought by my husband of adultery between myself and the Reverend Henry Ward Beecher was true." The letter was published by almost every newspaper in the country but evoked only a brief stir. Elizabeth Tilton had already confessed and recanted so many times that those who believed in Beecher's innocence were undisturbed by still one more reversal of Mrs. Tilton's story. Those who had been convinced of Beecher's guilt might feel renewed indignation against the minister as they considered Mrs. Tilton's plight, but the days were gone when every fresh revelation in the Beecher-Tilton scandal could echo like thunder and lightning across the nation. The storm that had raged so long was over and the air was different everywhere as a result.

This changed atmosphere would be, finally, the chief result of the scandal that had filled so many columns in so many newspapers. The "ventilation" of the Brooklyn matter did more, much more, than change the lives of the principals in the case.

Elizabeth Cady Stanton, whose comments from the beginning had had an unusual objectivity about them, made a summation of the change. The trial, she wrote, "has been a salutary medicine . . . it has knocked a great blow at the priesthood . . . struck a great moral blow at the weakness of women . . . taught men they need to be strong-minded and self-possessed." There was now a strong pull, Mrs. Stanton felt, "toward making the standard of tolerated behavior of men and women equal."

Victoria Woodhull had been directly responsible. With her insistence that sex be recognized as a fact of life for the godly as well as the ungodly, she had changed the thinking of her generation, and with it the thinking of generations to come. Men and women alike have achieved history-book status for less. One can evolve one's own theories as to why Victoria Woodhull did not. There may have been a lingering distaste for the way she chose to attain her goal, making a man of unquestioned stature her victim. There may have been a residual resentment at her violation of so many taboos—stripping the black robe from the man of God to show the phallus erect beneath.

And one can consider other factors as well. Her victim, having chosen to proclaim his innocence, never deviated from that stand for a moment so long as he lived, remaining true, so far as the public was concerned, to the principles he preached. Victoria Woodhull, who had challenged him, was unable to remain so steadfast. Whatever the human and understandable reasons that lay behind her abandonment of her principles, the world is never kind to the apostate or tergiversator and prefers to lay its laurels on the brows of the intransigents who are committed, truly or falsely, unto death.

At the close of the Beecher-Tilton trial, the *Weekly* had a few comments to make on its lessons. There was a mild recognition of the fact that some attitudes would never be the same again but there was none of the rejoicing that might have been expected at such a change. Clearer than ever was the evidence that Victoria had lost interest in the whole affair.

The chief matter in the magazine, still only eight pages in size, was almost wholly devoted to a new reading of the Bible, designed to reveal "newly discovered truths about Society." "Sexual Purity and Impurity" were discussed and the human body was described as "a holy temple." "The sexual organs are also part of it, and ought never to be defiled with an unholy touch or thought."

Cabalistic diagrams added a strange, new look to its pages. An equilateral triangle represented man's ideals of liberty, equality and fraternity. A second, upside-down triangle was balanced on the tip of the first, showing God's world and man's just touching. A third diagram showed the two triangles super-imposed to create a six-pointed star and to show man's world and God's intermingled.

Protests began to come in from astonished readers who asked the meaning of this sudden and unprecedented interest in religion. Was Victoria "going over to the church"? The *Weekly* denied any such step, but for the first time in its pages, it was suggested that there might be merit in some forms of organized religion, especially that of the Roman Catholic Church.

Stephen Pearl Andrews, who had been loyal in his detached, intellectual fashion through all of the turmoils of the scandal, now withdrew from any association with the *Weekly*. The "Bulletin of the Pantarchy" was no longer a standard feature. The *Weekly* noted Andrews' departure with regret. He was "the most learned and save one (in our esteem) the wisest of our friends." (The identity of the "wisest" was not revealed.) It was also reported with regret that Robert Hume, a well-known radical who had helped to write the *Weekly* "during Victoria's absences," was another who had left "when we made the new departure."

The tone of the *Weekly*, which had been, in general, crisp and matter-of-fact, was changing also and becoming rhapsodic as its columns examined apocalyptic phrases from *Revelations* and Victoria described some of the spiritualistic visions that had been hers since childhood. There was no hint that she might be sad, ill, despairing, a leader who had been cast aside as a revolution rumbled on without her. She was only entranced with a vision of a new heaven and a new earth and a spirit-promise that her "body would never know corruption."

Once again it was Elizabeth Cady Stanton who seemed to have the clearest earthly vision of what was happening. She had put it into words in a statement which she released immediately after Theodore Tilton, on the witness stand, had regretted abjectly his association with The Woodhull. Mrs. Stanton rebuked him.

"Victoria Woodhull's acquaintance would be refining to any

man. In her character and person there is never anything but refinement in word and movement. She has a beautiful face— the ideal of spirituality. Victoria Woodhull has done a work for Women that none of us could have done. She has faced and dared men to call her names that make women shudder. She has risked and realized the sort of ignominy that would have paralyzed any of us who have longer been called strong-minded. Leaping into the brambles that were too high for us to see over them, she broke a path into their close and thorny interstices, with a stedfast faith that glorious principle would triumph at last over conspicuous ignominy, although her life might be sacrificed; and when, with a meteor's dash, she sank into a dismal swamp, we could not lift her out of the mire nor buoy her through the deadly waters."

Still, in plain, dark dress, a rose at her throat, Victoria refused to drown and snatched at what support she could to help her out of the mire.

25 § *The Garden of Eden*

SMOKY torches, throwing a lurid, flickering glare across a clearing—preachers, their voices tolling like bells through the nighttime woods, "The Blood—the Blood—be washed in the Blood of the Lamb!"—an emotional response swelling like a tide through the listeners—figures rising and jerking in responsive ecstasy—"The Blood—the Blood—Amen!"—figures suddenly impelled into jerky, somnambulistic marches around the clearing to the mourner's bench—figures falling stiffly to the ground, crying out their pain, their sense of sin, in incomprehensible babble—this was the religion Roxanna Hummel Claflin knew and understood from the days of her childhood in Pennsylvania. It was the religion that had released and purified her during the early years of her marriage in Homer, Ohio. Perhaps it was the absence of anything like it in New York City that helped to make that city so offensive to her. Without that release she was left always on edge, forced to create her own exorcisms through public displays of emotion or hysteria.

Instead of the excitements Roxanna once had known, the kisses of brotherhood leading to embraces that could lead even further, but who knew exactly where, when it was all part of the communion of the saints, there were Victoria's friends, talking, talking, talking—making free love an exercise in emancipation, and votes for women more important than salvation. Perhaps it was no wonder that Roxanna shrieked at Colonel Blood, quiet and courteous no matter what the provocation, his name, with all its overtones of ecstatic cleansing, such a mockery.

And then, somehow, Roxanna Claflin found the Roman Catholic Church. In America, in the 1870s, it was a church even further from social acceptability than the most primitive backwoods camp meeting. It was a church of "foreigners," Irish and Italian immigrants, and so mistrusted by patriotic, Protestant Americans that they had, only a few years before, made opposition to the Roman church a tenet of a political party, the Know-Nothings. But the Roman Catholic Church emphasized the physical—Jesus' wounds and blood, the Virgin Mary's tears —and the drama and color and fragrance of the Roman Catholic ritual brought Roxanna Claflin closer to the reality of what religion meant to her than could the services in any proper city Protestant church. For Roxanna, after she discovered Catholicism, there were beads to finger, candles to light, crucifixes to adore and prayers to intone that, properly delivered could be even more transfixing than the free-wheeling imprecations of a revival preacher.

It must have been strange to Roxanna to discover that Victoria was listening to her when she talked about her new faith. But after Utica's death and during the winter that followed, when Victoria went off on lecture tours and then had to return, time after time, too ill to continue, Roxanna realized that Victoria was listening to her more and more.

For years Roxanna had felt that she had no influence over Victoria. She had not won Victoria to her bidding since the time when she had Tennie project her spirit-voice to summon Victoria, Canning Woodhull and the baby, Byron, back from San Francisco. After that, Victoria had insisted on her own course and influenced Tennie to follow her. Then there had been Colonel Blood and an end to any kind of life that Roxanna understood.

Now Roxanna found that Victoria was not only listening to her but commenting on what she said to Colonel Blood. Blood was not naturally sympathetic to Roman Catholicism, but forced an interest for Victoria's sake and contributed various historical and intellectual sidelights on the subject. More and more small items about the Roman Catholic Church's historic role and the validity of various points of its doctrine began to appear in the *Weekly*.

In the spring of 1875, when the *Weekly* made its "new departure," Roxanna may well have felt that she was having a direct influence on Victoria's public utterances for the first time. That June, when Victoria traveled to the West Coast for a series of lectures, Roxanna, as well as Tennie and Zulu Maud, accompanied her. And when they returned to New York the same new relationship between Roxanna and Victoria was evident.

Victoria's ill health probably played some part in her new dependence on her mother. The *Weekly* chronicled the various complaints that cut short Victoria's lecture trips—a weakness of the lungs, a pleurisy condition, and so on. But that there was something more which was troubling her became clear in the fall of 1875.

For Victoria, it was impossible not to force whatever engaged her own attention to the attention of the world. She took a cosmic view of herself, convinced that anything that concerned her must automatically be of universal concern. Her own interest in revealing herself and then winning approval of

the revelation was surely one of the reasons for her power to
win audiences when she addressed them from a lecture platform. "I would so gladly have you think well of me. . . ." she
had cried to the Steinway Hall audience in 1871. When they
ceased thinking well of one aspect of her, she went on to another.

And still another physical aspect was what she was revealing
in a new lecture in the fall of 1875. "The Garden of Eden, or
Paradise Lost and Found," was the title of the new speech. It
was a curious compound of Biblical scholarship, mystic interpretation and female physiology—chiefly the physiology of
menstruation. The nineteenth century was not an era when
anybody, male or female, talked publicly about menstruation.
But nobody had talked publicly about the glories of sexual intercourse until Victoria began doing so. And her sudden, almost obsessive concern with the subject of menstruation, her
elaborate theories as to why only human and ape females
showed this particular function, and her equally elaborate
theories about the waste of vigor and vitality caused by it, could
only point to some deep, personal concern.

Who helped her to write this particular speech can only be
surmised. Perhaps it was Colonel Blood, using some of Stephen
Pearl Andrews' medical books for research. Some Biblical
scholar must have been consulted as well, for the speech was
full of exegetical lore and translations from the Hebrew.

The lecture began with a reading of the second and third
chapters of Genesis, describing the Garden of Eden. It proceeded from that to an inquiry as to why, with such explicit
details given in the Bible, the Garden had never been located
geographically.

"And the Lord God planted a garden eastward in Eden. . . ."
read the Biblical description. "And a river went out of Eden to
water the garden; and from thence it was parted, and became
into four heads. . . . And the name of the first river is Pison: that
is it which compasseth the whole land of Havilah, where there is
gold; there is bdellium and the onyx stone . . . And the name of
the second river is Gihon: the same it is that compasseth the

whole land of Ethiopia . . . And the name of the third . . . Hiddekel . . . And the fourth river is Euphrates."

With scholarly care, Victoria located each of the named rivers, or the rivers assumed by Biblical geographers to be the ones named; then, tracing their courses, she arrived at the physical impossibility of their bounding or watering any real garden.

Was there no Garden of Eden after all, then? Oh, yes, Victoria insisted. But to find it, it was necessary to use the original meaning of the name of each of the rivers. With this as her key, she explained that in Hebrew Gihon meant "The Valley of Grace, or breast, or bursting forth as from a fountain"; and that Hiddekel meant "swift, which refers to the swiftness of the current"; that Euphrates meant "that makes fruitful or grows"; and Havilah, "suffers pain that brings forth"; and Ethiopia meant "blackness, darkness, heat, burning."

Suddenly then, she was making her revelation. "Where should the Garden of Eden be found if not within the human body?" She traced the river Pison, which entered at the mouth to water the land of pleasure and delight, bringing nourishment to the whole garden by way of "stomach, intestines, heart, lungs, arteries and veins." She came to the river Gihon—the "Valley of Grace" —and asked if there could be a more appropriate name than that of "grace" for the operations that are performed within the abdomen for the elimination from the body of the refuse that is gathered there. Hiddekel was the river that drained the system of another class of impurities, "a stream that runs with a swift current." Finally, there was the Euphrates, which means "fruitfulness, and this river, the last one in the order of physiological sequences, is the fruit or the result of the perfected action of all the others combined . . . a physical purity [from which] primitive man and woman fell by the improper use of the functions of the garden."

And so Victoria came to the fall of man, symbolized by eating the fruit of the tree of life—the fall that was not of a moral nature "but brought about by improper physical habits." She asked what these improper habits were and found them in the relations between the male and the female. In all the animal world, those relations were solely for propagation and the female was supreme mistress of when they should occur. Only among humans and monkeys was there copulation for purposes other than reproduction. And only among humans and monkeys was there menstruation.

Victoria cited a variety of medical authorities as she launched into specific details of the menstrual process, nor was any ignorance shown of the currently accepted physiological theories. It was only when Victoria went on to offer her own conclusion as to what had caused menstruation in the first place that she abandoned all authority. "An undue excitation of the ovaries . . . for other purposes than propagation . . ." had brought about the phenomenon, Victoria declared. She suggested that this "undue excitation" might have been caused by a shift in internal pressures when humans and apes assumed the upright posture. But once "undue excitation" had brought on purposeless male-female relations, the consequences now had to be faced—a wasting away of the river of life which would go on until the time of the New Jerusalem, "which is the purified woman."

She had once hymned the joys of free love and the glories of sexual embraces in which men and women alike should delight. Battered now by life and her own physical difficulties, she turned her back on the pleasures she had known, obliquely suggesting that they were to blame for her present unhappy state. The lecture concluded with a solemn warning against any defiling of the human body and a prayer for the day when perfect men and perfect women would join in perfect marriage for no other purpose than the propagating of perfect children.

"The Garden of Eden" was only one of the lectures prepared for the fall of 1875. In August, the *Weekly* announced that Victoria C. Woodhull and Tennie C. Claflin would receive applications to speak anywhere in the United States and listed seven lectures which formed "a regular course on the new religious revelations." Some of the talks bore familiar titles, "The True and False, Socially," and "Social Evils, Their Cause and Cure," but all of them had been reworked to follow the new themes—

the need for purity in men as well as women, the body as God's temple, and the horror of any abuse of it. Most dramatic evidence of all, however, as to the sweeping change in Victoria, was her new explanation of free love. The Victoria Woodhull who had once proclaimed to thousands in Steinway Hall her right to change her lover every day if she pleased now insisted that by free love she meant the sort of love about which she had learned in revival meetings as a child—the free love of God for all the world. And marriage, against which she had once raised her voice so firmly, declaring it "the most consummate outrage on women that was ever conceived," was now a "divine provision," her one qualification being that law alone could not make it divine.

She had changed. She was another Victoria. And were one to argue that she had to speak in this vein if halls were not to be closed to her, and that she had to speak if she and her family were to live, there would still be the same conclusion. For she never spoke without deep, personal feeling, herself as convinced as she sought to make her hearers.

Once again Roxanna was accompanying Victoria, Tennie and Zulu Maud as they set out on what would become the most grueling tour yet. Colonel Blood remained in New York, reporting the tour for the *Weekly* and coping as well as he could with the changed tenor of what Victoria was saying. "We won the battle with the ax," he wrote, "now we win with the plow. Harsh means are no longer required," he rationalized, "and if they were used they would destroy the tender blades of freedom that begin to show above the crusts of law and custom."

Still, readers who had been agitated by the onset of the *Weekly's* religious preoccupation were now in open revolt. A few, a very few readers remained loyal and sought explanations, even as Colonel Blood did. "Victoria has been condemned so severely for declaring unwelcome truths, that her yearning heart would burst ere long did she not soften some of her expressions . . . and plead for the love of the people," one correspondent surmised. But the majority of subscribers sent in cancellations of their subscriptions or simply allowed them to lapse. George Blood, worrying over the bills and looking at receipts, shook his head hopelessly.

In Albany, New York, where Victoria's tour began, the *Argus* reported that in her address she "outevolutionized the evolutionists by asserting that not only is the present intellectual and moral condition of man the result of progression but that the human organism is capable of further development that shall culminate in immortality here upon the earth." And the *Evening Post* commented that "earnestness is Victoria Woodhull's best friend, and her faith in her errors is so great that she becomes a power at once dangerous and fascinating."

"Dangerous and fascinating," Victoria traveled on, her stops almost a blueprint of the railroad schedules of the day. From Albany she traveled north into Vermont, from Vermont back to New York, where she spoke in Watertown, Utica and Binghamton, then on into Pennsylvania and thence to Wisconsin.

Everywhere the newspapers reported good audiences and many noted with surprise that her lectures could be "heard without shame by every man, woman and child in the city." In Chicago, "an immense concourse of people" listened to her and her words were "like a mountain torrent." In Fort Wayne, Indiana, her "audience was one of intelligence and respectability, such as any speaker might feel proud to address." In Cincinnati, Ohio, where Tennie had brushed with the police long ago, "one-fourth of the people in the house were ladies of the best families. ... We venture to say they went away well pleased with themselves for having had the grit to go."

Into Wisconsin, back into Pennsylvania, down into West Virginia, up again to Ohio, the travelers struggled on. Trains were slow and uncomfortable and arrived at their destinations at all hours. Hotels were dingy, disagreeable, poorly heated, and the kind of meals most of them served had long since become a standard theme of horror for those who partook of them. Roxanna Claflin was in her seventies by this time but she bore up under the trip's rigors as well as any in the group. She had an amazing store of energy and resilience and Victoria leaned on her more and more as the tour went on.

Sometimes rain reduced the size of Victoria's audience. As winter came, there were storms, snow, freezing weather to battle. In some towns ministers heralded Mrs. Woodhull's lecture with attacks from the pulpit. These attacks Victoria sometimes recognized with hurt but firm rejoinders, winning applause as she did so. "I came prejudiced against her," said a citizen of Greenville, Ohio, "and now think there was nothing said but what every man and woman in the world ought to hear."

Victoria was pale and drawn as she and her group traveled back to New York and then to Massachusetts. Most papers noted her look of fatigue as she stepped forward on the platform, but as always, once she was caught up in her subject, the fatigue seemed to vanish and her manner became magnetic.

She was in Washington, D.C., soon after the first of 1876— Washington, where she had known such triumphs in 1871. Several Washington newspapers called attention to the obloquy she had known in more recent years and congratulated her and her audience on having lived it down.

New Jersey, Pennsylvania, and then St. Louis, Missouri. "Her manners are cultured and refined and possess that poetical movement which is always the marked attribute of the true gentlewoman," wrote the St. Louis *Globe-Democrat*. If there were any memories for Victoria in St. Louis of how she had found both love and principle there, in the person of Colonel Blood, she gave no hint of it.

The image of Colonel Blood was changing in Victoria's mind. He was no longer the handsome, intellectual veteran who had opened the doors of the world for her with his theories and ideals. He was somebody sitting at ease, writing a few pieces for the *Weekly* each week, but otherwise doing nothing to comfort and support her as she expended such effort to keep herself, her family and the *Weekly* alive. Night after night, she moved audiences to tears as she spoke of the beauty of life with a perfect mate. And the more she talked of a perfect mate the less did Colonel Blood appear to fill the role.

After her lecture, back in another cold, uncomfortable hotel room, Victoria would be too weary to sleep and Roxanna sympathized with her for having such a husband. Roxanna had always wanted rich husbands for her daughters, men who would enable them to "ride around in their own carriages." She had never liked Colonel Blood. He was the only one left now of the group that had surrounded Victoria in her days of triumph. Stephen Pearl Andrews had vanished, and so had all the Pantarchy. So Roxanna talked and talked, during that long trip, of how little help Colonel Blood was to any of them. She began suggesting that the Colonel had been holding Victoria and Tennie in thrall all these years by means of evil spirits. Victoria was so tired, so receptive to some such explanation for her difficulties, that she was ready to believe it. She even agreed that when they got back to New York she would consult with some monks of whom her mother had heard, who were said to be skilled in the exorcising of evil spirits according to the church's old rituals.

Nashville, Tennessee; Memphis; Atlanta, Georgia; Dallas, Texas—the tour ground on. Finally, in April, the travelers were back in New York City.

Any hope that Colonel Blood might have wrought some kind of miracle in their absence vanished at once. Receipts from the *Weekly* had dwindled to nothing. Resentful radicals across the country had not only withdrawn their own support but were attacking Victoria in other radical publications, urging everyone to pay no attention to the *Weekly*'s appeals for financial aid.

Colonel Blood had other news for Victoria as well. During her absence the first Mrs. Blood had come to Brooklyn to live and had been in touch with him through his brother, George. She was ill and without funds. The Colonel confessed that he had been trying to help her financially with what money he could scrape together.

Gone entirely from Victoria's mind were any memories of the day when Canning Woodhull, her first husband, had stood, sick and penniless, at the door of the house on 38th Street and she had taken him in, deeming the act one of the most worthy of her life. Gone was any memory of how Colonel Blood had encouraged her in this humane gesture. She herself was a sick woman now, exhausted from months of traveling and lecturing. She needed money too. She flared in the kind of eye-blazing anger that most often filled her only on the platform, when she was denouncing her enemies. George Blood, who had been go-between for Mrs. Blood and the Colonel, was fired from the *Weekly*. The Colonel himself faced an unforgiving woman.

Victoria mustered strength for two more lectures, one in Brooklyn and one in New York. At the Cooper Union, on the stage where she had dramatically divested herself of Quaker cloak and bonnet to tell the "Naked Truth," she now stood with a morocco-bound Bible in her hands, near a large statue of the Virgin Mary. Zulu Maud began the evening with a recitation of Portia's "Plea For Mercy," from *The Merchant of Venice*. Then Victoria opened her Bible, read for her text the verses wherein God promised woman that her seed should crush the head of the serpent and launched into her thesis that humanity's redemption depended on women. Victoria asked women to fit themselves for this mission by studying the marital question in all its details; then, with male and female alike cultivating purity, crime and vice would cease to exist.

Her two speeches were fairly well attended and received, but the receipts were only a trifle compared to what was needed. The situation seemed hopeless. There was nothing more she could do, no one to whom she could turn. The newspapers carried reports of Commodore Vanderbilt's serious illness. There were rumors that he was dying. Once, years before, the Commodore had implied that Tennie and Victoria would be remembered in his will. There no longer seemed any likelihood of that.

With the issue of June 10, 1876, *Woodhull & Claflin's Weekly* ceased publication.

And even as the *Weekly* was expiring, Victoria was suing Colonel Blood for divorce. She charged him with adultery. A witness whom Colonel Blood had never seen before was produced and swore that he had accompanied the Colonel to a house of prostitution.

Adultery was the legal ground, but it was more as though Victoria, in the complete reversal that she had made of all her attitudes, had to rid herself of every reminder of her old beliefs.

The final decree was signed in September, making the divorce absolute and allowing at least one newspaper which remembered another Victoria to amuse itself with a lively item. "The High Priestess of free love gets a divorce for infidelity. Look out here, or the religion of unselfishness will tumble down."

The decree provided that Victoria could marry again but that the Colonel could not. The provision seemed a mere technicality. For the first time in years there was no man in Victoria's life. She had no eager, devoted male to whom she could turn for instruction, advice, the writing of articles, books or speeches. At thirty-nine she was her mother's daughter again, perhaps more completely than she had ever been. Roxanna and Buck, Tennie, and her own two children, Byron and Zulu Maud— these were her family now.

Twice divorced, she sought further lecture dates to speak on the sanctity of marriage and to deplore "the loose system of divorce now so much in vogue."

26 } *She Gathers Unseen Strength . . .*

JAMES BLOOD had loved Victoria from the moment that she said, "I see our futures linked." He still loved her when she divorced him and, from all the evidence, he would love her until he died. He was a man of principle, committed to free thinking in every area of human experience. He might have tried to change his very habit of mind for her if she had allowed him, rationalizing his changed opinions as he had hers. His friends remembered only one comment after he and Victoria parted. "The grandest woman in the world went back on me."

Once he had been a man able to make a living for himself and his family. When Victoria met him he had been City Auditor of St. Louis. After he and Victoria came to New York, he was the competent background figure, carrying on the day-to-day activities of the Woodhull, Claflin brokerage house. He had handled editorial and technical details in the publishing of *Woodhull & Claflin's Weekly,* and there would never be any way of knowing how much of it he wrote. He had become knowledgeable in a variety of fields as he helped Victoria toward her various goals—finance, the law and, lately, religion and medicine. But after their parting he seemed at a loss about what to do. He stayed for a while with his brother. George Blood had obtained a government job on Governor's Island after Victoria fired him from the *Weekly.* He got James Blood a job there also. But Blood did not keep it long. He drifted on to managing a bakery shop. Then he ran a refreshment booth at Coney Island for a while.

The boom times of six years before were over for the country generally. So much corruption in business—the wheeling and dealing of the railroad barons and stock manipulators—so much corruption in city, state and federal government, so much corruption among those swarming to take advantage of reconstruction efforts in the conquered South had finally brought on a reaction. There had been a Wall Street panic in 1873. It had passed almost unnoticed by Woodhull, Claflin & Company, already sinking into failure. The panic had worsened steadily into a general depression. A great many people aside from Victoria and Tennie were in need of money when the sisters began their desperate appeals for help in keeping the *Weekly* going. Railroad construction had slowed down; business failures mounted each year; industrial plants were closing. In 1876, a lavish exposition to celebrate one hundred years of American independence was being held in Philadelphia. There was a fine

showing of machinery, inventions, gadgets and densely ornamented architecture and artwork, but for at least some Americans,
there was a hollow pretension about the display. That same summer, the Democrats nominated as their Presidential candidate
Samuel J. Tilden, who had won a reformer's name when he
headed New York City's fight against "Boss" Tweed. The Republicans, seeking someone safe and innocuous, had nominated
Rutherford B. Hayes. Such a groundswell of desire for general
reform was building everywhere that Tilden would win the
popular vote in November. But so many possibilities for manipulation still existed that a specially selected commission was able
to award the election to Hayes, overruling the popular vote and
maintaining Republican control. And so a general bitterness
at one more instance of fraud would continue.

Colonel Blood, drifting in the currents close to the bottom
of this nationwide disturbance, had his own hopelessness to
further weigh him down. He followed Victoria's fortunes as
well as he could, but hers were plainly no better than his. In
the fall of 1876, he could have seen a letter sent out by Victoria
and Tennie to all the past subscribers of the *Weekly*, imploring
all who had ever believed in their causes to come to their rescue
now. "Let the widows send their mite . . . let others, their dollars—their fives, tens, twenties, their fifties, hundreds and thousands."

There was obviously little response, for soon a pamphlet,
signed by Tennie, was being circulated among both subscribers
and anyone even remotely considered a friend. Titled "What
Was Her Crime?" the pamphlet related in throbbing prose the
sufferings which Victoria had undergone and was still undergoing in humanity's behalf. Ignoring all of her past crusades,
the pamphlet focused on her current mission, which was to
solve the great mystery sealed in the pages of the Bible and to
find thereby the key that would unlock the tomb. "Pregnant
with this great problem," Victoria had withdrawn herself from
all contact with the world. She had found that even lecturing,
the activity by which she had hoped to support herself and her

family, was impossible. Her sensitive nature was so worked on
by the conditions of her listeners that she was pushed to exer-
tions beyond her strength when she essayed public speaking,
and then retired from the rostrum so exhausted that friends
had to work for hours to keep the breath of life in her. The
pamphlet concluded with instructions that all remittances
should be "made to her in post-office orders, registered letters,
drafts to her order (in no case sending money loose in letters,
for such letters never reach her) ... which will receive immediate and proper acknowledgment."

James Blood could remember a Victoria who had spoken in-
cisively on Constitutional law to members of the House of
Representatives. He could remember a Victoria who had spoken
out about life as she saw it—the condition of prostitutes, the
reality of passion, the need for recognizing sex as a fact. If he
felt a chill of fear now as he read these ramblings about revelation and wondered if Victoria was going to become quite mad,
there was nothing he could do about it. She had flouted whatever protection he could give her.

In January, 1877, old Commodore Vanderbilt, who had rallied again and again during the summer, suddenly weakened.
His wife, Frank, her minister, and the Commodore's doctor and
nurse gathered around his bed. The Commodore asked that
they sing hymns for him. Hymn-singing was a pastime to which
Frank had introduced him in recent years and one in which the
Commodore found comfort as he heard again the songs his
mother had sung to him years before. Frank and the minister
sang hymn after hymn for the old man. Just before he died
they sang his favorite, "I Am Poor, I Am Needy."

The newspapers, announcing his death on January 4, 1877,
reported that he left a fortune of $105,000,000.

The terms of the Vanderbilt will were awaited with curiosity
by everyone, including those millions of people who could not
be possibly affected one way or another by its provisions. Soon
it was learned that he had left the bulk of his fortune, $90,-

000,000, to his son William. His wife was provided for and his other eleven children remembered with what seemed to them token sums from the remaining $15,000,000.

Cornelius Jeremiah Vanderbilt, the son who had distressed his father all his life because he was prone to epileptic seizures and general instability, joined at once with two of his sisters to contest the will. These three heirs felt that it would be simple to prove that their father had been eccentric to the point of irresponsibility in his later years. It seemed to them that they needed little to prove this except evidence of his reliance on spiritualism and magnetic healers. Spiritualism, so much the rage in the 1850s, was now in disrepute. Thinking men and women who had been so impressed by the Fox sisters thirty years before had long since been apprized of the fraudulence involved in much purported spiritualistic phenomena. But the Commodore had never lost his faith. Even after his wife had presumably weaned him to orthodox medical men, he had pleaded for magnetism in his last illness. When a magnetic healer was summoned at last to press and push his aching limbs he said, "Why have you kept this from me so long? It does me such good."

And, of course, for the most telling proof of their father's gullibility, his dissatisfied heirs needed only to refer to Victoria C. Woodhull and Tennie C. Claflin. The whole country knew of Vanderbilt's association with them and the curious behavior which they had been able to inspire in him.

William Vanderbilt, a patient and practical man, wanted no contest. He talked with his brother and sisters and their lawyers in one conference after another. He was willing to make settlements with each of them which he hoped would relieve their discontent. But they remained obdurate, convinced that their chances of breaking the will completely were excellent, once the case came to trial and the Claflin sisters began testifying.

James Blood, following Victoria's course by whatever means he had, might have learned that in June, 1877, she was lecturing in Canada. An article in the *Mail*, in Toronto, sounded like something prepared for publication by Victoria herself. There was a survey of her career, "as singular as any heroine's in a romance," which touched lightly on some of the triumphs of her life but played down the suffering and persecution that she had known. And there was a new and surprisingly optimistic note in the article's conclusion. "When apparently about to be struck down she gathers unseen strength, and goes forward conquering and to conquer."

Colonel Blood also learned that soon after that, in August, 1877, Victoria, Tennie, Roxanna and Buck Claflin, and Victoria's two children sailed for England with no plans for returning.

"William H. Vanderbilt had no more to do with her departure than did the youngest child in San Francisco," Victoria would find it necessary to assert time and again in later years, varying the simile only slightly in the repeated statements. "Mr. William H. Vanderbilt had no more to do with her departure for England than a child unborn, although it has been published far and wide that he gave her and her sister handsome sums of money to quit this country at the time the old Commodore's will was contested before the Surrogate in New York."

There were indeed many rumors, both published and verbal, some with a definite ring of authority to them. Years later, Henry Clews, of the famous Wall Street brokerage house, would mention both Victoria and Tennie in his memoirs and tell of how he had brushed with them in their early days as lady-brokers. Then, quite matter-of-factly, he wrote of how "at the beginning of the celebrated case to break the Commodore's will, the sisters suddenly took a trip to England, lest they might be called as witnesses."

Colonel Blood could not have helped reading and hearing the rumors at the time. The ring of truth may have sounded unmistakably in his ears, but he made no comments. The facts beyond any rumors were that Victoria and her family were in

England and none of them would show any sign ever again of being troubled about money.

For Victoria, it was very like stepping into a new life. With money at her disposal, it is likely that she was able to afford good medical care at last, perhaps surgery, for the difficulties that had obsessed her through the last year. Her concern with the subject of menstruation gradually vanished in England. Her health improved and her old energy returned.

The apocalyptic note did not vanish nor did the determination to break "the seventh seal" of the Bible and discover the secret of everlasting life. As a child she had looked "beyond the veil," and mystic matters had concerned her long before her thinking was modified by Colonel Blood. When she rejected his influence she returned to her original concerns, but her hysteric insistence on her mission to redeem humanity was gradually muted.

She made arrangements to give lectures in several cities soon after her arrival in England. The lecturing habit was strong and the need to impress and sway listeners was basic. With Tennie functioning as advance agent and enthusiastically proffering vast sheafs of selected press clippings from the United States to managers of various English halls, it was easy to create the impression of wide and favorable American fame. So Victoria lectured in Nottingham in September, her subject, "The Human Body, the Temple of God." She must have modified some of the more clinical details of female function, for the Nottingham *Guardian* reported only that "Mrs. Woodhull appealed in the most impassioned and fearless language to her audience to awaken to the responsibilities of life, and especially of maternity. . . . The child too often gathers from ignorant and vicious companions knowledge which ought to be imparted by a loving, intelligent mother. . . . Mrs. Woodhull is unquestionably a great orator, and it is not difficult to understand how she has gained so remarkable a hold upon the people of her own country."

Victoria spoke again in Liverpool on the same subject and

"those whom from prurient motives imagined that they were to hear something *outré* were disappointed." She was in Manchester in October, and finally, in December, in London, speaking in St. James Hall.

Not all the London notices were favorable. London reporters had transatlantic files which they could check to discover that Mrs. Woodhull had been notorious as well as famous in America, and this in spite of the fact that the posters advertising her lecture in London spelled her name "Woodhall." Some newspaper announcements of her forthcoming appearance in London reviewed a few highlights of her past and mentioned her connection with the current Vanderbilt will case. And one London reporter who attended her lecture felt that "no man would dare discuss such subjects as Mrs. Woodhull is ready to discuss anywhere." He admitted, however, that "her half-nervous style of utterance, her little womanly ways, so out of keeping with the matter of her lecture, pleased the audience."

Present in the pleased audience that night was a slender, handsome, bearded Englishman named John Biddulph Martin. He was the younger son of Robert Martin and Mary Biddulph Martin, and a partner in Martin's Bank, a family concern that was one of the oldest banks on London's Lombard Street. Just what had led Martin, a quiet, conservative banker of thirty-six, to that particular lecture was never explained. He had taken classical honors as well as athletic trophies at Oxford and he had a taste for research, but he had no particular bent toward a religious interpretation of life or the human body such as Victoria was offering. Still, among those "spell-bound by her fervid and impressive eloquence," was John Biddulph Martin.

"I was charmed with her high intellect and fascinated by her manner," he was reported to have said later, "and I left the lecture hall that night with the determination that, if Mrs. Woodhull would marry me, I would certainly make her my wife."

Money had materialized for Victoria when she needed it most. Now a new love, and just the kind she needed, had suddenly appeared.

27 } *I Utterly Repudiate Free Love...*

YOUNG Henry James, the novelist son of the philosopher who had once argued "Love, Marriage and Divorce" with Horace Greeley and Stephen Pearl Andrews, had settled in London—"the place where there is most in the world to observe"—only the year before, to remain for the rest of his life. More than any other literary man of his time, James was fascinated by the collision of the innocent American, particularly the innocent American female, with the rich, dense and ancient culture of Europe. He was sensitive as few Americans were to the layered pattern of English society, and, tuned to the finest vibrations in the delicate play of manners in the middle and upper classes, he was as serious as any English dowager about the need for "marrying properly," and perhaps even more concerned with what was and was not "respectable."

There is no evidence that Henry James ever met Victoria Woodhull. But in 1882 he wrote a short novel, *The Siege of London,* which reads so much like a fictionalized account of Victoria's efforts to capture John Biddulph Martin that it is difficult to believe he was wholly ignorant of her story. On the other hand, it is also possible that Victoria, who always thought of herself as universal, was simply working out, in an archetypal fashion, the destiny of any American demimondaine in Europe.

James himself underlined the typical aspects of his story by giving his characters descriptive names in the style of Restoration comedy. Nancy Headway was the pretty and fascinating woman suddenly arrived in Europe with plenty of money to spend but only mysterious hints as to what had constituted her past in America. Sir Arthur Demesne was the infinitely correct and unimaginative young Englishman of property and tradition who was bewitched by her to the point of wanting to marry her. Lady Demesne, his mother, "gentle, tranquil, plainly dressed, yet distinctly imposing," was the chief antagonist, totally determined that her son be saved from such a disastrous marriage. And George Littlemore was the passive American observer (one of a gallery of such characters in James' fiction) who had known Mrs. Headway in America. He knew quite well that she was "not respectable," but he hesitated, as much from lethargy as sympathy, at giving Lady Demesne the information that she wanted so badly.

Lady Demesne explained her feelings about Mrs. Headway to a friend of Littlemore's: "She's very pretty, and she appears to be very clever; but I don't trust her." She puzzled over her son's infatuation: "I don't know what has taken possession of him; it is not usual in his family to marry people like that. I don't think she's a lady."

George Littlemore had a sister who had married an English squire and become Mrs. Dolphin. The transplanted American, Mrs. Dolphin, had adapted so well that she "knew as much about English society as if she had invented it," and she also was determined that "poor Arthur Demesne not be taken in by" Mrs. Headway. "You can see to look at Mrs. Headway that she's not a lady."

Nancy Headway, fighting her battle to win Sir Arthur Demesne in spite of such opponents, appealed to George Littlemore to vouch for her to Lady Demesne and to swear that he knew nothing against her.

Uneasily, George Littlemore tried to shift responsibility to Sir Arthur. "If he asks too many questions he's not worth marrying," he said.

"I beg your pardon," replied Nancy Headway, "he's worth marrying whatever he does—he's worth marrying for me. And I want to marry him—that's what I want to do."

Certainly Victoria Claflin Woodhull wanted to marry John Biddulph Martin. Proper, respectable and wealthy, he was not only the antithesis of everything she had known all her life, he was the complete answer to the reaction she had suffered when she challenged the pillars of respectability in America. But just as Nancy Headway had faced the hostility of her admirer's family in her "siege of London," so Victoria faced the unyielding disapproval of the Martin family and with that, the proper Mr. Martin's hesitation at defying his family and marrying her against its wishes.

There was no George Littlemore in Victoria's life, holding the secret of her past. There were newspaper files instead, many newspaper files, relating the doings of that past in detail. The London newspapers had referred only glancingly to any of that material so far, and only in connection with Victoria's lecture at St. James Hall. There was no reason for them to do more and to query their overseas correspondents in America about further material that might be available there about the newcomer on the London scene.

But the Martins were disturbed enough by the little that had been published already. Even a few hints that Victoria had been involved somehow with free-love theories at one time and a few hints that she was connected in some way with the Vanderbilt will contest were enough to start the bells of alarm ringing in their minds. There was also the undeniable fact that Victoria had been divorced twice, itself enough to mark her as less than respectable.

Victoria could explain everything to John Martin. Her earnest manner, her gift for quick, intimate, disarming speech, and her ability to leap swiftly from one subject to another, seeming to evoke connections or explanations even where there were none, satisfied him even as they bemused him. But he could not explain things to his family as Victoria explained them to him. His family became even more agitated when he undertook a defense of Mrs. Woodhull.

Victoria herself had to try to allay the Martin family's suspicions of her, at least to a degree where active opposition to a marriage would be withdrawn. She thought of the reams of newspaper reports on herself and Tennie in the United States, a mass of evidence that could become a lethal avalanche if once it were dislodged to come flooding down on her in England.

She made the acquaintance of an American newspaperman in London and threw herself on his mercy, begging him to help her.

"All between him and me is what those papers have said of me," she said, "Help me ... I love him better than life. He is my all, my everything. ... Stop those slanders in the American newspapers. Place me right with the world ... and my loved one will come back to my arms."

Victoria had changed while she was still in the United States. One way and another, the consequences of her ventilation of the Beecher-Tilton scandal had caused her to abjure all the beliefs that had made her "Mrs. Satan" to Thomas Nast and thousands of other Americans. Now she changed even more completely. The woman who had once confessed to wearing a verse from the Psalms embroidered on the sleeve of every dress she wore, asking the Lord to deliver her from lying lips, was now a woman not only abjuring the past but denying it in toto. Confronted by evidences of what had actually happened in years gone by, she called the evidences slanderous lies, inspired by the malice of enemies. (And if there was an echo here of Beecher's defense of his innocence when he was challenged, she would not have been the one to note it.)

Only three elements remained constant; her insistence that everything she did was inspired by principle, her conviction that any unfortunate events in her life simply proved her a martyr to her principles, and, above all, her belief that if the first two convictions could be made in print, preferably in newsprint, their validity would be established beyond any possibility of doubt.

The newspapers, therefore, were at once the overpowering threat to her future and at the same time her one hope of salvation.

Victoria did her best with what opportunities she had. A sketch of her appeared in a paper called the *London Traveler,* describing her as a "martyr woman," who was the victim of a conspiracy between the church and the state. All she had ever attempted to do, the article explained, was declare that women require the same chastity of men that men require of women, but because of this declaration she had been persecuted publicly and privately. She had to pay vast sums to give a lecture, "opening halls with keys of gold"; extortioners and blackmailers had pursued her. "The malice of enemies together with her opinions on the social question have combined to give her a reputation of sin, but no slanders have been heaped on any human soul with greater injustice. A more unsoiled woman does not walk the earth."

A similarly compassionate character study of her appeared in an English *Christian Union*. "That a woman who has devoted her whole life to doing angels' work should have been so maligned and persecuted, even up to the gates of justice, where alone she received a verdict of blameless, is one of those marvels which the pages of history only can explain, and which show that all those who have fought for a good cause, from Saints and Martyrs downwards, have had to pass through their Gethsemane of mental suffering too exquisite for human utterance."

Victoria could show these articles to John Biddulph Martin and urge that he take copies of them to show to his family. These would surely make his family realize how cruelly they were misjudging her. Still, there were Americans in London who had been in the United States in the early 1870s and read of Victoria Woodhull in the newspapers then. They were gossiping, when the occasion prompted, about what they knew of Mrs. Woodhull and her sister, Tennie Claflin. Victoria challenged these gossipers with a notice in the London *Times*.

"Mrs. Victoria C. Woodhull, being again compelled to commence libel suits against Americans who are constantly circulating malicious slanders, offers a REWARD OF FIFTY POUNDS for every letter that contains enough libel to enable her to proceed criminally and civilly, and Five Pounds will be given to any and every person who will give information that can be proceeded with legally against persons who are circulating foul stories by word of mouth."

This was another item that John Biddulph Martin could show to his family. And although no information that would allow her to "proceed criminally and civilly" was forthcoming, Victoria seized on the role of the libeled innocent who was ready to fight publicly for her vindication. Months were passing. A year and a half had passed since her first meeting with John Martin, and though he was as devoted as ever, the prospect of marriage was no nearer.

In November, 1880, Victoria, along with Tennie, Roxanna and Zulu Maud, sailed for the United States. Victoria's purpose in the journey was to confront and expose her libelers there and bring them to justice, or so she told Martin, but this was a project easier to announce in England than to pursue in the United States. Fortunately for her needs, some reporter gave an unfriendly account of the party's arrival in New York and the item was reprinted in a Chicago paper. Mrs. Woodhull and her sister were described as "two middle-aged women, *outré* in costume, with the sharp, eager look of the adventurous females that they are," and Roxanna Claflin was called "an old woman so withered and brown and wrinkled that she looks like one of the hickory nut dolls you find at county fairs." Such comments, along with one referring to the fact that "Mr. Wm. H. Vanderbilt had hurried Mrs. Woodhull and Miss Claflin to England," offered a perfect opportunity for public rebuttal. Letters, reputedly written by friends and defenders of Victoria, were sent to newspapers across the country, decrying these slanders and insisting that Mrs. Woodhull receive fair play. A review of her accomplishments focused on her efforts in behalf of the woman's suffrage movement.

These letters also suggested that there was one special agent, as opposed to slanderers in general, who was contributing to Mrs. Woodhull's martyrdom. Her "unfortunate marriage to Colonel Blood" was cited and then it was claimed that he and Stephen Pearl Andrews had "dragged her into the mire" by the views that they had promulgated in *Woodhull & Claflin's*

Weekly. "She had been led into endless trouble, it was evident, by the man who, as her husband, should have shielded her. Stephen Pearl Andrews and others wrote for *Woodhull & Claflin's Weekly.* The world at large was given to understand that these articles were written or dictated by Mrs. Woodhull, when the fact was that she had no more to do with writing or inspiring them than one of the great elms in the Green of your city." (That particular defense appeared in the New Haven *Union,* in New Haven, Connecticut.)

Most of the letters mentioned that Mrs. Woodhull had been "sick in mind and sick in body" when she defied doctors' orders to come to the United States to meet her defamers face to face. Finally, it was "ill health that prevented her from carrying out her intention of calling them to account." For, after only three weeks in America, Victoria sailed back to England, the various letters in her defense her only trophies.

As soon as she arrived in London, she sent a letter to the *London Journal,* where it duly appeared. Her name, she wrote in this letter, had been "unrighteously associated with what is known as Free Love. No viler aspersion was ever uttered. No greater outrage could be inflicted on a woman." She explained how it had come about. "For several years, I was the ostensible editor of a New York journal, the main object of which was the elevation of woman, politically, morally and religiously." She had done her best to keep it on a high plane but lecturing engagements all over the country had prevented her from the sort of supervision the magazine required. "Articles favoring free love appeared without my knowledge or sanction, which startled the readers of my hitherto spotless print. . . . I now openly avow, with all the earnestness of righteous indignation, that during no part of my life did I favor free love even tacitly." (In a very similar vein, Henry Ward Beecher had once "stamped as utterly untrue" all stories and rumors about him.)

To further prove her innocence, she announced that she was planning to recommence publication of her weekly in London. "Therein full particulars shall be given of the manner in which articles got into *Woodhull & Claflin's Weekly* bearing

my signature. Those articles I utterly repudiate, more especially
the one known as the 'Beecher Article,' the writers of which
acknowledged the authorship of the same at the Beecher trial
under oath." No testimony about the authorship of "The
Beecher Article" had been taken at the Beecher trial; Victoria
herself had claimed the authorship in testimony at the two
trials where she was a defendant because of the fact. However, everything of which she had once been most proud having
been denied, she signed herself "Yours faithfully, Victoria C.
Woodhull, 8 Gilston Road, West Brompton, December 29,
1880."

She was indeed readying an issue of a new magazine which
she was calling *Woodhull & Claflin's Journal,* but before it
came out she mailed a proof-sheet of her *London Journal* letter
to all the leading newspapers in the United States. It was not
the sort of document to which any editor would pay a moment's attention in the normal course of events, but Benjamin
Tucker, who had been Victoria's "boy lover" in 1874, was
currently an exchange editor on the Boston *Globe* and it was
into his hands that the proof-sheet was delivered.

Benjamin Tucker was still faithful to all the radical causes
which had engaged his interest when he first met Victoria, and
the scorn he had felt when he first heard of her apostasy to
those causes had deepened the satisfaction he felt for having
broken with her after less than a year's intimacy. Still, he was
amazed when he read the London proof-sheet and was impelled
to scrawl a heading for it—"As Big A Lie As Was Ever Told."
Then he routed it on to the typesetters. When it was published,
he sent a copy of it to Victoria in London, with a postcard telling her that now she knew what he thought of her.

Victoria would respond to this thrust when she was able.
Currently she was engaged in appealing to "the whole press of
the world to aid us in unearthing those vile traducers who
wanton with our good name," through the pages of an issue of
Woodhull & Claflin's Journal dated January 29, 1881.

"If anyone living can point to any corrupt or unwomanly
action in our life," she wrote in its columns, "now is the time

for him to disclose what he has to say." She attacked Colonel Blood again and wrote of a scurrilous pamphlet about her that had been circulated in New York in 1874. The pamphlet had been written by the lecturer and reformer Joseph Treat, who had once been one of Victoria's great admirers. Then there had been some break or quarrel, and Treat had taken his revenge through the pamphlet. But why, Victoria asked, had Colonel Blood not defended her when this "malicious, obscene and scurrilous pamphlet was hawked about the streets of New York? ... Upon what principle did he refrain from taking legal action against Treat, the vile, mendacious vendor and reputed author of such an outrageous publication?"

She had no pity anymore. Colonel Blood had been busy with the Challis libel trial just as she had been when the pamphlet came out. Two years later he had obtained an indictment against Treat, but the case had never been brought to trial. Blood had done his best to defend her in other ways as well. In the past, he had protested rumors that she did not write her own books or lectures. "I have always found my wife capable of putting her thoughts on paper or before the public on the rostrum much more brilliantly than either myself or anybody else could do it for her," he declared. (But that defense would hardly have interested Victoria now, busy as she was disclaiming authorship of almost everything printed over her name.) Blood had stood up for her against the radicals who claimed, after the *Weekly's* demise, that Victoria's extravagance had ruined it. He was still defending her. After a year of working on a newspaper in Auburn, Maine, he had begun drifting again, working sometimes as a spiritualist healer, sometimes as a hypnotist, sometimes as a lecturer. But his thoughts were of Victoria. Even in her new *Journal* Victoria admitted that "her husband, from whom she is divorced, has recently been sending around letters, wherein he stoutly protests against the imputations which were once cast on his former wife's honor." But that was not enough for her.

"It is not improbable," she suggested in the *Journal*, "that he —who should have been his wife's protector, may yet be proven to have been not only the author, but the person who actually furnished the money for the obnoxious publication."

This suggestion must have brought some pain to Colonel Blood when he saw a copy of *Woodhull & Claflin's Journal* in America. But he made no sign and simply wrote to London to enter a lifetime subscription to Victoria's new magazine.

That one issue proved to be the only issue of the *Journal*, however, for Victoria had found another outlet for her re-workings of the past, an obscure English publication called *The Cuckoo*. In a letter to this paper in April, 1881, she spoke of a "moral leprosy" that had broken out in New York City some years before, when a free-love club had been founded under the sponsorship of none other than Stephen Pearl Andrews. The club had been raided and publicity broke it up, but after this "Mrs. Woodhull . . . became the scapegoat for others' evil doings." Stephen Pearl Andrews began to take advantage of her long absences from the city to fill her journal with his doctrines. This "high priest of debauchery . . . actually had the audacity and unblushing effrontery to affix Mrs. Woodhull's signature to his filthy effusions. But, it will be asked, why did Mrs. Woodhull keep silent? The answer is simple and satisfactory. She acted thus to exculpate her husband, who was the responsible editor and who was threatened with lynching by an exasperated public. . . ." (One can almost hear the puzzled but bashful questions of John Martin prompting each new "simple and satisfactory" answer from Victoria.)

Having thrown Stephen Pearl Andrews into the arena along with Colonel Blood, Victoria set the lions loose on him. The next week she arraigned him again in *The Cuckoo*. "Stephen Pearl Andrews! I impeach thee before the judgment bar. Pure hearts, which might have communed with their Maker in the spiritual Sinai, hast thou by infernal wiles tempted to bow down before the idol of the flesh. . . . Arch-blasphemer! But none liveth to himself, none dieth to himself. All ye who love humanity, aid me in rescuing sons and daughters of men from him who would trample all that is ethereal, beautiful, incorruptible and immortal into a pestilential mire of sensual grossness. . . ."

She had been apocalyptic in her style when her thoughts turned to revelation and religion. Now she was becoming hysterical, her language a mixture of old-time revivalism, self-righteousness and pure raving.

Not all readers of *The Cuckoo* were completely unaware of some of the facts about which Victoria was weaving such a thicket of denial. One wrote to *The Cuckoo* to complain that her "barefaced mendacity has never been exceeded. . . . Would it be believed that even Mrs. Woodhull would have the effrontery to deny that she ever had sympathy for or was in any way connected with the doctrines of free love?"

The complainant to *The Cuckoo* was answered by a letter informing the readers of the magazine that Mrs. Woodhull was preparing her autobiography to show just how all her speeches had been distorted. Further, "It is well known that from the moment Mrs. Woodhull knew Colonel Blood he adopted towards her a course of deception and treachery. After she had returned from a long southern lecture tour, his conduct was so flagrant that she felt forced to apply for a divorce. Whilst this was pending in 1876, and she still his legal wife, he, under terrible pressure, essayed to defend her for the first time. The nature of this pressure was that if he did not perform so tardy an act of justice his whole history would be made public."

Then, in a vein reminiscent of Roxanna, Victoria went on to suggest that her ill health for many years might have been due to slow poisoning. She did not name Colonel Blood as the poisoner but the implication was clear. No longer the "Mrs. Satan" who asked the world to be saved by free love, she might have been accused, from some points of view, of still having satanic elements in her character, as she sought for any vantage point in her battle for a respectable reputation.

Just how Victoria managed to keep the quiet, scholarly English gentleman and banker John Biddulph Martin spellbound while she waged this battle was her own secret. It might seem logical that such a frenzied defense would have caused him to ponder uneasily on overprotestation. He might have wondered why, active as she was in the woman's suffrage cause in the United States, she made no move to join the similar movement in England. To concern oneself with such a cause may not have seemed the best form to his family, but a great many respectable ladies were concerning themselves with the matter during these years. Joining with them would not have put Victoria outside any pale. She might even have made acquaintances and friends that would have helped her personal cause to win Martin. But Victoria was too committed to the course she had chosen to have time for any other considerations. And it was easily the least boring of any course she might have followed.

Perhaps it answered what doubts Martin must have had from time to time to remember that Victoria was an American. Martin knew few Americans and little about their country. Perhaps it seemed to him that in that wild, brawling land across the sea, libelers and slanderers did run in packs like wolves, attacking any pure, innocent woman who, by some show of spirit and originality, had made herself a target.

Victoria sailed again for the United States in the fall of 1881, accompanied by Tennie. Her mission this time, she told John Martin, was to reactivate her campaign for the Presidency. After all, she had many press clippings and pictures from the days when she had indeed been the candidate of the Equal Rights Party. The project had a sound of importance which might help to impress his family.

She was also remembering the headline which Benjamin Tucker had put over her letter when he printed it in the Boston *Globe*. She and Tennie journeyed to Boston soon after they landed. Benjamin Tucker saw Victoria arrive at the *Globe* offices one afternoon, but he had no desire to meet again with the woman he once had loved and kept out of her sight while she called on the managing editor. Later, he learned from the editor that Mrs. Woodhull had come threatening a libel suit unless the "lie" headline was immediately and publicly retracted. The editor had talked with her until she grew calmer, and had finally promised to put a paragraph in the next day's paper, announcing her arrival in America and her intention to renew her Presidential campaign.

The paragraph appeared the next day, as promised, without any mention of the protested headline. Tennie made a visit to the newspaper's offices to pick up some papers that Victoria had left the day before. Tucker saw her from a distance also, but, as in Victoria's case, made no move to speak to her. Tennie's mission accomplished, she departed. And nothing more was said or done about that particular libel suit.

The sisters also spent some time in New York City. By chance one day, Victoria and Colonel Blood passed within a few feet of each other on one of the city streets. Colonel Blood saw Victoria, started and moved forward. But Victoria's gaze passed over him and she did not pause. The Colonel paled and faltered, taking the arm of the man who was with him. Victoria moved on down the street. Perhaps by now she wholly believed that he was the chief cause of all her difficulties, the one person who was keeping her from her heart's desire.

Victoria did very little about any Presidential campaign except talk about it with some of the crankier acquaintances from the *Weekly's* apocalyptic days. Returned to England, however, she issued a long manifesto to the English newspapers about her campaign, calling the people "of all Europe, America and all the world," to "rally around her standard and support her in her right to represent and work for the people of America." She suggested public meetings everywhere, the choosing of delegates and the passing of resolutions. She promised steamer tickets to all delegates for a convention that would be held in "Philadelphia, or New York or Boston." A nominating convention would be held in St. James Hall, Piccadilly, London, but no date was given for that event. All particulars could be obtained by writing to "H. T. Belmont, Secretary, 32 Thistle Grove, S. Kensington, London, England."

Talking importantly of this new venture, rustling papers and making plans, Victoria at least had an alternate theme to the obsessive one of persecution for her conversations with John Martin.

And then, before that project had dragged on through so many months as to become wearisome, something happened to bring John Biddulph Martin to the point of resolution. Did his family finally find its hostility to Victoria Woodhull too exhausting to maintain any longer? Had Martin, after so long, finally decided to act for himself regardless of the consequences? Victoria never said.

Elizabeth Cady Stanton was visiting in London late in 1882. On December 11, she wrote in her diary:

"For the last three days London has been visited by one of the blackest and most dense fogs ever known. It was dark as night. The gas was lighted in all the houses, and streets, carriage lamps were burning, and other conveyances had flaming flambeaux. It was considered dangerous to go out. I was surprised by the call of a heavily-veiled lady, who, when I entered the drawing room, threw off her concealment, and there stood Victoria Woodhull. She insisted on my going with her in her carriage to a beautiful house, where she lives, the legal wife of an Englishman of wealth and position. She has passed through great suffering. May the good angels watch and guard her. I will not condemn."

28 ❧ *Riding in Their Own Carriages...*

SOMEHOW Tennie had managed to avoid the limelight during the years of Victoria's campaign to become Mrs. Martin. And although she was often at Victoria's side, she was almost never mentioned in Victoria's appeals to the press in both England and America. Perhaps Victoria felt that she had enough to do in creating a public figure of one martyred victim without stretching the agony to cover two. Tennie seemed not to mind and quickly found her own ways of amusing herself in London. Roxanna and Buck Claflin were also quiet during those years, but since both of them had reached advanced ages their quiescence may not have been so remarkable.

Then Victoria was married and went to live at 17 Hyde Park Gate, a richly somber house on an exclusive and somber street and Tennie spent more time with her sister. Victoria indulged her love of elegance in the interior decoration of the house. There were blue and gold ceilings, white fur rugs on darkly polished floors, and many marble or silver busts of Greek deities —a tribute perhaps to Victoria's Grecian spirit-guide, Demosthenes.

Amidst this chill glory, Victoria and Tennie could sit and drink tea while Victoria waited, usually in vain, for friends of John Martin's to call on her. She had married into that level of British society just below the aristocracy whose members cherished hereditary wealth and position and guarded their ranks against all interlopers. Even the wealthiest industrialists seemed suspect to the bankers, military men and diplomats of this class, for the industrialists had made their money in trade and hence could not be considered gentlemen. Naturally the members of this group were even more inclined to avoid the new Mrs. Martin, who was American, a divorcée, with a past both mysterious and unsavory, and who had spent the years before her marriage in constant and unseemly appearances in the press.

Victoria seemed almost to take pleasure in the aloofness of her husband's friends, finding proof of their worth and of the high level which she had attained in their reluctance to welcome her. Always quiet and ladylike in her personal manner, however shrill her public utterances sometimes were, she took on a new dignity as Martin's wife, and she enjoyed discussing with Tennie the Martin family pedigree. The bank on Lombard Street dated back to the fifteenth century, when it had been a goldsmith's concern. In the sixteenth century, a Sir Thomas Gresham had made his family crest, a grasshopper, the emblem of the business. In the same century, the first Martin, Sir Richard, had become a member of the company. A century later, the goldsmith's company had become a bank and in 1703 the name Martin reappeared in its records. Ever since then a Martin had been one of the bank's partners.

Talk of such matters roused Victoria's latent craving for a pedigree of her own. From time to time in the past, she had told reporters about her mother's descent from the old German family of the Hummels, "whose ancestors were of royal blood." She had also indicated vaguely that her father came from an old, aristocratic English family.

Now she and Tennie busied themselves with the composition of what seemed to them a proper genealogical chart. Roxanna and Buck Claflin were consulted. A letter was sent off to Margaret Ann in New York, asking for any information she might have about the family background. Beyond that, Victoria and Tennie did little else in the way of research but exercise their imaginations.

The chart that they finally prepared was printed in a small folder, ready for instant distribution. It read rather loosely but impressively:

MEMO:
beneath
THE WASHINGTON PEDIGREE
as on the Chart, reads as follows:
JOHN DANDRIDGE HAD TWO DAUGHTERS

King Robert III of Scotland,	George Washington married
King James of England	Martha Dandridge.
from whom are descended	Penelope Dandridge married
The Dukes of Hamilton,	Michael Biddulph,
to whom was related	who died in 1800
Alexander Hamilton	Their son
the friend of Washington.	John Biddulph married

Thomas Hamilton married
Anna Underwood
Their grandson was
Rubin Buckman Claflin (born
in 1796 at Sanderfield,
Mass., U.S.A.), the father
of
VICTORIA CLAFLIN
WOODHULL and
TENNESSEE CLAFLIN

Augusta Roberts,
Their daughter
Mary Ann Biddulph married
Robert Martin.
Their son,
John Biddulph Martin
Married
VICTORIA
WOODHULL

A further paragraph explained that Victoria Claflin Woodhull-Martin and Tennessee Claflin, "who are descended on their
father's side from the kings of Scotland and England and on
their mother's side, from the Hummels and Moyers of Ger-
many, who also were of royal blood, are related to the famous
American legislator, Lieut.-Colonel Alexander Hamilton
(whose statue adorns the Central Park, New York City); and
they are connected by marriage with the family of Washington
himself."

After this appearance on the chart, Tennie generally returned to the original spelling of her name as Tennessee. Aside
from that, the folder had little effect except to further alienate
those whom Victoria wished to impress.

However Victoria may have felt about the scarcity of visitors
to 17 Hyde Park Gate, John Biddulph Martin showed no
signs of regret for the unusual marriage he had made. He was,
if anything, even more devoted once Victoria was his wife.
Probably he was filled with a sense of his own chivalry at having rescued her from a cruel and unprotected life, especially as
she continued her murmuring about enemies writing and talking against her. This preoccupation with persecution was the
easier to bear since Victoria also continued to enchant John
Martin with her soft and gracious ways and the loving glance
of her great blue eyes.

For a long while there was peace at 17 Hyde Park Gate.

The friends Tennessee found during the years in London did not belong to the class into which Victoria had married, but this did not mean that some of them were not wealthy. And it was only logical that some of them should have spiritualistic leanings, for Tennessee took her second sight and magnetic powers as much for granted as Victoria did and gravitated toward those who understood or sympathized with such matters.

Sometime in 1884 or 1885, Tennessee met an elderly widower named Francis Cook who was interested in spiritualism, just as Commodore Vanderbilt had been. Mr. Cook was not, perhaps, quite as many times a millionaire as the Commodore, but he was very rich, having made a fortune from his importing firm, Cook & Son. He lived in a magnificent home on the Thames called Doughty House, and he had a taste for collecting, manifested in an art gallery impressively filled with quite splendid old masters. Along with all this, he also had an estate in Portugal, near Lisbon, on which he had lavished so much money that the King of Portugal had given him the title of Visconde de Montserrate.

Tennessee, fifteen years older than when she had declined the Commodore's offer of marriage, brought a spirit message to Francis Cook from his dead wife. The dead wife advised the living Mr. Cook to marry Miss Claflin. No difficulties followed this pronouncement. There was none of the anguish that followed Victoria's recognition that John Martin was the man for her. Francis Cook's children were grown and married. He was lonely and eager for entertainment. And Tennessee was prettier these days than she had ever been, as well as gay and insouciant.

In October of 1885, Francis Cook married Tennessee Celeste Claflin and took her to live with him at Doughty House.

The marriage was widely announced. Reports of it reached the New York papers and at least one, the *World,* could not forbear reviewing a few highlights from Tennie's and Victoria's careers.

Just three weeks later, on November 19, 1885, Reuben Buckman Claflin died. Victoria was jarred by the shock but also found it a circumstance that enabled her to reply with hurt indignation to the recent press comment about her and Tennie in New York. She wrote to the New York *Sun*.

"Sir: My father, Reuben B. Claflin died of grief caused by the malicious libel published in the World of October 25th. Has not our family suffered enough? Please insert this notice for our heart-broken family. Victoria Claflin Martin." But this card served only to remind other United States newspapers of the Woodhull-Claflin story.

Then, as though any death in the Claflin family had to inspire rumors of foul play, someone wrote a letter to the Lord Mayor of London suggesting that Reuben B. Claflin's death had been very sudden. "His sickness and burial was very mysterious. It would be well to have this matter investigated at once by the proper authorities as delay may defeat the ends of justice."

Investigation, duly undertaken by Scotland Yard, showed only that Buck Claflin, at the age of eighty-nine, had died of a paralytic stroke. No definite clue could be found as to who had written the accusing letter, but after some time the investigators told Mr. Martin that they were forced to suspect that some member of the Claflin family was responsible. John Martin had surely gained some knowledge of the melodramatic propensities of the Claflins by this time. He could only greet such a suspicion with silence. But fortunately, however her mother or sister behaved, Victoria was forever beyond any doubt in Martin's mind, the spotless, blameless object of his protection and love.

It would be a long time before Victoria heard of another death that occurred only a few weeks after her father's, nor would she admit to any grief when she did hear of it, though the story was dramatic enough for any Claflin.

Colonel Blood, still pursuing his erratic and seemingly aimless course, had returned to Auburn, Maine, the previous spring and surprised everyone who knew him by marrying an elderly widow there. Immediately thereafter, he had joined with a Portland sea captain named Jackson in a project almost as glamorous as some of Victoria's had been. They were going to Africa to claim and work a gold mine about which the captain had heard on previous voyages to the African coast.

All went well on the voyage. The captain let Colonel Blood off the ship at a small coastal port in Africa and then sailed farther down the coast to a larger port which was needed for unloading the heavy mining machinery they had brought. Colonel Blood traveled some hundred miles inland, found the mine just as reported and went to work.

Several weeks later, Captain Jackson arrived with the machinery. The first news he heard was that the Colonel was dead—dead and already buried. He tried to learn details but the native stories, told in varying dialects and translated into broken English, did not tell him much. Colonel Blood had taken ill of an "African fever." Some "black medicine" had been given to him. That was all. He had died on December 29, 1885.

One could find a small irony in the fact that the man of principle, whose life had once been joined with Victoria's "by the powers of the air," perished in pursuit of a commodity for which he had never cared at all when Victoria knew him. He had found some too. When a friend arrived from Maine to take his body back to the United States for burial, he was also given to take back a small vial of gold that the Colonel had mined.

In London, after the flurry caused by Buck Claflin's death, Roxanna went to live with Tennessee at Doughty House, and remained there until her death in 1890, aged 85. It must have filled her with satisfaction to be there and to watch Tennessee and Victoria go out driving every fine afternoon in Hyde Park in splendid carriages behind sleek horses. After all the incomprehensible years with Colonel Blood, both girls were now "riding around in their own carriages," as Roxanna had always wanted them to be, the pampered wives of millionaires.

Tennessee's husband soon acquired another distinction, which Tennie was able to share. The art-loving Francis Cook used some of his fortune to endow an artists' home in London. The opening was a grand occasion, made even grander by the appearance of the Prince and Princess of Wales.

Tennessee and Victoria were both beautifully dressed for the event, but Victoria's manner was cold and subdued, her dignity as Mrs. John Biddulph Martin giving her an almost forbidding air. Tennessee, on the other hand, was as animated as she had been years before, at the opening of the Woodhull, Claflin brokerage firm in New York and she made an excellent impression. Always herself, she had one talent for pleasing bored and conventional Londoners which Victoria lacked. She could make them laugh. The opening was a triumph for Tennie.

Soon afterward, Francis Cook was rewarded for this lavish gesture toward the arts by being made a baronet. He became Sir Francis, and Tennessee, the "Wonder Child" of long ago in Ohio and Illinois and Indiana, was Lady Cook, mistress of Doughty House and of a marble castle at Montserrate, in Portugal, as well.

Sir Francis took Tennie to visit this other home. As their carriage drove through the village below the hill on which the castle stood, the natives sang and danced and pelted Tennie with flowers. Sir Francis had showered many blessings on the village and so his arrival with a new bride was the occasion for a general fiesta, with rockets adding to the celebration. Then the carriage drove on up the winding road to the hilltop where the castle, surrounded by exotic gardens, gleamed in the sun.

It was all like a fairy tale come true for Tennessee, one that in her come-day-go-day approach to life she had never bothered even to imagine, but it did not delight her any the less now that it was hers to play with as she would.

Victoria's life had its fairy-tale elements also. Her husband was young, handsome and adoring. Her home in London, if not as lavish as Doughty House, was splendid enough. And the Martins had a country seat as well, at Bredon's Norton, a rustic, almost medieval village in Worcestershire, near Tewksbury. There, amid the charms of unspoiled rural England, were the grassy park, the great trees, the small old manor house and the stately main dwelling to round out the scene from romance.

A fairy tale come true for both sisters—Rose Red and Snow White—who, after fearful adventures in the dark and menacing forest of the world, had been rescued at last by proper princes. Could anything spoil the proper fairy-tale ending "And so they lived happily ever after . . ."?

Nothing but the fact that they were still Victoria and Tennessee. And whether or not the royal blood of Robert III of Scotland, James of England, the Duke of Hamilton and even Alexander Hamilton, coursed in their veins as "The Washington Pedigree" claimed, it was undeniable that the fighting, vital, attention-craving spirit of the Claflins and Hummels burned in their hearts. That was a spirit that no luxury or protection could smother.

29 ⧙ *Two Noble Women, Nobly Planned* ...

SOME of the troubles of the next ten years could be traced legitimately to the activities of others. Members of the Claflin clan periodically raised public rows that caught Victoria and Tennessee in the updrafts. In 1886, sister Mary Sparr in New York (who had formerly called herself Polly, and who had, along with her husband, helped precipitate a public washing of Claflin dirty linen back in 1871) hit the newspapers in both America and England with a lawsuit contesting the will of one of her daughters by her first husband. The details of the poor girl's life and death, and the reasons for her having bequeathed her legacy from her father to someone other than her mother, were so unsavory and shocking that the newspapers devoted a great deal of space to the story. Mary Sparr, intoxicated by her prominence, began defending her own purity by reminiscing about the wild free-love life that her sisters Victoria and Tennie had led in New York in the 1870s.

John Biddulph Martin buckled on the armor of Don Quixote and wrote a stern letter to the New York *Herald* in defense of his Dulcinea. "Referring to reports in the case of Sparr vs. deMartin that recently appeared in your columns, it is impossible to remain silent or to refute seriatim the innumerable falsehoods and malignantly libellous statements and insinuations that have been directed in that law suit against my wife, Victoria Woodhull Martin. . . . They originated, to our certain knowledge, in personal malice. . . ."

Other troubles arose as various figures in Victoria's past themselves tried to establish new and blameless lives. In 1888, the Reverend Henry Ward Beecher's authorized biography appeared, and in the course of explaining away the great Beecher-Tilton scandal, now twelve years past, there were various references to how Beecher had been blackmailed by Victoria Woodhull.

Responding to this, Victoria summoned reporters and said, "I don't believe Mr. Beecher ever made or wrote such a charge. . . . At any risk of personal annoyance my husband and I are prepared to bring the libellers to book." No action was taken, however.

Some attacks came from people unknown to either Victoria or Tennessee, who saw in the contrast between the sisters' present respectable affluence and their past activities various kinds of opportunities for themselves.

John Biddulph Martin, again playing Don Quixote, helped Victoria track down a certain Miss Schonberg, who had written a "spicy and telling" article for a New York newspaper about "Two Sirens of New York." Tearfully, Miss Schonberg confessed that she had been the tool of "bad wicked men who had hatched the plot to destroy . . . two noble women." She named as one of her sources for details about their lives a Mrs. Clara Warner.

Victoria and her husband found Mrs. Warner in a London

hospital, and Martin made a patient memo of all that Mrs. Warner had to say. She was a former resident of New Jersey and for some years had been claiming that her husband had been ruined by Mrs. Woodhull and Tennie Claflin in the days when the sisters lived on 23rd Street in New York. When Victoria dramatically revealed her identity and declared that everything Mrs. Warner had said about her was a lie, Mrs. Warner hastily retracted all that she had said. Before the interview was over she dictated a statement to Martin in which she confessed that she had been totally misinformed about Mrs. Martin.

These echoes from a past that was gone, buried and denied were exasperating. But if Victoria, and Tennie too, following her lead, could have remembered Victoria's own brave advice to the Reverend Mr. Beecher some years before, the echoes might gradually have faded to nothing. Victoria had told Beecher that he should "not admit the right of anybody to question or compel him to plead by stooping to answer what anybody might charge against him." She had counseled him to insist that "the public had no business" with his private affairs.

But such a course had become impossible to Victoria. And so she and Tennie, in their eagerness to confound any possible charges or questions, themselves contributed to their difficulties. They began issuing a stream of pamphlets from 17 Hyde Park Gate, pamphlets detailing the confessions of those who had slandered them, pamphlets defending their characters and accomplishments, pamphlets headlining the sisters as "Two Noble Women, Nobly Planned."

Such a storm of self-vindication only fanned the distaste of the members of society whom they were hoping to impress, and the snubs grew more pronounced. One of John Martin's clubs gave a dinner to which ladies were invited. Martin asked his wife and sister-in-law. A certain Mrs. Taylor, wife of an army officer, convinced the other wives that Mrs. Martin and Lady Cook were not "proper persons to be associated with." As a result, the day after the affair the society press reported that Mrs. Martin and Lady Cook had been the only women present at the dinner.

This crushing snub brought forth a new rush of pamphlets from Victoria and Tennie. "A Page of American History" reprinted some of the newspaper articles that had praised them during their days of activity for the suffrage cause. Still another pamphlet reprinted the *Weekly's* account of Victoria's "Naked Truth" speech at Cooper Union. William Cullen Bryant's poem "The Naked Truth" was also reprinted, as it had appeared in the *Post,* but set just above the account of the speech so that it appeared as if both items had been printed in the *Post* originally.

But naturally, being Victoria and Tennie, they could not consider what Mrs. Taylor and her friends were saying to each other about them without beginning to talk to their respective husbands about the possibilities of a libel suit against the slanderous ladies.

It was probably hearing talk that such a suit was threatened that drove Mrs. Taylor and her group to a new and more active attack. They arranged for some private investigation into Victoria's and Tennie's earlier lives to be done in the United States. The first result of this was that Mrs. Taylor was soon able to do some pamphleteering of her own. After receiving some old issues of *Woodhull & Claflin's Weekly* she published a leaflet reprinting excerpts from some of the *Weekly's* more arresting articles on sex.

Victoria had managed to achieve, during trips to the United States before her marriage, a few press clippings that seemed to vindicate her as a "noble woman" wrongly used. She probably felt that now, with a husband like John Martin at her side, she could achieve even more. In 1890, she, Martin and Tennessee embarked on the first of what would become a series of voyages across the Atlantic to clear the sisters' names.

They had an immediate objective in New York. An article about various adventuresses, among whom Victoria Woodhull and Tennie C. Claflin were included, had recently appeared in the Brooklyn *Eagle,* signed by New York's Police Inspector,

Thomas Byrnes. John Martin was determined to deal with that "foul aspersion" first. Soon after their arrival in New York he and Victoria called on the Police Inspector.

The interview was unrewarding if not actually alarming. The Inspector refused the gambit that was offered him of saying that he had not written the piece himself and so had been unaware of subscribing to untrue statements about Victoria and Tennie. Instead, as a public official he insisted on standing by his public statements and told Victoria that if she wanted to dispute him she had a recourse in the courts. Somehow, Victoria managed to explain away this attitude to her husband before they were interviewed by some reporters. Victoria told the reporters that the Police Inspector had admitted to knowing nothing of her past life and that he had said that the use of his name had been unwarranted.

The next day, the Police Inspector read this version of his meeting with the Martins with "no little surprise" and held a press conference of his own. He gave the reporters his version of what he had said and suggested that the Martins had visited him and then talked to newspapermen so that they would have a story that could be cabled to England.

John Biddulph Martin, bewildered by another storm arising out of something that had promised to be straightforward, issued a statement denying that he and his wife had sought any publicity. Reporters had called on them. They had talked to the reporters briefly and then had been misquoted. After this, Victoria did summon some reporters and this time she told them that Byrnes had made a "manly apology."

The minor flurry thus being created had already irritated the Police Inspector. Queried about his reactions to Victoria's remarks, he shrugged and said he had no more time for such people. After that, someone asked Victoria if she did not plan to sue and she said no. She had heard enough about the Police Inspector's power, she said, to know that she could not expect justice if she took him to court.

Two days later there was a news item in several papers announcing that an old indictment against Tennessee Claflin for manslaughter had been revived in Ottawa, Illinois. In this instance there seemed little doubt that the private investigations undertaken at the behest of the righteous Mrs. Taylor and her friends had at last borne fruit. Lady Cook was reported prostrated by the news at first. Then she recovered enough to see two reporters.

Tennie had grown slimmer in recent years. She was pale and fragile now and it only made her more attractive. And her excitable manner had not changed.

"My God," she said, "so they are to fulfill their threats. Well, let them do it. Now that they have begun their attacks anew, I will insist on going to the bottom of all the foul charges. But why have they not brought this up before! Manslaughter—and after twenty-six years. It is all persecution. All the old filth throwing, all devilish malignancy, and hate and envy because now we are rich and up in the world!"

More expostulations, more explanations, more talk of how young Tennie had been, and how exploited, even more tears and collapses, were required in the intimate family circle, to make things clear to John Biddulph Martin. Even so, it was decided to cut the American trip short and return to England at once.

As soon as they arrived in London, Victoria fell gravely ill, just as she had fallen ill once before, in 1873, when it seemed she was hemmed in on every side. She was so sick and remained that way for so long that when she recovered, the hostilities, the threats, the revelations that had been looming so closely had been pushed aside and almost forgotten.

Tennessee liked to give garden parties and sometimes she invited more people than she kept count of so that she had to entertain the overflow in adjoining fields. Such misadventures did not trouble her, and she was so cheerful and offhand about them that they did not trouble her guests either. She soon learned that her American slang amused her English guests (just as it had once pleased Commodore Vanderbilt), so she sprinkled her conversation with Midwestern colloquialisms.

Tennessee went again and again to her husband's castle in Portugal. She was queen there without any need to echo Victoria. Following her husband's lead, she took an immense interest in the village and enjoyed playing Lady Bountiful. She established a school in the village and sent several of its children to a convent in London. She enjoyed the rich, tropical gardens around the castle so much herself that she had them opened to tourists. But she did not forget principle and the fact that life must have its lessons. The gatekeeper was provided with a stack of pamphlets to distribute to departing visitors. Some spoke of the perils of "The Primrose Path," and some told of the battles she and her sister had waged in the United States that women might be free. News stories about her when she was in residence at the castle always delighted her. One such, titled "On Cintra's Far Rock," appeared in the Nottingham *Express and Journal*. A clipping of that article found its way to the United States and various newspapermen who had known Tennie in days gone by read, in a happy daze at life's wonders, of the "blond, spirituelle Lady Cook," moving graciously among her "rare and gorgeous plants."

Tennessee, it seemed, could enjoy the glories of the present without comparing them to the glories of the past that had tarnished.

Perhaps it was because Tennessee did not regret the past importance of the *Weekly*, with its world-saving intent, that Victoria did not ask her sister's help in a new venture. She was planning to publish a new journal, on a monthly basis, which she was calling the *Humanitarian*. Instead of having Tennie as an associate, Victoria chose her daughter, Zulu Maud. A quiet and attractive young woman of twenty-eight by this time, Zulu was hardly the child that Victoria still liked to call her sometimes. But she was devoted to her mother, did not rebel at the way Victoria shielded her from romantic entanglements and busied herself with all the details of the magazine for the next few years.

The *Humanitarian* was handsomely printed on fine paper,

just as *Woodhull & Claflin's Weekly* had been, and it also dealt with social themes, but in no way as lively a fashion as the *Weekly* had. Stirpiculture, actually a sort of theory of planned parenthood, which had been one of Stephen Pearl Andrews' pet topics, was one of its continuing concerns. (Stephen Pearl Andrews was dead now—he had died the year after Colonel Blood, but Victoria offered no eulogies for him either.)

Life was busy and dignified for Victoria once the *Humanitarian* was launched. Her husband had his responsibilities at the bank. He was interested also in the doings of the Royal Statistical Society, was on the boards of various philanthropic organizations and the member of several clubs. From time to time he immersed himself in research for a book that would trace the history of his family bank.

All battles seemingly over, Victoria managed to persuade John Biddulph Martin of the necessity and propriety of her running again for the Presidency of the United States, in 1892. They sailed for America in early summer, once again accompanied by Tennessee. (Sir Francis always seemed to have convenient business commitments elsewhere when these junkets were planned.)

Each of her visits brought Victoria to a changed country. New York had doubled in size since the year when her spirit-guide led her to 17 Great Jones Street. Mechanical marvels were everywhere—telephones, typewriters, electric lights, elevated railways. The Brooklyn Bridge now spanned the river that "Beecher's ferries" had crossed on Sundays. Only Victoria had not changed in her need for attention. She announced that she had come to America to ask her people to put her in the White House, where she would have the power to inaugurate "a system of education which will waken people to the responsibility of creating a race of gods instead of inferior human beings. . . ."

She had further announcements, interviews, copies of speeches or articles for the newspapers each day. From the start of her career in New York she had the instincts of a good press agent. Now that she was able to afford a secretary, or even secretaries, if she wished, there seemed no limit to the amount of copy she could furnish, and the papers, still rather unsophisticated in the ways of personal publicity, printed a great deal of it. It was only two years since the flurry with Police Inspector Byrnes and the publicity about the old indictment against Tennie, but somehow no reporter was inspired to look into back Woodhull or Claflin files.

Then the Martins and Lady Cook went on to Chicago, and in Chicago the announcement of their arrival did prompt one newspaper, the Chicago *Mail,* to revive some memories in a lively piece called "Tennie and her Vicky."

The next morning John Biddulph Martin was at the Criminal Court building instituting a suit for criminal libel against the newspaper. And at once the *Mail* put its best reporters to work on the Claflin pasts and was soon publishing a long and detailed story with names, dates and circumstances, beginning with Buck Claflin's activities in Homer, Ohio, and including all the police complaints against Tennie in Cincinnati and elsewhere.

Again Victoria and Tennessee met the attack with expostulations, explanations and cries of persecution, which seemed to satisfy Martin. He did not press the libel case, however, and soon the little party was on its way back to England.

Two months later the Martins were again in the United States, bringing Zulu Maud with them. Victoria was obviously determined to see this Presidential campaign through to the finish. In Washington, D.C., she managed to gather a group of fifty women who nominated her as the Presidential candidate of the Humanitarian Party. Announcing this to reporters, Victoria also said that she was accepting the nomination of the National Woman's Suffrage Association as their candidate. It hardly mattered that Miss Frances Willard, speaking for the NWSA, promptly denied that the association had any Presidential candidate. Victoria had managed to link her name with the NWSA in print in connection with the Presidential campaign.

She was in New York on election day and she sat in the pleasant drawing room of the house her husband had rented sipping tea and talking to a reporter. She confessed to him that she did not expect to be elected.

"The truth is that I am too many years ahead of this age and the exalted views and objects of humanitarianism can scarcely be grasped as yet by the unenlightened mind of the average man."

She was not dismayed to learn later that the Humanitarian ticket had not received a single vote and that Grover Cleveland had been returned to the Presidency for a second term. Her campaign had been only educational. And also, an enlivening interlude in a life of respectability that she plainly found rather boring now that she had achieved it.

She stepped out onto the lecture platform again in 1893, speaking in St. James Hall in London, and then, on another trip to the United States, in Carnegie Hall in New York. She was still a beautiful woman and looked well, wearing a violet dress with violets at her throat for her New York appearance. But she no longer had any deep personal concern like sex or pain which was driving her to revelation and persuasion and with that gone her old compelling magnetism was gone. She read her speech on "The Scientific Propagation of the Human Race" from a manuscript and the applause was only polite when she finished.

After that she gave up a contemplated lecture tour "in compliance with the wishes of her husband," and accompanied John Martin to Chicago. He was one of the British commissioners to the World's Fair being held there. Only a year before the Chicago *Mail* had spread her past and Tennie's on its pages and the Martins had left the city in agitation and distress. This year the stir seemed entirely forgotten. Newspapers and Chicagoans in general were much too interested in the wonders of the great fair to spare a thought for old items about Woodhull and Claflin.

Returned to England, Victoria continued the publication of the *Humanitarian,* filling it with essays culled from all over.

And then, as though irked herself by its dullness, and overcome once again by boredom, she suddenly provoked her prince and protector, John Biddulph Martin, to one more dramatic defense of her name.

She had hired a man to do some research for her in the British Museum. Before long he had discovered that the shelves of the Museum held not only the Henry Ward Beecher biography which mentioned Victoria Woodhull as a blackmailer but various other books and pamphlets about the Beecher-Tilton case which referred to her in unfavorable terms. Presumably these had not been the object of the researcher's efforts but once they had been discovered Victoria forgot everything else and soon had her husband as agitated and determined as she. Together, the Martins brought an action against the trustees of the British Museum to recover damages for libel.

Victoria had scored another first. In the United States, she had been the first woman to address a Congressional Committee, the first woman to run for President, the first lady broker, and managed a variety of other unique achievements. Now, in England, she and her husband became the first people in history to sue the British Museum for libel. As a result, the case was covered widely by the London press.

For Victoria, the trial had the novelty of British trappings and traditional courtroom ritual. In almost every other way it was like all the other courtroom dramas in which she had figured. She looked gracious and composed on the witness stand. Her testimony, given in an earnest voice, took off from counsel's questions to range far afield, touching on those whom she had trusted who had betrayed her, the work she had done for women and humanity, and the endless sufferings she had known as a result. The counsel for the defendants was more severe with her than her own counsel, but she eluded him also, managing to win sympathy from both spectators and jury as she did so.

The trial lasted five days. The jury, after due deliberation, found that the documents complained of did libel the plaintiff, but since the defendants did not know that the books contained libels, they were not guilty of negligence, merely of not using proper care, caution or judgment. The defendants were fined twenty shillings.

The Martins appealed the case and that kept the matter in the news a while longer, but at last their counsel assured the court that "since the character of Mrs. Martin has been thoroughly vindicated during the trial," which was all that was desired, the plaintiffs did not propose to press the case further and were willing that the appeal be dismissed. It was then so ordered by the court.

And still unsought notoriety pursued Victoria and Tennie along with the more desired "vindicating" publicity. Soon after Victoria had wrung her concession from the British Museum, Tennessee's husband, Sir Francis Cook, was hailed into court by a former housekeeper who charged breach of promise and seduction. Sir Francis frankly admitted the seduction but denied any promises and the case was soon settled in his favor.

Another Claflin storm blew up the next year in New York. Zulu Maud (who now spelled her first name Zula) had been there for some months, supervising an American edition of *The Humanitarian* and, hopefully, conducting a literary salon in imitation of the one over which her mother had reigned twenty-five years before. In New York, Zula stayed with her cousin, Ellie Celeste, a younger daughter of Margaret Ann Miles (who had married a Mr. D. W. O'Halloran in 1889). Cousin Ellie was married to an intelligent, personable young doctor, Charles Steuart Welles. They lived in a pleasant house, were parents of a little girl named after the beautiful and unfortunate Utica, and Dr. Welles helped Zula considerably with putting out *The Humanitarian*.

Just what went wrong in this seemingly comfortable situation was never clear. But once again John Martin found himself in America, this time defending his wife against her family as well as the press. Victoria denounced her sister, Mrs. O'Halloran, her niece, Ellie, and her niece's husband, Dr. Welles, with impartiality. She burned some furniture and papers in the Welles' house and this made the newspapers, along with her declaration that she and her husband had helped the Welles until the burden became too great. John Martin concurred, saying, "Frankly this family disturbance is caused by money. We became tired of being played." Margaret Ann, on the other hand, denied this. She said that Victoria sent her money from time to time certainly, but only so that she, Margaret Ann, could put it in a private account for Victoria, from which she could withdraw it as she wished without her husband's knowledge. Margaret Ann insisted that the only real aid or payment for their services that the O'Hallorans and Welles received was from Tennie, Lady Cook.

When the Martins finally disengaged themselves and were able to sail for England, John Martin admitted that America was a country that he did not understand and that once he had returned to England he was planning to stay there permanently.

Home again in England, where life was more comprehensible, John Martin completed his history of the family bank, and his book, *The Grasshopper of Lombard Street*, was published. He became president of the Royal Statistical Society. Victoria undoubtedly manifested the proper gentle and wifely pride in these accomplishments of her husband, but her own life again began to seem empty and constricting.

She began her autobiography. "Sitting here today in this north room of 17 Hyde Park Gate, London—dreary, smoky, foggy, insulated as you are in the customs and prejudices of centuries—I am thinking with all the bitterness of my woman's nature how my life has been warped and twisted out of shape by this environment...." It was an environment which she had fought fiercely to become part of, but success always seemed to have a frustrating effect on her. She progressed no further than one chapter in this disenchanted mood but issued the fragment as a pamphlet.

Not many months thereafter, John Martin became dangerously ill. When he began to recuperate he went on doctor's
orders to Las Palmas in the Canary Islands. For once, Victoria
did not accompany him on a journey. In Las Palmas, John
Martin died, on March 29, 1897.

Victoria wrote a eulogy for him in *The Humanitarian*, prais-
ing the loyal way in which he had defended her from persecution. The weeks he had spent in Las Palmas without her had
been their longest separation in all their years of married life.
"Theirs was a perfect union, marred only by persecution."

Indeed it seemed to have been. Year after year, Martin had
been dragged into one incomprehensible drama after another
and never ceased loving his wife or believing whatever fantastic tale she told him. When he died he left her an estate
of 171,779 pounds sterling, and asked that he be cremated and
his ashes scattered, "or otherwise dealt with as my dear wife
sees fit."

In 1901, Tennessee's husband, Sir Francis Cook, died. He
did not leave her as large a sum as John Martin had left Victoria but she was amply provided for. Certainly Tennie was
not impelled by any financial motive but simply reacting in
typical Claflin fashion to death when she suddenly demanded,
a few weeks later, that Sir Francis' body be exhumed. She said
his relatives were circulating "infamous stories" about how he
had come to his end.

The horrified relatives managed to forestall any exhumation,
but by that time Tennessee had said so much to the press that
an old family servant sued her for slander. Tennessee was
pleased, foreseeing an opportunity such as Victoria had enjoyed with her suit against the British Museum of having her
character "thoroughly vindicated" in court. When the case
came to trial, however, Lady Cook's counsel refused to put her
on the stand and the whole matter was settled summarily.

Tennie flew into a tantrum. "I have been had by my
counsel and jury," she cried. "Oh, cruel, cruel, cruel—after
thousands of pounds! I brought it to go into the witness box,

and I gave those instructions, but they did not want me to go into the box."

Not long after that a coolness developed between Victoria and Tennie. Neither of them, usually so voluble, gave any reason for their estrangement. They had moved side by side through triumph and disaster, melodrama and comedy, for more than forty years. They would never be quite so close again.

Tennessee, at fifty-eight, was slender and delicate and still very pretty, with a Dresden china look. She dressed exquisitely in pastels that accented her fragility, and now began a peripatetic career of travel, back and forth from England to the United States. Often she had nieces and nephews with her, or grand nieces and grand nephews. Niece Ellie Celeste's husband, Dr. Welles, was first secretary at the United States Embassy in London for a while. Tennessee could enjoy this family importance and also take young Utica Welles on shopping expeditions and advise and comment on proper clothes for her first flutters in London society. These flutters would result, in 1903, in Utica's marriage to a brilliantly talented young musician, Thomas Beecham, eldest son of Sir Joseph Beecham of Ewanville, Huyton, Lancashire.

Tennessee would also fling herself, periodically, into activity for the woman's cause as it was being pursued in England. Mrs. Evangeline Pankhurst, leader of the struggle in England, had a charm and eloquence to match or surpass what Victoria's had been in America. But Mrs. Pankhurst had a husband, daughters and her own group of devoted followers to stand beside her and march with her in the more dramatic manifestations of her crusade. And so, although Tennie could be generous financially, her contributions in the way of drama often seemed frivolous, wide of the mark, and were more likely to win her personal publicity than to aid Mrs. Pankhurst's endeavors. At one time she announced a plan to build a home for unmarried mothers in Richmond, and again, she planned to open a bank. Nothing came of either announcement but news stories. On one of her trips to the United States, she managed an interview with President Theodore Roosevelt to speak with him about the woman's cause. And she also arranged a nostalgic trip to Ludlow Street Jail in New York, with reporters following her as she reminisced about the days when Cell No. 11 had been the focus of national attention.

Such dramas and excursions into the limelight had all been left behind by Victoria. She had made one nostalgic visit to her birthplace, Homer, Ohio, on one of her last trips to the United States with John Martin. After his death she did not visit America again. In 1901, she gave up London and its excitements also. She suspended the publication of her magazine, *The Humanitarian*. It had lasted one year longer than the *Weekly* without making even a ripple to compare to the *Weekly's* tidal wave. Then, with Zula Maud and Byron, she retired to the country seat at Bredon's Norton that had become hers after her husband's death.

30 § *I Could Get Out of This . . .*

"You will know wealth and fame. You will live in a mansion in a city surrounded by ships and you will become ruler of your people." Fifty years before, the spirit of Demosthenes had made the prophecy to Victoria. She had achieved most of what he had promised. Now, in the lovely house called Norton Park, she was at last fulfilling even the final goal as she reigned over the little realm of Bredon's Norton, a gracious but imperious lady of the manor.

Bredon's Norton, in Worcestershire not far from the abbey town of Tewkesbury, was an ancient village nestled at the foot of Bredon Hill, that gentle elevation with its panoramic pastoral views that A. E. Housman would one day hymn in his lyrics. Up a winding road from the village lay Norton Park. Victoria was at home at once in the great house with its gabled façades, its ivied walls, leaded windows and shadowed library, lined with richly bound books. A smaller and far older building on the estate, which had been built before Shakespeare's time and was called the Manor House, pleased her also. And there was an old tithe barn, as picturesque as something painted by Constable.

Victoria soon acquainted herself with some of the history of the area. Local legend held that Queen Boadicea had built the village road, and so, before long, Victoria was seeing herself as a latter-day Boadicea who had "fought against the hosts of wickedness and corruption in high places and prevailed."

She was still Victoria. As the months and then the years passed, she became even more herself, without the shrill distortions to which some of her battles had led her. Colonel Blood had given her the banner of principle to wave over anything she chose to do. Now she waved that banner over her responsibilities to the inhabitants of her little realm. The thatched cottages of the villagers were charming to behold but unsanitary dwellings in which to live. They needed repairs and improvements, so Victoria arranged for the repairs and improvements to be made. She had the roads in the village repaired and kept in condition. She arranged for a lighting system, imposing her will in these matters with the quiet authority of any enlightened despot.

Her missionary zeal, her desire to teach and preach and reform, at last had more practical outlets than *The Humanitarian* had provided. She talked to farmers around the country about new methods of agriculture. She divided up one of the farms on her estate into small acreages to be rented to women only so that they might learn to farm.

She built a school on the estate where the latest educational methods could be tried. The county school authorities balked at using public funds for strange new systems and Victoria responded by paying for trained kindergarten teachers herself and also providing a bus to collect children from the villages

296] MRS. SATAN

roundabout. She assured the authorities that their withdrawal of support would be brought to the attention of Parliament.

She established a flower show at Bredon's Norton, which became, over the years, an annual agricultural show. She turned the old tithe barn into a village hall, where pageants, lectures and Christmas parties for the villagers were held.

And still she was the Victoria who wanted public recognition for these services to humanity. Pamphlets continued to stream from Bredon's Norton. Through all her years of pamphleteering, she had called on various writers or would-be writers to help her. Now the ancient Manor House became the center of a new literary salon, where these helpers could gather around her and take note of her interests and projects. A few spiritualists were part of the group, for her belief in her visions never waned. Some of the cabalistic signs and symbols that had decorated the *Weekly,* after its "departure" from free-thinking and radicalism in the 1870s, were added to the decor of Norton Park. Palmists and astrologists also interested Victoria these days. A regular series of pamphlets, called "The Manor House Causeries," was instituted to report on Victoria's causes and opinions. One such pamphlet contained a lengthy analysis of her character as deduced from the unique lines of her palm.

She had moments of glory. Soon after her move to Bredon's Norton, the Prince of Wales, who would later become Edward VII, traveled through the district and stopped for lunch at Norton Park. Victoria was not dismayed at entertaining a prince. She intertwined an American flag with the British Union Jack in the dining room and greeted royalty with the same charm that had won congressmen, suffragists and John Biddulph Martin. The day after the luncheon the Prince of Wales sent his compliments for Mrs. Martin's hospitality with a gift of grouse.

The American flag in the dining room reflected her continuing pride in being an American. She talked frequently to the writers and spiritualists around her about the "Anglo-American relationship," to which she gradually gave almost the same importance she had once saved for the male-female relationship. When a committee was formed in London to purchase Sulgrave Manor, the ancestral home of George Washington's family in England, which was located not many miles from Norton Park, Victoria appeared dramatically and promised a gift of one thousand pounds. Her association with the Sulgrave Manor Committee continued over the years, giving her much pleasure and affording much material for "The Manor House Causeries."

Zula Maud, loyal and loving as ever as she grew into middle age, helped her mother in all her activities, a second Tennie in devotion, but without Tennie's tendencies to unpredictable drama. Tennie came for visits now and then, bringing with her acquaintances of the moment, writers who were going to write her biography, social workers, spiritualists, minor members of the nobility. But Tennie never stayed for long. Tennie still had some of the free and easy ways of her youth. Some days she would like to stay curled up on a chaise longue, clothed in a dainty wrapper, and reading penny dreadfuls. This disturbed Victoria's sense of what was proper and dignified.

Still, Victoria had her own impulsive ways of keeping boredom at bay. She loved the twentieth-century invention of motorcars and had one of the first automobiles in the county. She liked to have her chauffeur drive as fast as the car could go, disregarding all hazards and even elementary caution. She was thrilled by the new conquest of the air. In 1912, through the Women's Aerial League of Great Britain, she announced that she would give an award of $5,000 and a piece of sculpture from Norton Park to any man or woman who would fly the Atlantic from America to any point in the British Isles or make the same flight in the opposite direction.

Then the war came and Victoria had a new cause to engage her. She was so anxious for America to enter the conflict at England's side that she prepared and sent off a new Memorial to the United States Congress in Washington, D.C. This Memorial did not arouse any of the attention or response which had attended her famous Memorial of 1871. So she concentrated on local activity, organizing sewing sessions for the Red Cross in the tithe barn, and arranging for lectures, pageants, even milking contests—anything that she thought might help the war effort. She gave hats to the Village Land Army.

Tennessee was stimulated by the war also. She announced plans for organizing an amazon army of women who would wear khaki uniforms like men and she planned a trip to America to talk to President Wilson about it. She did go to America but did not meet the President, nor did she lecture widely on conditions in Belgium as she had also announced she would do.

When America did at last enter the war, Victoria flew the Stars and Stripes over Norton Park and was more assiduous than ever in the organization of sewing sessions, lectures, pageants and other helpful projects.

Victoria was eighty when the war ended. She was smaller than she had been and frail in appearance, but she still had a profile like a cameo. And she was still fiercely resistant of death, determined to "break the seventh seal" and find the key that would unlock the tomb.

Brother Hebern, older than she, had died during the war. In true Claflin style, he had managed to make a few headlines in Chicago before his last illness by becoming involved in a tangle of spiritualist and matrimonial difficulties. His obituary described him as a pioneer physician of great wealth. The spiritualist who considered herself his fiancée at his death was publicly disturbed when she learned that the last claim was untrue.

In January, 1923, London suffered under one of its recurrent wintry fogs. Tennie, now the Dowager Lady Cook, was staying with Sir Thomas Beecham and his wife, her grand niece, Lady Utica, at their home at 32, Upper Hamilton Terrace. Seventy-seven years old, Tennessee had not been well for some time. Still, her death on January 18 was unexpected.

The London *Times* called her Tennessee Claflin in the heading to its obituary. But all that had been frivolous, and perhaps even irritating sometimes, about Tennie as she lived was forgotten. Forgotten too, were the tumults of her early life when she had "supported thirty or thirty-five deadheads." Instead, the *Times* noted her "strenuous campaign for woman's rights" in the United States. Her early career as a magnetic healer in Ohio, Illinois and elsewhere was transformed. Ahead of her time, she had "studied law in her father's office," and then forged on to study medicine and surgery as well. She was "a hard and conscientious worker," according to the *Times*, with a natural gift for public speaking, and she had always been a "strong advocate of equal purity for both sexes."

In America, the New York *Times* also ran a long obituary for the woman it called "Lady Cook." The *Times*, which had once found two sisters like Victoria and Tennessee, "jointly operating in one family," almost surpassing belief, now referred to Lady Cook as a "banker and journalist," and an advocate of woman's rights who had aided the Pankhursts in England. Her editorship along with her sister, of *Woodhull & Claflin's Weekly* was noted, and it was recalled that some "disagreeable" articles in that journal, in connection with the Beecher-Tilton case, had brought the sisters some criticism. Her arrests, along with Victoria, and the nationwide storm they had aroused, were forgotten. In New York, as in London, Tennessee Celeste Claflin was memorialized as a sober, courageous pioneer in the battle for women's rights.

If Victoria, eighty-four when Tennie died, murmured nervously about foul play when she heard the news of her sister's death, sure that no Claflin, particularly not Tennie, could succumb at such an early age to the workings of natural laws, only Zula and the servants who cared for her heard her. If she felt an emptiness and sought to fill it by communing with Tennie's spirit "beyond the veil," that too was privately expressed. The one reaction that was plainly evident was a stiffening of Victoria's resolution that death was not for her. Her heart had begun to give her difficulties. She had to go to Brighton for the sea air. But lying back on her cushions in the rear of the car, she insisted that the chauffeur continue to drive at top speed.

"A splinter of the indestructible" was what a reporter had called her years and years before. She held to that description as if it were another prediction of Demosthenes.

On September 23, 1923, her eighty-fifth birthday, a reporter from an English newspaper interviewed her. Through the alchemy of time and under the drifts of her own and Tennie's pamphlets, much had been forgotten and buried. The reporter did not know that Victoria Woodhull had once been notorious, an advocate of free love, and the woman who had aroused America with her revelations about the private love life of a famous minister. To him, she was someone who had worked for the cause of women in the United States, a cause that had once been disreputable but was now quite respectable. He called her "The United States Mother of Woman's Suffrage," but was not coining the title, even so, for other English newspapers, not exactly sure of her role, had already dubbed her that. There was no one to protest. Elizabeth Cady Stanton was dead. Susan Anthony was dead. And every newspaper in England had in its files a pamphlet that Victoria had sent it, reprinting the "Victoria C. Woodhull Memorial to the United States Congress of 1871." The reporter asked the aged Mrs. Woodhull-Martin what she thought of the current English bill to give the vote to women of twenty-five.

"I want women to have the vote as soon as they are fit to use it," Victoria said, "but I do not believe in forced maturity." In the manner of the aging, she remembered early scenes most clearly and recalled now the confused unhappiness of her youth. She told the reporter that she had become a wife when little more than a child. But she also said that she had been making history at twenty-one.

A few months later, an American writer, compiling a history of the American Labor movement, visited her at Norton Park. He saw her across a long room—a small, fragile old creature who lifted a hand as he advanced. She had developed a crochety dislike of physical contact in her later years.

"Not any closer," she said.

The writer had done research on those aspects of her American career that dealt with labor—her membership in Section Twelve of the International Working Men's Association, her speeches on capital and labor, the *Weekly's* original publication of Karl Marx's *Manifesto*. He expressed admiration of what she had done for the cause of labor in America.

"In England too," Victoria said. Then she looked about her. "If more people knew about it, I could get out of this."

"If more people knew. . . ." Recognition was what had mattered to her always above all else. The great battle of her life, for the recognition and acceptance of sex, she had forsworn long since. The consequences of that battle had helped to change a nation's attitude toward the relations between men and women. She was not even aware of that. She was hardly aware that in the 1920s a great many people in both America and England were beginning to behave sexually just as she had once preached that they should. Marriage was no longer the yoke on women that she had once protested so violently. Divorce, if not a great deal easier to obtain, was far more socially acceptable. Any woman with enough spunk could "change her lover every day if she wanted to," and only stir up minor alarms. The years were over when only Victoria Woodhull had dared to say publicly that she would do so and had earned a nation's horror as a result.

"I could get out of this. . . ." Old age had forced her into a corner with death at her back. But she was still sure that recognition would free her and save her—recognition of principle, recognition of herself, just as she was, whatever she was—recognition of a life force burning so fiercely that even death must withdraw from the flame.

For four years after that she refused to go to bed at night. Lying down might give death an advantage. She slept sitting

upright in her chair. For four years she had her chauffeur drive
her more and more swiftly about the countryside. In May
of 1927, young Charles A. Lindbergh flew the Atlantic Ocean,
alone in a small plane. Victoria Woodhull-Martin had forgotten
about the prize that she had offered for such a feat fourteen
years before. All her energies were focused on just one goal,
outwitting death. Then, on the morning of June 9, 1927, she
was found dead in her chair.

In the London *Times*, she was given an obituary as sober,
and even longer, than Tennie's. She was recalled as a pioneer of
woman suffrage, as Tennie had been, an advocate of Anglo-
American friendship and a worker for the Sulgrave Manor
institution. Both sisters were remembered in the obituary for
their championship of "what used to be called women's rights,"
but Tennessee, four years dead, seemed to have made the deeper
impression in England. "Miss Tennessee especially studied subjects then regarded exclusively as the province of men, law,
medicine, surgery and banking. Miss Victoria contented herself
with banking and scientific agriculture." The *Times* noted that
Mrs. Martin had been a speaker for thirty years, and the editor
of *The Humanitarian, Woodhull & Claflin's Weekly* and a
number of books and pamphlets.

In America, the New York *Times* was full of a welcome
for Lindbergh on his return to the United States after his
triumphant flight. Headlines, news stories and advertisements
all focused on his imminent arrival in Washington, D.C. The
obituary of Victoria Martin, on the page opposite the editorials,
noted that she had been a pioneer suffragist in America, that
she had been a banker and the author of a Memorial to Congress, that she had been the writer of several books, and had
contributed to the Sulgrave Manor movement in England.
There was not even a hint, as there had been in Tennessee's
obituary, to link her with the great Beecher-Tilton scandal of
fifty-five years before.

No one could have guessed that half a century earlier, Victoria Woodhull had been America's Mrs. Satan, the incarnation of passion—luring men and women to a new acceptance of one of life's delights.

Victoria's daughter, Zula Maud, who inherited her mother's fortune, stipulated in her will that the residue of her estate should go to the Royal Institution of Great Britain to be applied for research work in eugenics—the subject into which Victoria's concern with sex, with stirpiculture, with the breeding of finer men and women, was finally channeled.

Before Zula Maud Woodhull's death in September, 1940, however, she had arranged still another memorial for her mother. The historic Abbey in Tewkesbury, not far from Bredon's Norton, had long been obscured from view by a private house, garden and wall on one side. Miss Woodhull provided a sum sufficient to purchase and tear down this private obstruction, so that, after centuries, the beauties of the Abbey might be plainly visible from the main street of the town.

In the midst of the blitz in December, 1940, Robert Holland Martin, a relative of John Biddulph Martin, wrote an appreciation of this gesture to the London *Times:* "The donor, a local resident, Miss Zula Woodhull, had long wished to erect some permanent memorial to her mother, Mrs. Victoria Woodhull-Martin, whose husband's family had almost continuously represented Tewkesbury in Parliament during the eighteenth and nineteenth centuries. What, then, could be a fitter and more enduring memorial than to give back to the public forever this wonderful view of one of the great shrines of English freedom, within whose walls lie two signatories to Magna Carta and many of the warrior knights of the Crusades and of the French wars, who fought at Sluys, at Crecy, and at Agincourt?"

It was a fitting gift in more ways than Robert Martin mentioned, for surely, however she denied it later, Victoria Woodhull-Martin had always been concerned with pulling down structures that obscured the view.

BIBLIOGRAPHY

Newspapers and Periodicals

The files of: *Woodhull & Claflin's Weekly.* New York, 1870–1876; New York *Democrat;* New York *Evening Telegraph;* New York *Post;* New York *Herald;* New York *Sun;* New York *Times;* New York *Tribune;* New York *World;* Brooklyn *Argus;* Brooklyn *Eagle;* New York *Independent* Scrapbooks, New York Public Library; London *Times;* and others, as cited. *The Golden Age,* New York; *Harper's Weekly,* New York; *The Humanitarian,* London and New York; *Frank Leslie's Illustrated Newspaper,* New York; *The Revolution,* Boston; *The Christian Union,* New York.

Pamphlets

Stephen Pearl Andrews, Henry James, Horace Greeley, *Love, Marriage and Divorce, A Discussion.* New York, Stringer and Townsend, 1853.

A Review of the Evidence in the Beecher Trial. Reprinted from the New York *Times,* July 3, 1875.

The Great Scandal, The Historical and Famous Beecher-Tilton Case. Distributed by the American News Company, 1874.

Edward H. G. Clark, *The Thunderbolt.* Troy, N.Y., 1873.

G. S. Darewin, *Synopsis of the Lives of Victoria Woodhull and Tennessee Claflin.* London, J. H. Corthesy, 1891.

M. F. Darwin, *One Moral Standard For All.* New York, Caulon Press, 1895.

E. B. Fairfield, *Wickedness in High Places.* Ohio, L. D. Myers and Brothers, 1874.

James W. Nelson, "America's Victoria" (article in *Historical and Philosophical Society of Ohio,* University of Cincinnati).

The Downfall of Henry Ward Beecher. New York, 1874.

Madeline Legge, *Two Noble Women, Nobly Planned.* London, Phelps Brothers, 1893.

Theodore Tilton, *The Constitution: A Letter to Charles Sumner.* New York, A *Golden Age* Tract, 1871.

Theodore Tilton, *Life of Victoria Claflin Woodhull.* New York, *Golden Age,* 1871.

Victoria Claflin Woodhull (Martin), *The Alchemy of Maternity.* Manor House Club, Bredon's Norton, 1889.

————*The Argument for Woman's Electoral Rights Under Amendments XIV and XV: A review of My Work at Washington, D.C. in 1870–1871.* London, G. Norman & Son, 1887.

————*The Elixir of Life, or, Why Do We Die?* New York, Woodhull, Claflin Co., 1873.

————*Brief Sketches of the Life of Victoria Woodhull.* London, 1893.

————*Breaking the Seals.* New York, Woodhull, Claflin Co., 1875.

————*And the Truth Shall Make You Free.* London, Blackfriars, 1894.

Zulu Maud Woodhull, "Affinities" *Westminster Review,* 1899.

Books

Lyman Abbott, *Henry Ward Beecher.* Boston, Houghton Mifflin Co., 1903.

Stephen Pearl Andrews, *The Basic Outline of Universology.* New York, D. Thomas, 1872.

Wayne Andrews, *The Vanderbilt Legend.* New York, Harcourt, Brace, 1941.

————*The Science of Society.* New York, T. L. Nichols, 1854.

Katharine Anthony, *Susan B. Anthony, Her Personal History and Era.* New York, Doubleday, 1954.

William C. Beecher and the Rev. Samuel Scoville (assisted by Mrs. Henry Ward Beecher), *A Biography of Henry Ward Beecher.* New York, C. L. Webster & Co., 1888.

The Official Report of the Trial of Henry Ward Beecher, with notes and references by Austin Abbott. New York, G. W. Smith & Co., 1875.

Heywood Broun and Margaret Leech, *Anthony Comstock, Roundsman of the Lord.* New York, A. C. Boni, 1927.

William B. Carpenter, M.D., F.R.S., F.G.S., *Principles of Human Physiology.* Philadelphia, Henry C. Lea, 1868.

Tennessee Claflin, *Constitutional Equality.* New York, Woodhull, Claflin, Co., 1871.

Tennessee Claflin (Lady Cook), *The Evils of Society and Their Remedies.* London, University Publishing Co., 1895.

————*Talks and Essays.* London, The Roxburghe Press, 1897.

Henry Clews, *Fifty Years in Wall Street.* New York, Irving Publishing Co. 1908.

Rheta Childe Dorr, *Susan B. Anthony.* F. A. Stokes, 1928.

Leon Edel, *Henry James.* Philadelphia, Lippincott, 1962.

Robert H. Fuller, *Jubilee Jim, The Life of Colonel James Fisk, Jr.* New York, The Macmillan Co., 1928.

Johann Wolfgang von Goethe, *Elective Affinities.* English trans, with intro. by Victoria C. Woodhull. Boston, D. W. Niles, 1872.

William Harlan Hale, *Horace Greeley, Voice of the People*. New York, Collier Books, 1961.

Ida Husted Harper, *The Life and Work of Susan B. Anthony*. Indianapolis, Bobbs-Merrill Co., 1899.

Paxton Hibben, *Henry Ward Beecher*. New York, George H. Doran Co., 1927.

Ada Louise Huxtable, *Classic New York*. New York, Anchor Books, Doubleday, 1964.

Henry James, *The Great Short Novels of Henry James*, ed. and intro. by Philip Rahv. New York, Dial, 1944.

Gerard W. Johnson, *The Lunatic Fringe*. Philadelphia, Lippincott, 1957.

Alma Lutz, *Created Equal, The Life of Elizabeth Cady Stanton*. New York, John Day Co., 1940.

Eduard Friedrich Wilhelm Pflüger, *Ueber die bedeutun und ursache der menstruation*. Berlin, 1865.

Ishbel Ross, *Charmers and Cranks*. New York, Harper & Row, 1965.

Emanie Sachs, *The Terrible Siren*. New York, Harper & Bros., 1928.

Robert Shaplen, *Free Love and Heavenly Sinners*. New York, Alfred A. Knopf, 1954.

Arthur D. Woden Smith, *Commodore Vanderbilt, An Epic of American Achievement*. New York, Robert M. McBride & Co., 1927.

Matthew Hale Smith, *Sunshine and Shadow in New York*. New York, J. B. Burr & Co., 1868.

———*Twenty Years Among the Bulls and Bears of Wall Street*. New York, J. B. Burr & Co., 1870.

Elizabeth Cady Stanton, Susan B. Anthony, Matilda Joslyn Gage, eds., *The History of Woman Suffrage*. Fowler & Wells, 1881–1902.

Theodore Stanton, Harriot Stanton Blatch, *Elizabeth Cady Stanton, As Revealed in Her Letters, Diary and Reminscences*. New York, Harper & Bros., 1922.

Charles E. Stowe, *Life of Harriet Beecher Stowe, Compiled from Her Letters and Journals*. Boston, Houghton, Mifflin Co., 1889.

Harriet Beecher Stowe, *My Wife and I*. New York, J. B. Ford & Co., 1872.

Lyman Beecher Stowe, Saints, Sinners and Beechers. Indianapolis, Bobbs-Merrill Co., 1934.

Theodore Tilton, *Tempest Tossed*. New York, Sheldon Co., 1874.

Edward Wagenknecht, *Harriet Beecher Stowe, The Known and The Unknown*. New York, Oxford, 1965.

Irving Wallace, *The Square Pegs*. New York, Alfred A. Knopf, 1957.

Forrest Wilson, *Crusader in Crinoline*. Philadelphia, Lippincott, 1941.

Victoria C. Woodhull, *The Tendencies and Principles of Government*. New York, Woodhull, Claflin Co., 1871.

———and Tennessee Claflin (Mrs. J. B. Martin and Lady Cook), *The Human Body, The Temple of God; or The Philosophy of Sociology, and Other Essays,* also press notices. London, 17, Hyde Park Gate, S.W., 1890.

INDEX